This is a very significant book – m
on parenting. Jim McNally, a m(
friend, has embraced and taugh
for decades. But not until I rea
Flesh *did I realize how fully I*
important topic. I have gained immensely from -
profound truths that leap from its pages.

– John D. Beckett
Chairman, The Beckett Companies
Author of *Loving Monday*
Mastering Monday

The book is profound. Sometimes I think writers take a fifty-
page book to five hundred pages; you have done the opposite.
It could be a textbook. I will certainly highly recommend it. It
meets a great need.

– Charles V. Simpson
Founder, Charles Simpson Ministries
Senior Editor: *One-One Magazine*
The Covenant & The Kingdom
Author of *Courageous Living*
The Challenge to Care
Take Your Hat Off, Son

What you will find in this book is not a method or program but
a way of life. Since being touched by Jim and this sonship
message, I have gained far more confidence in who I am in the
Lord. The truths laid out in this book will liberate you in your
walk with the Lord. It will change your understanding of
authority. If you want a fresh perspective on God's fatherhood,
this book is a must. It will transform your life as it has mine.

– Dr. Bradley Stuart
Founder, Yada International
Author of *Destiny, An Intimate Journey*

SONSHIP:

THE WORD MADE FLESH

by

Jim McNally

Editors: Roger Shipman, Eric Samuelson and Glenda Head

Contributing editor: Michael Puffett

Editing assistance: Kathy McNally

Cover Design: Sean and Wen McNally

Layout assistance: Roger Shipman

For further information please contact:

> **Jim McNally**
> **c/o Harvest Christian Fellowship**
> **5 Serene Court**
> **Stafford, VA 22556-1641**
> **Phone: [540] 286-1560**

Dedication

It is only fitting that a book on sonship would begin with a tribute to one's own parents. My father, Bertram McNally, spent his life in Michigan as a Methodist minister. My mother Bessie raised ten children—I was number seven. In 1945, at the age of four, I was struck with appendicitis. The surgical team at the hospital mistakenly thought my kidneys were the problem and opened up my lower back. My kidneys were fine, but in the midst of this exploratory surgery, my appendix ruptured. The surgeon told my parents, "If Jim lives for two weeks, we will give him a fifty-fifty chance." My parents could do nothing but dedicate me to the Lord.

I am persuaded that my Lord Jesus Christ honored my parent's dedicatory prayer—on April 22, 1968, I knelt in the living room of my home in Marlette, Michigan, as Pastor J.P. Murray introduced me to Jesus Christ. Therefore, I have chosen to honor my parents by dedicating this book to them. One day, I will thank them face-to-face.

Secondly, I would like to dedicate this book to my wife Kathy, my "Proverbs 31 woman." She has been the greatest source of support and encouragement to me in this endeavor. On April 2, 2010, I suffered a major heart attack, known to the medical staff as the "widow maker." Upon learning from the cardio-surgeon that I had but a fifty-fifty chance to live through the night, Kathy gathered a number of my friends and family in the waiting room, and prayed this prayer. "Lord, Jim is in your hands, and there is no better place for him to be. I know that you are good, and I accept your will for his life. However, if you are taking requests, please don't make me a widow." Once again, I believe God answered this prayer of dedication, the result of which was the opportunity to finish this book.

Table of Contents

Acknowledgments

It has been a privilege and an honor to work with so many people while authoring this book. I want to express my sincere gratitude to everyone who has prayed for and/or contributed, especially to some who have supplied technical help, inspiration and encouragement.

Bradley Stuart was the catalyst for me to begin writing. Michael Puffett spent weeks working with me at the onset of this endeavor. Both Eric Samuelson and Glenda Head were of tremendous help in proofreading and editing the first draft. Marlin Eller gave me some great insights into the Son of God/Son of man paradigm. Roger Shipman labored through the tedious tasks of not only the final edit but also laying out the format. Charles Simpson and John Beckett, authors both, took time from their busy schedules to proof the content and to supply suggestions and encouragement. Tony Fitzgerald graciously agreed to write the foreword. My natural sons, Sean and Matt, lived in the laboratory of this experience. My spiritual sons and daughters throughout the world were also instrumental in practically validating my hypothesis. Finally, no person has sacrificed more than Kathy to release me and allow me the freedom to pen these thoughts. To each and every one of you I am indebted and eternally grateful.

In sum, I wish to present all the trophies and crowns, the kind and wonderful words of praise I have received throughout the process of writing this book, unto God. May the Father who conceived it, Jesus who demonstrated it and the Holy Spirit who revealed it receive all the glory.

Foreword

No subject is closer to my heart than knowing the father heart of God. Understanding God as a father allows us to grow to be sons in His Kingdom and to father others who will experience the same joy. Walking with God as his son has been a lifelong journey for me. In recent years, Jim McNally has magnified my understanding of this rich and meaningful subject.

When God created the earth, he placed Adam in the midst of it as a son. The first man, made in the image of his heavenly father, powerfully illustrated the spiritual principle of father and son as the foundation of creation. God and Adam walked in covenant—in a deep, trusting relationship. God said, "It is not good for man to dwell alone," (in this natural realm) so out of Adam He created Eve. Together, they reflected the fullness of God; together they were awarded a dominion mandate to rule the earth. Their ability and authority to fulfill this mandate depended on the quality of their ongoing relationship with Father God. Most of us reading this book recall that sin entered the world, breaking man's relationship with his heavenly father. After this break, all relationships became a struggle. Adam and Eve lost their right to rule—rulership of the earth was taken over by the enemy. The battle for control raged on for thousands of years until a savior, Jesus, was given. In the Bible, Jesus is referred to as "the last Adam." To validate the principle of father/son relationships, the first words uttered at the beginning of Jesus' three-year ministry were, "This is my beloved son in whom I am well pleased." Ultimately, through His death and resurrection, illegitimate rulership of the earth was taken away from Satan and placed back in the hands of Adam (mankind).

God's original intent has never changed. His will is the same today as in the beginning. He desires to have a generation of sons on the Earth living in relationship with their heavenly father and ruling his creation.

I was raised by a wonderful dad. I am very thankful for being raised in a home where I never needed to doubt my father's love. My dad did not have the same luxury; when he was only around two years old, his father was killed on the battlefields of France. Many years later I had the joy of standing with my father at his father's grave in France. As I stood and held my dad, I could hear him say through his tears, "I really did have a father." Something increased in my heart that day. It was a desire to let many people know that they really do have a father—a heavenly Father. Knowing this can release us to full lives as sons.

Unfortunately, many of our churches continue to be run by CEOs, not fathers. The cry of our hearts—for authentic fatherhood—goes unheard in modern churches. Program-based, not family-based, they are performance-driven and not relational, built on a Hellenistic mindset rather than on Hebraic thought patterns. As a result, we are stuck in an evangelical/charismatic form of the problem, rather than the answer.

I was humbled a few years ago when Jim McNally asked me to fulfill a spiritual father role in his life. Jim not only writes books on the subject and models it in his family and with spiritual sons, but also walks it out in his own life.

If you want to finish your race strong, then understanding the principles outlined in this book is essential. Read these pages with an open heart and grow in your sonship and your ability to father others. Live out your God-given destiny to be a part of his government on earth. This will not just be an academic reading exercise but rather a life-changing experience as you learn more about your heavenly father and his relationship with you. Allow the Holy Spirit to instruct, heal and restore.

My life is richer through knowing Jim and the power of his fatherhood message. Yours will be, too, as you touch Father's heart through him in these pages.

Tony Fitzgerald
Apostolic Team Leader
Church of the Nations
March 2011

1

Preparation for Our Journey

The magnificent obsession of Jesus the Messiah is that all of humanity would know God as a Father. To overemphasize the importance of the Fatherhood of God would be impossible. It is one of the principal revelations of the New Testament (or the New Covenant) and a central theme of Jesus' message. I am aware that numerous books have been written on the subject of fathers. Many of these contain great insight and are useful resources for us. Nevertheless, I have chosen to address this theme again, because I believe that my approach to the subject of fatherhood requires a paradigm shift. As we all know, when God wanted to reveal Himself as a father, He did not send a father, He sent His only begotten Son Jesus Christ.[1] Since Jesus Christ must always be the archetype for us, we are required to look at His example. **In this book, I will attempt to convince you that one becomes a father by setting an example as a son.** Therefore, I have attempted to address what is required of us as sons. As we begin, let me state clearly that this is not a book about parenting.

The apostle Paul wrote, "But in the fullness of time, God sent forth His Son..."[2] The definitive question in life for each

---

[1] John 3:16
[2] Galatians 4:4

of us is found in the words of this Son, "Who do you say that I am?"[1] To enable us to know God as a Father, Jesus came as a Son. We must know Jesus Christ before we can know our Father God, because it is written, "No one comes unto the Father but by Me."[2] If this book does not give a deeper revelation and appreciation for our Lord Jesus Christ, it will be of little value. As we come to know God as Father, it will help equip us to shape our personal life, structure our family and order the church. As we attempt to bring our personal lives, our families and the church into proper order, our Father can use us to positively influence and affect our respective communities and even the nations.

What you are about to read is a summary of my lifelong journey. In writing this book, I am forever indebted to the inspiration, urging and encouragement of my wife Kathy, my sons Sean and Matt, and my "spiritual sons and daughters" throughout the world. The hypothesis of this book has been tried and tested in the laboratory of life. Kathy and I have raised our two sons, with whom we have walked closely for the majority of four decades. Sean and Matt are married men and are fathers themselves. Their lives have demonstrated, authenticated and therefore validated what you are about to read. Having said this, however, please allow me to concede a few things here.

First, I am fully aware that the success of any endeavor, including raising children, is utterly and absolutely dependent on the grace of God our Father. There is no substitute for the unmerited and ill-merited favor of God. There is no formula to insure our success apart from it. Without God's grace, any suggestion or guarantee that this

---

[1] Matthew 16:15; Mark 8:29; Luke 9:20
[2] John 14:6

book will make you a successful father is absurd. The Scriptures tell us, "God gives grace to the humble."[1] Walking in humility simply puts us in the best position for us to receive God's grace.

Secondly, Kathy must receive much of the credit for raising the boys, especially when they were young. As with most fathers who have young children, I was busy pursuing a career. In my case, I served as a high school teacher and athletic coach. In addition, I was providing pastoral oversight to a growing congregation. During that time, I set a goal to have a relationship with the boys that they would want to duplicate with their own children. Kathy left her career as a registered nurse to dedicate herself to being a homemaker, wife and mother. In my frequent absence, she was faithful to continue to knit the relationship of the boys and me together. Sharing the burden for the boys that I carried in my heart, she skillfully and carefully translated the message of fathers and sons to them.

Perhaps some of you who have selected this book are familiar with its predecessor, *Sonship: The Path to Fatherhood*, which was first printed in May of 2001. It was laid out and written in the format of a seminar manual. Over the next five years, it went through many alterations, not only due to typographical errors but also due to additional content. To my surprise, the manual has been circulated on six continents, resulting in numerous opportunities for me to share on this subject. Since composing the manual, my prayer has been that God would give me—and therefore my readers—further revelation and deeper insights into the subject of fathers and sons. I believe that God has answered my prayer. This book is my endeavor to explore this theme

---

[1] James 4:6; 1 Peter 5:5

more thoroughly and to greatly expand and elaborate on the material found in that manual. Furthermore, I have had the desire to make the material more readable by including personal experiences. Kathy summed up perfectly my effort in rewriting. She said it is like a tailor taking the suit of a small father, and trying to remake it to fit a larger son. I have attempted to carefully take each seam apart stitch by stitch, press each crease out, and even add some material, while making every effort to remain true to the original pattern.

As we begin our journey together, I feel it is not only expedient but also essential for us to agree upon certain elemental criteria. It seems obvious to me, as we travel this path, that we are best served to be guided by an identical map. The map I have chosen to use is the Bible. For me, the Bible stands alone as the ultimate source of authority and frame of reference for all of life and practice. The course for our journey will not be set using current sociological trends, cultural norms, popular practices or even church traditions, no matter how successful they might appear to be. We will not set our compass by opinion polls or Biblical commentaries. In fact, I have heard it said that the Bible can shed a lot of light on the commentaries.

I have chosen to use Jesus Christ as the utmost example and supreme standard for any revelation we discover on this journey. I think it would be futile to venture any further unless we agree to use the Bible and the example of Jesus Christ as our "global positioning system" to navigate this expedition. Let me assure you, this book is not meant to be a critique of the structure others might choose, but rather it is my sincere, if inadequate, attempt to offer an alternative. Charles Simpson, whom I deeply respect as a mentor and friend, said, "We must not elevate criticism to the level of achievement." Therefore, I invite you to join me in rediscovering what I believe is the Biblical model for fatherhood and sonship.

Biblical truth is not something that can be merely studied and learned; it is completely dependent upon revelation. Every author or teacher who attempts to bring spiritual understanding faces one common and seemingly insurmountable obstacle. "The natural man does not receive the things of the Spirit of God, for they are foolishness to him; nor can he know them, because they are spiritually discerned."[1] Even though I write this book and use many Scriptures to support my premise, the truth it contains will still require revelation from the Holy Spirit. Biblical truth is much greater than information and concepts. Jesus did not simply say that He would give us or tell us the truth. He said, "I am the truth."[2] Truth was incarnated and still remains embodied in the person of Jesus Christ. John stated, "... the Word became flesh and dwelt among us."[3] Jesus Christ came as the living truth, the Word of God.

I believe that one's ministry should not be his life, but that one's life should be his ministry. For this reason, every follower of Jesus Christ is called to be in "full time ministry." Some of us, however, have received the calling, grace and privilege to be in "full-time paid ministry." I have spent over three decades in full-time paid ministry. During these years, I have traveled extensively, not only in the United States, but I have also made well over a hundred trips to over thirty nations on six of the seven continents. Sadly, I can testify with complete confidence that the *greatest and most frequent problem I have encountered is the lack of genuine*

---

[1] 1 Corinthians 2:1
[2] John 14:6
[3] John 1:14

fatherhood. Consequently, my primary purpose for writing this book is to address this problem. My objective is to help us understand and walk down a path that will lead us into healthier father and son relationships. **What I have aspired to lay out in this book is not a program to be initiated; rather it is a lifestyle to be lived.**

For nearly four decades, I have had the privilege of walking with Dan Wolfe. He has been a mentor, a pastor and a spiritual father not only to me, but also to many of my colleagues. He has walked before me as an example of integrity and faith. I have attempted to behave as a spiritual son toward Dan, and then to lead my two sons, Sean and Matt, on the same path. As I have focused on being a spiritual son to Dan, God has given me the privilege of sharing this message to many men and women around the world. As I recount some of the things that I have learned along the way, I hope I can challenge you, encourage you and dramatically affect the way that you view fatherhood, sonship, family, and the church. To assist us on our journey, I will touch upon the lives of such great men as Abraham, Isaac, Jacob, Eli, Elijah, Samuel, David, John the Baptist, Jesus and Paul.

In the course of my travels, I have had the privilege of seeing and touring several of the great cathedrals, some of which required centuries of construction. Those who laid their foundations were well aware that they would never see the completion of these edifices. Years ago, I heard Bob Mumford speak about those persons who began to build these magnificent structures. He said that during the time they laid the foundation for the structure many of those builders planted seeds for trees. They knew that these trees would mature over many years, in fact, well beyond the lifetime of those who sowed them. However, they also knew that a time would come when they could be used as rafter beams for the ceiling. Today, modern techniques and materials allow us to construct buildings in a matter of weeks. They may be beautiful, but few would refer to them as magnificent. Besides, I rather doubt that they will still be standing centuries from now.

One of the saddest accounts recorded in the Bible is the story of King David's son Absalom. "During his lifetime Absalom had taken a pillar and erected it in the King's Valley as a monument to himself, for he thought, 'I have no son to carry on the memory of my name.' He named the pillar after himself, and it is called Absalom's Monument to this day."[1] The Scriptures say that Absalom, convinced that he had no son, built a monument to himself. As I hope to show you later, there is a difference between male children and sons. Absalom had four children, three of which were male.[2] However, I contend that Absalom was unable to have a son, because he refused to be a true son to David. His legacy would be chiseled upon a stone marker, instead of being inscribed on the heart of an heir. If we do not build for the next generations, like Absalom we are simply busy building a monument to ourselves.

Obviously, to set our focus on building for three or more generations will challenge our endurance. Our life is made up of many roads and crossroads. The noted American poet Robert Frost wrote about two roads and said, "I took the one less traveled by, and that has made all the difference."[3] This book has been my attempt to present the road I chose to walk. Once again, it is not a program to be implemented; it is a lifelong journey to walk. Lewis Carroll wrote, "If you don't

---

[1] 2 Samuel 18:18 (NIV)

[2] 2 Samuel 14:27

[3] "The Road Not Taken" by Robert Frost, published in 1916 in the collection *Mountain Interval*.

care very much where you are going, any road will get you there." I have attempted to present what I believe is a Biblical model for structuring the family and church in the context of Christ's kingdom. How and what we build will have implications for the generations to come. So, how will we structure our families and the church? Will they stand the ultimate test of time?

Many today are writing and speaking of the imminent return of Jesus Christ. Without question or compromise, I hold to the certainty of His coming once again. I do not know when He will return, nor does anyone else. The last command I received from my Father and my King was to advance His kingdom and occupy until He comes. Therefore, I will continue to attempt to establish a legacy, a heritage and an inheritance for the generations that may follow. If He returns in my lifetime, and finds me doing this, I believe He will be happy with me. Perhaps Paul's words can best express the urgency of this message. "For the anxious longing of the creation waits eagerly for the revealing of the sons of God."[1]

Finally, if what I have written is truth, it should give us a greater sense of freedom, since John wrote that the outcome of truth is freedom.[2] Solomon, who was noted for his great wisdom, wrote, "Listen to your father who begot you, and do not despise your mother when she is old. Buy truth, and do not sell it, get wisdom and instruction and understanding. The father of the righteous will greatly rejoice, and he who begets a wise son will be glad in him. Let your father and your mother be glad, and let her rejoice who gave birth to you. *Give me your heart, my son, and let your eyes delight in my*

---

[1] Romans 8:19
[2] John 8:31-32

ways."[1] In light of our total dependence on the gracious revelation of God, Paul's prayer for the church in Ephesus expresses my heart's desire: "May the God and Father of Our Lord Jesus Christ give to us the spirit of wisdom and revelation in the knowledge of Him."[2]

[1] Proverbs 23:22-26
[2] Ephesians 1:17

2

Biblical Roots and Principles

*I*t has been said, *"Those who navigate at sea understand that neglecting small variants at the beginning of a journey can require serious course corrections later on."* One of the great tragedies repeatedly witnessed in history is the world's proclivity toward anti-Semitism, leading to the extremes of persecution of the Jewish people. Anti-Semitism did not begin nor end with the rise of the Third Reich. Centuries before the holocaust, Jewish people were harassed and even massacred by nominal Christians and organized Christianity. Paul, referring to our Jewish heritage and warning us not to despise it, admonished the Christians in Rome, "Do not become arrogant toward the branches..."[1] It would be irrational and erroneous to dispute the fact that Christianity has its origin in Judaism. Clearly, the Bible has its basis in Judaism. We know that the Old Covenant patriarchs and prophets were Jews and the New Covenant apostles were Jews. By the Father's own design, Jesus was born as a Jew into a Jewish family and culture. He lived and died as a Jew. His followers called him Rabbi, and it is likely that He dressed as one having tassels which hung from His prayer shawl. Even after His resurrection and ascension, Jesus remains a Jew. In the Revelation to John, Jesus is called "the Lion of the

---

[1] Romans 11:16-18

tribe of Judah."[1] Centuries of anti-Semitism has robbed our families and therefore our churches from this understanding of the Hebraic roots of our faith. Therefore, to rediscover Biblical sonship and fatherhood, we must return to these Hebraic roots.

One of the basic characteristics of Judaism is that it is fundamentally patriarchal. Webster defines the word *patriarchal* as "a state of social development characterized by the supremacy of the father in the clan or family." **Fatherhood is a central feature of Judaism, and therefore it should be a central feature of Christianity.** God's decision to take the name and the title of Father gives both this title and role supreme importance. In fact, fatherhood is one of the primary roles and purposes for which God puts men on the earth. However, fatherhood in the scriptural sense is more than just procreation. Human fatherhood is an opportunity for man to reflect the very character of God. The word *father* in both the Covenants comes from the Hebrew and Greek words meaning *source* and *sustainer*. The Biblical father was supposed to function as the source of life and the source of provision, protection, acceptance and love. Sadly, what passes for fatherhood in today's world is far from a reflection of God's character. Abusive, absentee and perverted men have used the position as an opportunity for exploitation, thus smearing the reputation and glory of our Heavenly Father.

Very little is known about Jesus' childhood, except that He followed the traditions and customs of His Jewish parents. Along with His half-brothers and half-sisters, Jesus lived under the discipline of His earthly parents. The method for instruction commonly used among Jews is the practice of

---

[1] Revelation 5:5

apprenticeship. In the Bible, it is referred to as discipleship. We can surmise from the Scriptures that Jesus had a working relationship with Joseph, his "foster father." We assume that he learned His trade as a carpenter from him.[1] As a Jewish boy He learned by listening, observing, and then by doing. Jesus not only had a natural working relationship with His earthly foster father, but He also had a faithful relationship laboring with His actual Father, that is, God. Both in heaven and on earth Jesus worked for His Father.[2]

Having dealt with the issue of the Biblical roots of Christianity, let us now move on to some key principles of Biblical interpretation and exegesis. Webster's dictionary defines exegesis as "an exposition or a critical explanation of a portion of Scripture." We should all recognize that if we take passages of Scripture out of their context we could do great damage to their meaning. Having established that the Bible must be the map for our journey, here are some principles or tools that I have learned to use when studying the Scriptures. As we continue our journey together, we will use certain laws like a sailor's sextant to keep us on course.

During the first decade of my service as a pastor, I had the enormous privilege of fellowshipping with and sitting under the ministry of the late Dr. Derek Prince. Derek was a brilliant scholar and a world-renowned and respected Bible teacher. Apparently, he could read Hebrew and Greek like you and I read the newspaper. Few men could compare with Derek in his ability to exegete Scripture. One of the principles of exegesis that he taught us was *The Law of First Mention*. More clearly, the first time a word or idea is mentioned in the Scriptures it carries a seed. This seed holds the genetic code,

---

[1] Matthew 13:55; Mark 6:3-4
[2] John 5:36; John 17:4

or the DNA, of that word or idea. Any use of a word from the point that it is introduced [its first mention] requires that all the following uses of that word must remain true to the seed or DNA. In layman's terms, if the word or term used to describe a tomato in Genesis was "red thing," then "red thing" must describe a tomato in Revelation.

Now let me illustrate how the Law of First Mention relates to our theme of sonship and fatherhood. An experience between Abraham and his son Isaac, recorded in Genesis, serves as a shadow, or antecedent, of an occurrence on Calvary some millennia later. In Genesis we read, "God tested Abraham, and said to him, 'Abraham!' And Abraham said, 'Here I am.' God said, 'Take now your son, your only son, whom you love, Isaac, and go to the land of Moriah, and offer him there as a burnt offering on one of the mountains of which I will tell you.' "[1] I was stunned when I first discovered that the first mention of the word *love* is found in this text. It is not found in the relationship between husband and wife, but rather in the relationship between a father and his son. It refers to Abraham's love for Isaac: *i.e.*, a father's love for his son. Continuing on, we read, "So Abraham arose early in the morning, along with Isaac his son, and took two of his young men with him. Abraham split wood for the burnt offering, and went to the place where God had told him. On the third day, Abraham raised his eyes and saw the place from a distance. Then, Abraham said to his young men, 'Stay here with the donkey, the lad and I will go over there; and we will worship and (we will) return to you.' "[2] Careful scrutiny of this passage will reveal the first mention of the word *worship*. As Abraham speaks to the two young men who accompanied

---

[1] Genesis 22:1-2
[2] Genesis 22:3-5

him and Isaac, he says, "Wait here... my son and I will go, and we will worship..."[1] This forever links the first use of the word *worship* with a ceremonial event involving a father and a son. Observe that the pronoun indicating who would go up to worship is *we*, not *I*: "We will worship..." In addition, the antecedent for return is we, "and [we] will return..." Here is one of the most explicit examples of Abraham's faith. He said, "We will worship and [we] will be back." Since the promise to Abraham was to him and to his seed (not seeds), and Isaac carried the seed of that promise, Abraham was assured that even if he killed and burned Isaac on the altar, God would have to raise him up.

A second law of exegesis is what I will call the *Law of Pattern*. This refers to the principle of binary mention where repeated references are made to certain pairs of elements or things. In the Bible, there are patterns that are as common as salt and pepper. A case in point would be the pattern found in the mention of water and fire. Water and fire are commonly paired together in the Bible. For example, water was used in Genesis to destroy the world; fire will be used in Revelation to destroy the world. Water (in the form of a cloud) and fire (in the form of a pillar) were used to lead Israel in the wilderness. On Mount Carmel, we see Elijah pouring water over the sacrifice before the fire fell from heaven to consume it. The relevance of all these illustrations is found in water baptism and the baptism in the Holy Spirit expressed in the words of John the Baptist. John said to them all, "As for me, I baptize you with water; but One is coming who is mightier than I, and I am not fit to untie the thong of His sandals; He will baptize you with the Holy Spirit and fire."[2] John said that

---

[1] Genesis 22:5
[2] Luke 3:16

he was authorized to baptize in water, but Messiah would baptize in fire. The backdrop for this event was not only the baptism of Jesus, but also His authorization and release into public ministry.

One more example that may help us to understand and appreciate the Law of Pattern is the recurrent use of the couplet bread with wine, sometimes referred to as grain or flour and grapes. I suppose to all of us bread and wine have become symbols of the Lord's Supper. They signify or correspond to the elements of covenant, bread representing the body and wine the blood. Let me mention a few important incidences in Biblical history where this pair emerges. In Genesis, we find the first mention of the bread and wine couplet. "Melchizedek king of Salem brought out bread and wine; now he was a priest of the Most High God."[1] By the way, this is also the first mention in the Scriptures of the word *priest*. Numerous Bible scholars consider Melchizedek to be a theophany (a pre-incarnate appearance of Christ). Here Melchizedek, as a priest, offers Abram the elements of covenant and then of blessing.

"So," you may ask, "what does this have to do with fathers and sons?" As we all know, Abram became Abraham, an earthly father who became the spiritual father of all who call themselves Christians.[2] What's more, we know Melchizedek, the spiritual Son of God, became the earthly Son of Man. Relating this to our theme, we see that the spiritual Son of God, Melchizedek, blessed and offered covenant to the earthly father Abraham. One of the most significant and primary roles of a father is to perpetuate his lineage in the covenant community through his sons. The Old Covenant

---

[1] Genesis 14:18
[2] Romans 4:16

practice of confirming the covenant through circumcision of male children demonstrates and verifies this. In the New Covenant, circumcision is performed by cutting away the "flesh" in the heart. The Hebrew word for covenant is *b'rith,* meaning a cut where blood flows. Under the New Covenant, the Holy Spirit circumcises the heart of both men and women; thus, the perpetuation of the New Covenant is no longer gender-specific.

A further illustration of the couplet of grain and grapes is the call of Gideon. Notice that when the angel of the Lord visits Gideon, he finds Gideon beating out wheat in a winepress. As God looked down and witnessed the pogroms of the Midianites against the Israelites, perhaps wheat (the primary ingredient in bread) in the winepress reminded God of His covenant with the people of Israel. It is rather humorous that the angel of the Lord addresses Gideon hiding out like this as "mighty man of valor."[1] The Bible states that the Lord called Gideon to save the Israelites from the Midianites. First, look at what was required of Gideon. "And the angel of God said unto him, 'Take the flesh [body] and the unleavened cakes [bread], and lay them upon this rock [a name for Jesus], and pour out the broth [blood].' And he did so."[2] Like David when he faced the "uncircumcised" giant Goliath, Gideon went forth and was victorious in the power of God's covenant faithfulness. Pertinent to our theme of fathers and sons, notice that Gideon's valor in pulling down the images of Baal emboldened his father Josiah to stand and defend his son in the face of the multitude who were demanding that Gideon die.[3]

---

[1] Judges 6:11-12
[2] Judges 6:20
[3] Judges 6:31

A further understanding needed for the exegesis of scripture is the _Principle of Paradoxical Truth_. Western culture and mindsets cannot fathom the idea that two opposing truths can occupy the same space. Recently my son Sean shared, "Our cup is half full, and overflowing." He was speaking of the grace that fills the empty spaces of our shortcomings. Jesus is at the same time the Lion and the Lamb. The Principle of Paradoxical Truth hits us head on when we attempt to settle the issues of predestination, election and the sovereignty of God with the doctrine of moral agency and freedom of choice. Perhaps it is best to think of coins having two sides; we refer to these sides as heads and tails. When buying something, whether you place the coin on the counter with the head or tail facing up, the value of the coin remains the same. Since both Wesley and Calvin have Biblical support, I believe that if we are going to lean one way or the other, we should err on the side of grace and the sovereignty of God. **Personally, I believe in eternal security; that is, "once saved always saved." However, I would not encourage you to test it.** In other words, in our theology lean toward John Calvin, but in walking out our personal lives lean toward John Wesley. Making room for paradoxical truth is not relativism. Both grace and mercy, with justice and truth, came in the person of Christ Jesus. When it comes to the question of being a son and/or being a father, these are indivisible.

3

In the Beginning, God

Scientists have emphasized the vital role that genetics play in the development and function of life. I believe that we as Christians should take time to examine again our spiritual genetic makeup. In a previous chapter, I have implied that it is essential for Christians to recognize and appreciate their genetic connection to Judaism. The first five books of the Bible are also called "The Pentateuch." These books are attributed to Moses, and Jews and Christians alike consider them sacred works. Genesis is the first book of the Pentateuch. The word *Genesis* is defined as "the origin, the source or the coming into being of something." Words such as gene, genetic, genealogy and generation all relate to genesis, *i.e.*, origins.

I am constantly amazed at the hidden treasures that lie in familiar passages of Scripture. A couple of years ago, Kathy and I decided to splurge a little and take a vacation in Hawaii. While relaxing on the beach, I began to reflect on the first four words of the Bible recorded in Genesis – "In the beginning God..."[1] Unexpectedly these words took on new significance for me. Most of us in our finite reasoning view time as a linear dimension. Therefore, everything must have a beginning, a commencement, a starting place. As

---

[1] Genesis 1:1

mentioned, the first verse of the Bible states, "In the beginning God..." At that moment, I thought to myself, "But God and eternity have no beginning." We know that which is everlasting has no end, but that which is eternal has neither end nor beginning. Eternity consists of a dimension outside of time. We know that God is eternal; therefore, God was, is and always will be the pre-existent and ever-existent one. God existed prior to the beginning. He lived and He continues to live outside of the dimension of time. Creation was the first act recorded of God, but God existed before creation. Consequently, the Bible does not begin with creation, but it begins with God: "In the beginning — God!" Subsequently, everything that exists has its beginning in God. God is the creator, the originator and the source of all that comes into being. All existence, all reality, all creation and all things have their beginning with God. For my part, I believe that only a fool questions the existence of God. The Biblical definition of a fool is a person who says in his heart, "There is no God."[1] This book is not intended to be an apologetic for the Christian faith. It is not written for the agnostic or atheist, whom the Bible dubs fools. Therefore, I shall from this point on assume that you concur with the statement, "In the beginning God." For those who question the existence of God I can only say with pity, "Ignorance can be enlightened, but stupidity is hopelessly dark."

With this in mind, the Hebrew word for God used in Genesis 1:1 is **Elohiym**. Interestingly, *Elohiym* is the plural form of the Hebrew word **Elowah** that translates as God. Later in the first chapter of Genesis we read, "Let *us* make man in *our* image and after *our* likeness..."[2] We see in this

---

[1] Psalms 14:1
[2] Genesis 1:26

passage that God refers to Himself with the plural words "us" and "our." Rest assured, I am not proposing some form of heretical polytheism. Instead, while holding to the Scriptural truth of monotheism, I believe that the Pentateuch substantiates the reality of the Trinity. That is to say, prior to creation, prior to the beginning, God existed in three persons: Father, Son and Holy Spirit. They lived and continue to live in divine communion in absolute peace, unity and harmony with one another, co-existent and co-substantial; that is to say, they are of indistinguishable and identical substance. Only in a feeble and futile attempt to explain the unexplainable might one refer to co-substantiality using water, ice and steam.

The first letter of the Greek alphabet is alpha, and the final letter is omega. Four times in the book of Revelation Jesus is revealed to John as the "Alpha and Omega."[1] The passages say of Jesus, "I am the beginning and the end." The beginning and the end are not simply a concept or a thing, but are embodied in the person of Jesus Christ. Jesus is "the one who is and was and is to come."[2] These Scriptures then correspond with the words of the Apostle John who wrote, "In the beginning was the Word, and the Word was with God, and the Word was God."[3] Jesus was with God the Father in eternity, before creation. John continues by saying, "All things came into being through Him [that is, Jesus] and apart from Him nothing came into being."[4] The Son was totally involved with the Father in creation. In His great intercessory prayer, recorded also by John, Jesus said, "Father, glorify Me together with Yourself, with the glory which I had with You before the

---

[1] Revelation 1:8; 21:6; 22:13
[2] Revelation 1:8
[3] John 1:1
[4] John 1:2-3

world was."[1] Not only was Jesus with the Father during the act of creation, but also Jesus was with the Father before the world was. Therefore, all that we know prior to creation and the existence of things is that there was God. Taking into account the above, we can conclude that the DNA, or the divine atom and nucleus of the cosmic and celestial realm of eternity, consists of a relationship between a Father, a Son and the Holy Spirit. The relationship between fathers and sons is interlaced like a golden thread throughout the Bible as well as throughout this book. A primary effort of God, recorded throughout the Scriptures, is the recovery and restoration of fathers and sons in fellowship and communion with the Holy Spirit. God is at work restoring humanity to his original DNA. The ramifications of this work of restoration have enormous implications. It is a scientific fact that if we alter the DNA of something, we create a mutation. As we move forward, I aspire to help us see why our understanding of sonship and fatherhood is so significant and remains so relevant. **In so doing, we shall see that family, ministry, and the Kingdom itself are perpetuated through the reproduction of sons.**

A quote attributed to Billy Graham reads, "If we aim at nothing we'll probably hit it." My premise for this book is that, like Jesus, we become fathers by modeling sonship.[2] Fatherhood therefore is our destination, while sonship is our journey. As we progress along our journey, let us take a closer look at our target. In this manner, we can envision the magnificent, while building from the minute. So, before we examine the theme of sonship, let us first attempt to unveil the mystery of fatherhood.

---

[1] John 17:5
[2] Isaiah 9:6

4

The Renegade Son

A humorous story is told about a little boy who was drawing a picture in Sunday School. The teacher asked him, "Who are you drawing?" The little boy responded, "I'm drawing a picture of Father God." The teacher replied, "Child, you can't do that, nobody knows what He looks like." The boy said, "Well, Ma'am, they will when I am finished."

Actually, the Bible does say, "No man has seen God at any time...," but continues, "...the only begotten God, who is in the bosom of the Father, He has explained Him."[1] Jesus, the only begotten of the Father, has both seen Him and has painted a word portrait of Him for us. Jesus used a parable to "explain" what our Father is like. If I were to select the signature message of my life, it would be what I am about to share with you. It is popularly recognized as the parable of the prodigal son.

Much of what Jesus taught, He taught as parables. A parable is a riddle told as a story containing hidden truth. The gospel of Luke sets the scene for us at the beginning of chapter 15. "Now all the tax-gatherers and the sinners were coming near Him to listen to Him. And both the Pharisees and the scribes began to grumble saying, 'This man receives

---

[1] John 1:18

sinners and eats with them.' "[1] Jesus, as He did so often, gathered a crowd that included backsliders and sinners. The tax-gatherers were likely to be Jews who sold out to the Romans. It is interesting that they came to listen, not to mock or argue. Amazingly, sinners appeared to be comfortable in His presence. Also, included among the crowd gathered, were Pharisees and scribes.

The Pharisees were a religious sect of fundamentalist Jews, who became Jesus' most zealous antagonists. Scribes were those who copied that portion of the Holy Scriptures that existed in that day. Both the Pharisees and the scribes were given to memorizing these Scriptures. In this particular incident, Jesus disgusted them by associating with the unruly crowd He had gathered.

Their grievance was that this man Jesus "receives sinners and eats with them." The response to their indignation is probably the most familiar of all Jesus' teachings. "And He told them this parable, saying..."[2] Jesus used parables extensively. Not to make things easier to understand—on the contrary, he did so to conceal the true meaning of His message. It is interesting to note that this passage reads, "He told them _this_ parable." Actually, Jesus shared with them a triad, which consists of three parables in one.

The first parable in this triad is the parable of the lost sheep. The second parable is that of the lost coin. The third, commonly referred to as the parable of the prodigal son, is a story of two sons. We will begin with it.

I would like to suggest to you that the two sons play a supporting role in this story, because the parable begins, "A

---

[1] Luke 15:1-2
[2] Luke 15:3

certain man had two sons..."[1] Jesus used the two sons to symbolize the two groups gathered around Him. The younger son represents the sinners and backsliders; the older son symbolizes the scribes and Pharisees. I believe that the main character of this parable, however, is a metaphorical figure of His Father. Jesus, a third Son who also characterizes the Father, is the narrator. So let us now examine the word portrait He paints of His Father. For the moment, we shall only deal with the first half of the third parable, which recounts the experience of the Father with the younger of the two sons.

In the opening passages we learn that the father is affluent because he has slaves, he has an estate, he has sheep and cattle, and his banquet hall will accommodate many from the community. And, as mentioned, he has two sons. Jesus continues, "A certain man had two sons; and the younger of them said to his father, 'Father, give me the share of the estate that falls to me.' And he divided his wealth between them."[2] Under Jewish law, if there were two sons, two-thirds of the estate would be passed down to the older son; one third fell to the younger son.[3] This request made by the younger son was quite unthinkable. A son might ask for a gift, if the father was living. However, normally, an estate is passed down upon the death of a father. Therefore, this request is comparable to the son saying, "Dad, I wish you were dead, so I could have what's coming to me." We must remember that Jesus is addressing a Jewish audience, specifically responding to the grumbling of the Pharisees and scribes who have contempt toward the company He was keeping. It is to be expected that

---

[1] Luke 15:11a
[2] Luke 15:11-12
[3] Deuteronomy 21:17

a Jewish father would strike the boy across the cheek and angrily dismiss him by sending him out of the house. More than likely, the father would not allow him to return without a sincere, heartfelt apology, and perhaps because of the pleading and tears of the boy's mother. In violation of all tradition, the father grants the request. Imagine the shocked reaction of the religious half of his listeners.

"And not many days later, the younger son gathered everything together and went on a journey into a distant country, and there he squandered his estate with loose living."[1] "Not many days later" indicates that he had planned everything, including his journey, in advance. Many youth desire freedom but desire for others to pay for it. Since an estate would be impossible to transport, we may infer that he turned the estate into cash. Yet again, it would have been unthinkable to sell a portion of his father's estate while his father still lived. This adds an additional shock factor to his Jewish audience, especially the fundamentalists. Further-more, the son heads out from the restraints of home to a distant country. To a Jew any territory inhabited by gentiles is a distant country. There he squandered his estate with loose living. He is learning the hard way that there are people in the world whose full-time career is to separate him from his money. We should take notice, however, that the parable emphasizes the boy's poverty, not deficiency in character. It speaks of his financial destitution rather than moral corruption. It speaks of his lostness, not of his guilt.

Now a further reality check comes. "Now when he had spent everything, a severe famine occurred in that country, and he began to be in need. And he went and attached himself to one of the citizens of that country, and he sent him

---

[1] Luke 15:13

into his fields to feed swine."[1] It is not a good thing to be flat broke in the middle of a famine. This boy is about to receive a full-ride scholarship, room and board, to Pig Pen University. This is the world's training center for fools. We know from the parable that it he was in a gentile land, because they were raising pigs. The university cafeteria has a menu limited to pods that the swine were eating. Besides this, his roommates are real pigs; and pigs are pigs. They are not cute and cuddly little characters like Walt Disney portrayed. They are filthy, slop-eating, mud-wallowing swine. The boy is sharing their food at their table. In fact, carob pods come from a Palestinian tree and provide little nutrition for humans. Imagine the boy thinking, *I wish I were a pig*. Remember, once again, that the complaint of the Pharisees and scribes was that Jesus ate and drank with sinners. Imagine the grave horror and revulsion they felt as they listened to this riddle. The younger son had reached the lowest possible rung on the social ladder. Here is a Jew, not only feeding the pigs but also eating with them. Thus, we are reminded of the complaint of the religious leaders. Nevertheless, at least he had a job; perhaps he could earn the money that he had squandered away.

One might inquire at this point, "Why was it not the boy's first thought to return home?" Important and interesting research attributed to Kenneth Bailey gives us a possible answer. The Jerusalem Talmud of the time of Jesus had a simple but special ceremony, known as a *qetsatsah*. Any person that lost their family inheritance to gentiles was a prime candidate for this ceremony. The *qetsatsah* is equivalent to excommunication in Roman Catholicism, or the Amish practice of shunning. However, apparently the

---

[1] Luke 15:14-15

qetsatsah was more severe than these, since it was a total ban on any and all contact between the violator and his family or community. According to Bailey, the elders of the community would have a jar of clay filled with burnt corn and grain. They would have the boy stand before the entire community, and as they smashed this jar, they would say, "This boy is forever banned from this community." A *qetsatsah* awaited the prodigal if he returned without the money he had squandered. We may therefore assume that the boy had become a pig herder in an effort to save enough money to pay back what he had lost. Ironically, Jesus said, "And he was longing to fill his stomach with the pods that the swine were eating, and no one was giving anything to him."[1] The desperate plan of the younger son to earn this money was a disastrous failure, because no one was giving anything to him.

It is at this point, I have become convinced, that many are mistaken in their interpretations of this riddle. The following verse reads, "But when he came to his senses..." (Some translations say, "He came to himself."[2]) Many interpret this passage by concluding that the boy repented in the pigpen. I assert and maintain that coming to yourself or to your senses is not repentance, but rather it is self-realization—and self-realization is not repentance! In fact, self-realization awaits every man in the pigpen. This is where the obsession for autonomy took the boy, and this is where it will take us. In the pigpen we will look in the mirror and say, "Hello, self! This is the real you. All the other things, the things that you squandered, were your father's possessions." Notice that as Jesus continues with the boy's thoughts, "How many of my father's hired men have more than enough bread,

---

[1] Luke 15:16
[2] Luke 15:17a

but I am dying here with hunger!"[1] In essence, the younger son shows absolutely no remorse for the grief or embarrassment that he has caused his father. Instead, he said, "I am hungry and my father's hired servants have bread." His self-centeredness is revealed in this statement. His concern is not about the father but about himself. Banning could be no worse than where he finds himself now. As a matter of fact, what does he have to lose?

You may contest, but wait...the boy goes on to say, "I will get up and go to my father, and will say to him, 'Father, I have sinned against heaven, and in your sight; I am no longer worthy to be called your son; make me as one of your hired men.' "[2] However, this only allows me to illustrate my position more clearly. A hired man would be above a servant in rank and would receive wages. Remember that Jesus is addressing the scribes and the Pharisees who had criticized Him for fellowshipping with sinners. They had memorized the Scriptures. The boy says, "I have sinned against heaven and in your sight." The satire and irony in this is that Jesus was quoting from the Pentateuch, a passage familiar to the religious conservatives listening, one that they would have memorized. "Then Pharaoh hurriedly called for Moses and Aaron, and he said, 'I have sinned against the Lord your God and against you."[3] He was pinpointing a conversation between Moses and Pharaoh. Obviously, Pharaoh did not repent. What is happening is that our hero has come up with another plan to work off his debt. The essence of religion, as opposed to Christianity, is that one must work off one's debt. Here lies the great difference between genuine Christianity

---

[1] Luke 15:17b
[2] Luke 15:18-19
[3] Exodus 10:16

and all other religious beliefs. Religion emphasizes man's efforts to reach up to God, while Christianity alone emphasizes God's efforts to reach down to man. In other words, Christianity is not about what we do as much as it is about what God has done. By this point in the parable, I can imagine that the religious side of His audience is furiously fuming with anger and indignation. The brighter ones would have become conscious that He was speaking to them.

The above, too, describes the way we once were. Sin separates us from God. Due to the separation caused by the original sin, each person either attempts to deny that there is a God or must make the effort to reconcile with Him. One who acknowledges His existence often makes the effort to reconcile with God on his own. The boy still has not learned. Still, I will say this for the younger son: he got up and came to his father. His desperate state was a catalyst for action, even if he was motivated by self-preservation. However, thankfully the parable does not end with this picture.

5

The Gracious Father

*I*n the preceding chapter, I have attempted to paint a picture of the way each person begins the journey of life. Let us continue by trying to imagine meeting this boy on the road. More than likely, he was barefoot, wearing filthy and shredded clothes, reeking from the odor of pig manure, unshaven, unkempt, with matted hair. Being half-starved, perhaps he was gnawing on a kernel-less corncob. He was a penniless garbage picker, humiliated beyond shame, and a disgrace to his friends and family. I suggest that this is a prototype and spiritual image of all who are outside of the grace of our heavenly Father. Nevertheless, of all the scriptures of the Bible, the next passage is perhaps the most powerful and meaningful to me.

"While he was still a long way off, his father saw him and felt compassion for him, and ran and embraced him, and kissed him."[1] Along the shores of Lake Michigan lie homes that have a fenced platform atop the roof. Sadly, these fenced areas have come to be known as a widow's walk. It is said that the wives of sailors would climb to the roof to stand and stare at the horizon, watching for their husbands or sons to return from the oft-treacherous waters of the lake. Now imagine with me the young lad's father. Envision him daily

---

[1] Luke 15:20

walking through the village, headed for the highest hill from which he might scan the horizon. Oblivious to the scorn of his neighbors, with tears and sweat blurring his vision, day by day he climbs to the peak and patiently watches and waits.

Allow me to picture the moment with you. While the son was still a long way off his father sees him. Rubbing sweat and tears from bloodshot eyes, he recognizes his son from a distance. The Bible says that he felt compassion for him. He does not fold his arms in indignation and disgust, thinking, *Look at him! He is a disgrace to the family and me.* Instead, his father runs to him. Notice it is not the boy who runs to the father; rather, the father runs to the boy. Perhaps he desires to reach him before the self-righteous members of the religious community do. Once again, breaking the rules of Jewish custom, he draws up his robe and runs to meet this derelict youth. Ken Bailey wrote that for an elderly Jewish man to show his legs in public is analogous to someone dropping his pants today. Tears streaming down his weathered face, laughing and crying, stumbling and winded, he throws out his arms like a sprinter at the finish tape. Like Joseph when he revealed himself to his brothers, when he reaches the boy he hugs him and kisses him. Filthy as he is, the father hugs and kisses his unshaven face, seemingly unaware of the boy's condition. The boy has not showered or changed clothes. This is not the *qetsatsah* that the boy could have expected. What follows is the decisive moment, the clincher.

The father did all of this before the son said a word. This is grace! "And (then) the son said to him, 'Father, I have sinned against heaven and in your sight; I am no longer worthy to be called your son.' "[1] Paul wrote, "Do you think

---

[1] Luke 15:21

lightly of the riches of His kindness and forbearance and patience, not knowing that the kindness of God leads you to repentance?"[1] In the entire text of the Bible, I know of no finer portrait of the grace of our Father God than this. It is not merit but mercy. Do not fail to notice what has been dropped from the son's planned confession. He leaves out this phrase, "... make me as one of your hired men." After a reception like this, he no longer offers to work. As stated in the previous chapter, this is what differentiates Christianity from all other faiths on the face of the earth. Finally, the father's response demonstrates this grace further by giving little heed to the boy's confession, in that he gives no response to it. Instead, He calls out to his servants, "Quickly bring out the best robe and put it on him, and put a ring on his hand and sandals on his feet; and bring the fattened calf, kill it, and let us eat and be merry; for this son of mine was dead, and has come to life again; he was lost, and has been found. And they began to be merry."[2]

Let us take a brief look at what the items he called for symbolize. The robe is a symbol of righteousness.[3] The father's spotlessly clean robe covered the boy's filthiness. The ring is a credit card or, better yet, the power of attorney, the legal authority to use the name of his father. After the youth squandered his portion of the estate, the father looks upon this as another opportunity to give. The sandals on his feet will prepare him for the rest of the journey. Roman law prohibited a slave to wear sandals; only sons and soldiers could wear them. Moreover, as if this was not a sufficient welcome, he orders that they prepare a feast for the boy. The

---

[1] Romans 2:4
[2] Luke 15:22-24
[3] Isaiah 61:10

fatted calf was an animal set aside for the possibility that nobility might visit, especially the king. This feast, a symbol of communion, is the banquet that replaces the *qetsatsah*. However, I wish to propose that the banquet is not for the boy. It is to celebrate the gracious reception of the father. Who has ever seen a father like this?

There is a popular legend in American folklore that may give us a greater appreciation for this boy's journey. The version I learned was of a young juvenile delinquent, who after a time of debauchery, drugs and varied criminal activity, finally was arrested, tried and sentenced to several years in a penitentiary. As the date for his release approached, he wrote a note to his father, which read like this: "Dear Dad, I know that we have not communicated in years. I realize now that I have brought a great deal of shame and embarrassment to you and to our family in the community. In a few days, I will be released from prison. There is a train that runs close by here, and stops at the train station in our town. Beside the station is a large old oak tree. If it is okay for me to come home, tie a yellow ribbon in the old oak tree." The young boy, now a grown man, boarded the train that headed for his community. His palms sweating, his stomach churning, and his nose pressed against the window, he stared down the track as it drew closer to the station. In a moment as it slowed going around a corner, there was the old oak tree. Upon it had been tied a thousand yellow ribbons. Jesus Christ nailed upon the cross is the Father's way of tying yellow ribbons to His throne for us. The door has been reopened to fellowship with Him. The message is clear: *Welcome home, son!*

In relating the parable of the prodigal son, Jesus used him to address the sinners and the tax collectors who were eating and fellowshipping with Him. Still, the parable does not end with this wonderful scene. A second part to the third parable describes the older son. The older son is a caricature of the religious conservatives, the scribes and Pharisees, who were upset that Jesus would be so uncivilized, so uncouth as to eat and drink with sinners. Therefore, Jesus continues His parable.

6

The Self-righteous Son

I have concluded that people have a natural aversion toward grace because it violates their sense of fairness. The nature of grace is that it is not fair. Grace prohibits us from using the Law of Sowing and Reaping as an absolute applied during this lifetime. However, grace does not eliminate eternal accountability. We must understand that although the Law of Sowing and Reaping cannot always be applied in the temporal, there will be eternal consequences to temporal behavior. The story of the older son will help us understand this antipathy toward grace more completely.

Let me remind you that the triad of parables begins in Luke 15. Jesus' audience became the target for His remarks. He spoke three parables: (1) the parable of the lost sheep; (2) the parable of the lost coin; (3) the parable of the father who had two sons. The two sons represent the two types of people that made up His audience. Up to this point, we have concentrated on the relationship between the father and the younger of the two sons. The younger son is often referred to as the prodigal son. Now, let us examine the older son, whom I will refer to as the dutiful son.

Jesus continues, "Now his older son was in the field, and when he came and approached the house, he heard music and dancing."[1] In other words, the older son had been out in the field, where he should have been, doing what he should have been doing. He appears to be responsible, obedient and devoted. However, as we shall see, he is a Pharisee. Dirty, sweaty and tired, he returns from the field after a long day, only to hear a celebration going on. More than likely, there had not been much celebrating in the house since the younger brother had left. Think of it – he has been out in the field working while there is a party going on at home. Probably, the music and dancing were loud enough to capture his attention. Remember that the scribes and Pharisees were grumbling about Jesus eating and drinking with the sinners and backsliders.

"And he summoned one of the servants and began inquiring what these things might be."[2] Rather than investigating it for himself, he summons one of the servants to ask, "What's going on?" I presume he was suspicious, probably figuring out, *He's back!* Perhaps he thought, *He always was Dad's favorite son,* or, *I suppose now I will be required to share my portion of my inheritance with my delinquent brother.* It is obvious that Jesus understands our antipathy toward grace, knowing that any of us can become a Pharisee in twenty-four hours or less.

The servant responded, "Your brother has come, and your father has killed the fattened calf, because he has received him back safe and sound."[3] The servant's response might be considered naïve. He assumed the older brother would rejoice, since his younger brother had returned home. Assuredly, he assumed that the older brother would

---

[1] Luke 15:25
[2] Luke 15:26
[3] Luke 15:27

understand that any genuine father would simply have longed for the return of his son. The servant assumed that people would always rejoice when God's grace touches someone else. He may even have assumed that strife ends with brothers. However, the truth is that, more often than not, envy and competition have deep roots in the relationship between brothers. In fact, the first murder recorded in the Scriptures was fratricide; Cain killed his brother Abel. Perhaps, we too are naïve about this. Maybe we think that our brothers will always welcome us home, too. Remember, the Pharisees were angry when Jesus healed people on the Sabbath. Now, they are angry that He is fellowshipping with sinners.

"But he became angry and was not willing to go in; and his father came out and began entreating him."[1] Therefore, he is furious that his brother has not only returned but has been treated with dignity and honor. What the older brother was expecting, and even hoping for, was a *qetsatsah*, not a welcoming banquet. He was indignant with his father's grace. He may have been dutiful and responsible, but he certainly did not have his father's heart in this. He may have remained at home, but his heart was in a distant land. Still, in this instance look at the father's response. The older son was not willing to go in, so his father came out and began to entreat him. In the same manner as he had handled the younger son's return, he handles the older son's refusal to become a part of the celebration. He leaves the party to appeal to an incorrigible and insolent son. As he had run down the road to receive his gentile-like child, now he runs out of the house to receive his Jew-like child. Once more, a shocking reaction to the religious listeners, since no Jewish father they knew

---

[1] Luke 15:28

would countenance the embarrassment of his son's refusal, even leaving the celebration to do so. If we are to become like this father, we must be prepared to behave like this as well.

"But he answered and said to his father, 'Look! For so many years I have been serving you, and I have never neglected a command of yours; and yet you have never given me a kid, that I might be merry with my friends.'"[1] Notice the insolence and disgust in this statement. It is as if he is saying, "Look here, old man!" He presupposes that his father cannot see. However, earlier in the parable it says, "While he was a long way off his father saw him." This should serve as a caution to all of us as to how we address our fathers and leaders. He continues his disrespect by rehearsing how faithful he has been. "For so many years I have been serving you." No servant would use this tone of voice toward a master. He may have been serving, but he obviously was not a servant. He was simply doing what he ought to be doing. His self-pity plunges him into a victim mentality and a martyr's spirit. In a clear display of self-righteousness, he continues, "...and I have never neglected a command of yours." I rather doubt the veracity of this statement, noting the manner in which he is now speaking to his father. People who wallow in the mire of self-righteousness set themselves up as models for all others. Even if he obeyed in every way, he did so with a wrong spirit.

Now he attacks his father with these words: "And yet you have never given me a kid..." He has the audacity to accuse his father of being miserly. He says, You never gave me even the smallest of festive animals to share with my friends. Notice, here is a party going on for the family, but he will not join in. If he had his way, he would party outside the family with his

[1] Luke 15:29

friends. Dan Wolfe has taught me that comparisons are routinely evil. If we consider ourselves to be better than others, it will lead to pride. Considering ourselves less than others leads to envy and jealousy.

Remember, Jesus is using the older son to address the Pharisees. Referring to their indignation with Jesus' reception of sinners, Jesus continues the parable. "But when this son of yours came, who has devoured your wealth with harlots, you killed the fattened calf for him.[1] Herein, he disowns his younger brother by referring to him as "this son of yours" and not "this brother of mine." Furthermore, like a little child, he tattles on his brother, reminding the father that the younger son has squandered the inheritance given to him. I contend that the older son is not concerned with the father's interests and well-being; rather he is masking an effort to preserve his own self-interests. Besides, a Pharisee would always prefer to be right than to be rightly related. Therefore, when any of us prefer to be right rather than to be in right relationship, we too sit in the seat of the Pharisee. Genuine righteousness is relational. It requires a right standing with God, and a right standing with men. That is why the cross consists of a vertical and horizontal symbol.

With amazing demonstration of patience, Jesus concludes the parable triad with these words: "And he said to him, 'My child, you have always been with me, and all that is mine is yours. But we had to be merry and rejoice, for this brother of yours was dead and has begun to live, and was lost and has been found.' "[2] Jesus, continuing to address the Pharisees, uses the phrase, "My child." Instead of using the word *huios*, which translates as son, Jesus uses the word

---

[1] Luke 15:30
[2] Luke 15:31-32

teknon, meaning child. The importance of this designation will be addressed later. When Jesus said, "You have always been with me..." He is telling his son (and by extension, the Pharisees) that His mere presence should have brought them great joy and celebration. Yes, the younger boy gets a fatted calf, but every day you may eat at my table. Of course, we should rejoice in the health of our children, but it brings even greater joy when a gravely ill child recovers, let alone one "who was dead." As we know, Jesus was sent initially to the lost sheep of Israel,[1] and He sent His disciples to the same.[2] Paul wrote that the gospel was to the Jew first,[3] so here Jesus reminds them that even though the brother was welcomed home, they were the original chosen ones. The inference is that God does not reject us, but we can reject Him. Redemptive grace was offered to both sons. The younger brother had returned home unharmed, safe and sound. The older brother is at a loss for words, hushed by the wisdom of this Rabbi. Sadly, we are not privy to the choice the older brother makes.

I believe the first two parables of the triad are significant in drawing my conclusion. Jesus uses a shepherd and a woman, prior to telling the story of this swine herder. The first parable of the triad is about a lost sheep. The lost sheep is probably representative of the younger son. The sheep left home, was lost and did not know the way back. The shepherd went out and found the sheep, and celebrated the return of it. The lost coin likely refers to the older brother, whose story does not have a conclusion. Derek Prince suggested that the coin was likely one of ten coins the woman possessed,

---

[1] Matthew 15:24
[2] Matthew 10:6
[3] Romans 1:16; Romans 2:9 & 10

probably related to marriage, and representing her dowry. The coin remained at home but was lost. Unlike sheep, coins have no life in them. Therefore, like the older brother, the coin was lost in the house and did not know it. Still, the woman found the coin and celebrated. In the parable, Jesus the Son is speaking as Jesus the Father. The sheep did not find its way home; it was found by the shepherd, and the shepherd celebrated. The coin did not find the woman, the woman found the coin and the woman celebrated. What's more, the younger son did not find the father. While he was still a long way off the father saw him, had compassion on him and ran to him. The prodigal son, representing you and me, did not come to the Father. The Father came to him and to us in the person of His Son.

In his parable, Jesus is the third son, not the younger or elder son. He not only is describing His Father, but He is speaking about Himself. He is at the same instant the Son reflecting the Father. He spoke to members of his audience who were of the staunchest and strictest sect of Judaism. They were those who had said about Him, "This man eats and drinks with sinners."[1] Essentially, Jesus responds to them as if He were thinking, *Boys, you don't know the half of it. He not only eats and drinks with them, he runs down the road to get them, and brings them back to a banquet.* Moreover, to the sinners and backsliders that He described so graphically, He proclaims, *You may have spent all you have, but you have not spent all the Father has!*

---

[1] Luke 15:2

7

The Word Made Flesh

*O*ne of the greatest mysteries of time and eternity is found in the two natures of God and man blended in the person of Jesus Christ. Centuries before the incarnation of God as a man in the person of Jesus, Isaiah wrote, "Behold, the virgin shall conceive and bear a Son, and shall call His name Immanuel."[1] The Hebrew name Immanuel is translated by Matthew as "God with us."[2] In fact, the humanity of Jesus is emphasized throughout the New Testament. The author of Hebrews wrote, "Forasmuch then as the children are partakers of flesh and blood, He also Himself likewise took part of the same. For verily He took not on Him the nature of angels: but He took on Him the seed of Abraham."[3]

Several years ago my son Sean captured a sound bite from one of my recorded messages and put it on a website he had designed for me. The phrase that he captured: **"It has always been the will of God for the word of God to become flesh."** Lately, through a series of discussions with a spiritual son, Marlin Eller, this concept has taken on a much deeper meaning to me. Marlin's insights have been invaluable

---

[1] Isaiah 7:14
[2] Matthew 1:23
[3] Hebrews 2:14 & 16

to what follows.

Genuine orthodox Christians would commonly agree that Jesus Christ was eternally the Son of God, existing in a dimension outside of time, and having no beginning or end. Then, into a time-space world, the eternal Son of God entered the world as human flesh, born as a baby to Mary, His mother. Jesus the pre-existing, uncreated co-equal and co-substantial member of the Trinity would be the incarnation of God on earth. John wrote, "In the beginning was the Word, and the Word was with God, and the Word was God."[1] He continued, "And the Word became flesh, and dwelt among us..."[2] The full significance of this would be impossible for any of us to comprehend, let alone explain. However, let me suggest what I feel are some of the important points to ponder.

The dynamic that resulted from the above event was that the Son of God would become the Son of Man. As mentioned above, Jesus was eternally the Son of God, but He became the Son of Man. As a descendant of Abraham, Jesus would be also a descendant of Adam. Rather than taking on the nature of an angel, He took on the human nature. Derek Prince taught that the genealogy of Jesus recorded in the Gospels is in harmony with the presentation of Him. Emphasizing His identity with Israel, Matthew traces Him back to Abraham.[3] To stress His identity with the human race, Luke traces Jesus back to Adam.[4] Since Mark emphasizes His servanthood, he does not include a genealogy for Christ. According to ancient custom, a slave or servant needs no genealogy. John alone captured the God-man nature of Jesus. John presents Jesus as God without any human genealogy, as the eternal Word of God, who

---

[1] John 1:1
[2] John 1:14
[3] Matthew 1:1-17
[4] Luke 3:23-38

coexisted with God before creation.[1] However, a few verses later John emphasizes both the divinity and the humanity of Jesus by writing, "And the Word became flesh and dwelt among us and we beheld His glory, glory as of the only begotten from the Father, full of grace and truth."[2] Because of the above, the Bible has labeled Jesus with two titles: He is the Son of God, and He is the Son of Man. Evidently, God the Father, through the writers, wished to drive home the point that I have made above—essentially, that sonship was something that needed a physical expression on earth. In reference to this statement, let us look carefully at a conversation between Jesus and His disciples recorded in the book of Matthew. As readers of the New Testament, we have the privilege to be made aware of this private conversation.

"Now when Jesus came into the district of Caesarea Philippi, He began asking His disciples, saying, 'Who do people say that the Son of Man is?' "[3] Notice carefully His question, "Who do people say that the Son of Man is?" Obviously, He is speaking of Himself. We see that in His question Jesus refers to Himself with the distinctive title mentioned above, as "Son of Man." It was a surprise to me when I discovered that the name or title Jesus applied to Himself more than any other (over eighty times) was "Son of Man." By so emphasizing this name, He identifies Himself with Adam (mankind) as a member of the human race.

The disciples's response is in reference to the crowd's perception of this unusual Rabbi. "And they said, 'Some say John the Baptist; and others, Elijah; but still others, Jeremiah, or one of the prophets.' "[4] The disciples said that some

---

[1] John 1:1-2
[2] John 1:14
[3] Matthew 16:13
[4] Matthew 16:14

thought He was John the Baptist, while others said He was Elijah. As you will see later in this book, these two men are mentioned as linchpins between the Old and New Covenants. Others speculated that perhaps He was Jeremiah, or one of the other prophets. If they were right in their thinking, we must conclude that they were seeing Jesus as some sort of reincarnated Old Testament saint, since all whom they mentioned were dead by the time this conversation took place. What's more, it would imply that at least a number of the people were thinking that Jesus might be someone raised from the dead.

Then Jesus asked the disciples a second question: *"But who do you say that I am?"*[1] I believe this to be one of the most vital questions for all humanity. Peter's response is of tremendous importance both to us and to our theme. This time His question is not, "Who do you say the Son of Man is?" but rather He simply asked, "Who do you say that I am?" Still, using the previous question as the antecedent, we can assume that He is asking the disciples who they believe that the Son of Man is. Simon Peter answered and said, "You are the Christ, the Son of the living God."[2] In answer to Jesus' question, Peter alleged that Jesus was the Christ (the Jewish Messiah), the Son of the Living God. More simply, Peter said that the Son of Man is the Son of God. Jesus Christ, the only Son of God, has come into the world in flesh and blood.[3] Essentially Peter said that this is the Word made flesh. Sonship was not just an invisible or mystical relationship that Jesus held with His Father, but it was being modeled, manifested and demonstrated in human flesh. This is one of

---

[1] Matthew 16:15
[2] Matthew 16:16
[3] John 1:14; Hebrews 2:14

the greatest revelations of the New Covenant. When He became flesh, He emptied Himself of His divinity and became like one of us.[1] Although Jesus was and is eternally the Son of God, He **became** the Son of Man. By so doing, He lived His life in this world as a son both to Joseph and Mary and to His Father God.

Paul tells us, "There is one God and one mediator between God and man, the Man Christ Jesus."[2] Still today and forever, a man sits on the throne of God. Many of us have spiritualized our sonship and have accepted our position as sons of God. However, the majority of us refuse to live in the son-of-man paradigm. Jesus did both and then said, "As the Father has sent me, so send I you."[3] When He says, "Follow Me," I believe He means that we demonstrate our spiritual sonship through walking out our natural sonship. A major purpose of this book will be to support this position. The passages of Scripture mentioned above have been a source of major controversy, especially between Catholics and Protestants. To the question, "Who is the Son of Man?" Peter answered that the Son of Man is the Son of God. Peter had a revelation of the miracle of the incarnation.

Jesus responded to Peter by saying, "Blessed are you, Simon Barjona, because flesh and blood did not reveal this to you, but My Father who is in heaven."[4] Interestingly, this is the only time in Scripture that Jesus addresses Peter by his natural father's name. In all other passages Jesus calls him Simon, or Simon Peter, but here He calls Peter, Simon Barjona, or in English Simon Johnson. Perhaps Jesus is reminding Peter of His humanity here, because Jesus said

[1] Philippians 2:6-8
[2] 1 Timothy 2:5
[3] John 20:21
[4] Matthew 16:17

that as Simon Barjona he did not come to this conclusion from any human wisdom or knowledge he possessed. Jesus said that Peter was blessed because his answer had come through a divinely inspired and spiritually discerned revelation from the Father in heaven. The understanding of the Son-of-God/Son-of-man paradigm does not come to us by intellectual inquiry; it requires a spiritual revelation. Notice also that Jesus refers to the Father as "My Father."

8

Upon This Rock

*T*here is a beautiful old hymn of which the chorus reads, "On Christ the solid rock I stand, all other ground is sinking sand..." After He told Peter that it was a spiritual revelation that He was the Son of God and the Son of Man, Jesus continued, "And I also say to you that you are Peter, and upon this rock I will build My church."[1] It might be important that Jesus now uses the "spiritual name" that He gave to Simon Barjona instead of his natural name. He calls him a stone. The metaphorical use of this passage has been greatly misunderstood. In Greek, as in English, the word for *rock* differs from the word for *stone*. The name *Peter* derives from **petros**, signifying a stone or fragment of a rock, whereas the term for *rock* is **petra**. Herein we see the controversy. Many Roman Catholics believe that the rock on which Jesus would build the church is Peter. However, most Evangelicals or Protestants believe that the rock upon which the church must be built is Peter's testimony that Jesus Christ is the Rock. Paul seems to agree with the Protestant view when he wrote, "For no man can lay a foundation other than the one which is laid, which is Jesus Christ."[2] So permit me to ask, "What was the testimony?" The testimony that was to

---

[1] Matthew 16:18
[2] 1 Corinthians 3:11

stand as the foundation for the church is that Jesus is both Son of Man and Son of God. The point I wish to make is this: the fundamental building block and chief cornerstone of the church must be the testimony and the witness of the Word of God becoming flesh.

Restating the above, Peter's confession included two points. First, Peter understood that Jesus was the Christ, the anointed one, spoken of by the prophets as the Messiah. Secondly, and relevant to our theme, Peter realized that the church of Jesus Christ is founded upon the testimony of the natural and the spiritual sonship of Jesus. Recognizing and confessing that the Son of Man and the Son of God are embodied in the person of Jesus Christ are essential elements when we speak of the church. Consequently, I contend that in some manner all believers should reflect that they are sons of God by fleshing it out as sons of men. That is to say, if we are to follow the example of Jesus, we must live out our sonship in human bodies with human fathers.

Furthermore, Jesus said, "...and the gates of Hades shall not overpower it."[1] In the Bible, gates symbolize authority. No natural gate has ever attacked anyone. The promise here is that Satan and his outlaw band of demons will never overcome the church that is founded on the testimony that the Son of God is the Son of Man. This is confirmed in Jesus' words when He said, "All authority has been given to Me in heaven and on earth."[2] Heaven, you see, is the spiritual realm, and earth is the natural realm. Jesus lived and triumphed in both of these arenas as the Son of Man and the Son of God.

Then Jesus continues, "I will give you (Peter) the keys of

---

[1] Matthew 16:18b
[2] Matthew 28:18

the kingdom of heaven..."[1] Notice, Jesus gave Peter the keys of the Kingdom, not the keys of the church. Jesus said, "*I* will build My church."[2] We often see, even among Evangelical Christians, that we have preached the gospel of the church in an effort to advance the kingdom of God. However, from this passage we can see clearly that we are to preach the gospel of the Kingdom and allow Christ to build His Church. Apparently, due to Peter's understanding of the Son-of-God/Son-of-man paradigm, he was given the keys to open the door to the kingdom of heaven. I conclude from this that those who build the church on the testimony of this paradigm are the ones who should have the keys to the Kingdom.

Furthermore, we are amiss when we speak of the Kingdom or of the church if we disregard the issue of sonship. And to the ones who have the keys Jesus gave this authority: "Whatever you shall bind on earth shall be bound in heaven, and whatever you shall loose on earth shall be loosed in heaven."[3] When Peter made his confession that Jesus was the Christ, the Son of the Living God, Jesus gave him the keys to the kingdom of heaven.[4] Again, Peter was given the keys to the Kingdom, not the keys to the church.

We continue to read, "Then He warned the disciples that they should tell no one that He was the Christ."[5] Remember His initial question: "Who do people say that the Son of Man is?"[6] The secret that the disciples were to keep was the revelation that Peter had received; that is, that the Word of God had become flesh and dwelt among us. Since Jesus is the

---

[1] Matthew 16:19a
[2] Matthew 16:18a
[3] Matthew 16:19b
[4] Matthew 16:19
[5] Matthew 16:20
[6] Matthew 16:13

archetype for all of us, it would be appropriate for us to conclude that our responsibility is to live out our lives in the dual role of being sons of God, and manifesting it as human sons to human fathers. Many Christians would make the claim that they are the sons of God; however, few wish to flesh this relationship out as sons of men. Later, we shall see in greater depth that Timothy's relationship with and service to Paul were his credentials for ministry, and were equated to his service to Christ Jesus.[1]

Finally, I find it very interesting and spiritually coincidental that after Peter's revelation, our Lord began to talk about going to Jerusalem to die. It is as if He had to wait until someone understood that sonship must be more than a concept; it needs to be embodied and worked out in a time-space world. So, in the remaining passages of Matthew 16 we see that Jesus now sets His face toward His pending crucifixion.

Following the conversation above, we read in John 17 Jesus' great intercessory prayer. "Father, the hour has come; glorify Your Son, that the Son may glorify Thee, even as You gave Him authority over all mankind, that to all whom You have given Him, He may give eternal life. And this is eternal life, that they may know Thee, the only true God, and Jesus Christ whom You have sent. I glorified Thee on the earth, having accomplished the work which You have given Me to do. And now, glorify You Me together with Yourself, Father, with the glory which I had with Thee before the world was. I manifested Your name to the men whom You gave Me out of the world; Yours they were, and You gave them to Me, and they have kept Your word."[2]

---

5 Philippians 2:19-22
2 John 17:1-6

Of particular interest to us in Jesus' great intercessory prayer is the emphasis that Jesus puts upon the word "name": He mentions it four times. Perhaps the most significant verse for our purposes reads, "I glorified You on the earth, having accomplished the work which You have given Me to do. I have manifested Your name to the men whom You gave Me out of the world."[1] Several things stand out to me in this passage of Scripture. First, I suppose it would be beneficial for us to understand what Jesus meant when He said, "I have glorified you on the earth." God's glory is the manifestation or materialization of His divine attributes and perfection. God's glory relates to his holiness. It is His holiness coming into a visible expression. The primary concern of Jesus was not His own glory. Jesus sought to glorify His Father on the earth. Maybe I can express it better in this way. God chose the name "Father," and desired to be known as such. That name, through casual, slipshod or even vile use, has been tarnished and stained on the earth. God's glory relates to His reputation. Jesus viewed glorifying His Father as His highest accomplishment. The manner in which Jesus glorified His Father was by manifesting His name to the men that God gave Him. Therefore, we are to pray, "Hallowed (sacred, sanctified, consecrated, or holy) be your name."[2] *Father* is the name that Jesus manifested and glorified. His disciples would be the men God gave Him out of the world.

From the text taken from John 17:1-6, we can glean some of the following conclusions:

Verse 1: The glory that the Son receives is given back to the Father. Jesus' great concern was His Father's reputation. It has been said that God is most honored when honorable

---

[1] John 17:4 & 6
[2] Matthew 6:9

men honor God.

Verse 2: Jesus was given authority over all mankind, because of a Father-Son relationship. His authority was a direct consequence of His relation.

Verse 3: Eternal life only comes through knowing the Father through the sonship that Jesus demonstrated.

Verse 3: Jesus knew the purpose for which His Father sent Him; so when his work was accomplished, He began to speak of His coming crucifixion and the manner by which He would depart from this earth.

Verse 4: Jesus glorified the Father by accomplishing the work that He was given. Take note here that this is before the crucifixion.

Verse 5: Jesus qualified Himself as the Son of God prior to creation, and as the Son of Man in creation. That is to say, "The artist stepped into the painting."

Verse 6: This is the linchpin of that which is stated above and that which will follow. The glory that Jesus was to receive was because He had accomplished the work His Father sent Him to do. The work that His Father sent Him to do was this, "I have manifested Your name (Father) to those whom you gave to me out of the world."

Verse 6: And they have kept the Father's word. In other words, Jesus reproduced His life in His disciples, and His life was walking as a son.

Therefore, will we allow Jesus to be visibly seen in each of us as sons?

There is an old saying that you and I may be the only Bible some people will ever read.

For several years now, as a consequence of studying this passage, I have prayed that I would recognize, welcome and honor those whom God has sent to me. What's more, I have prayed that I might make His Fatherhood known to them by behaving as a son.

9
What's in a Name?

*T*he noted British playwright William Shakespeare authored the tragic play "Romeo and Juliet." In it he wrote, "What's in a name? That which we call a rose by any other name would be as sweet." At the cost of the lives of these two lovers, the Capulets and the Montagues discover that names make a difference. In the Bible, names often carried a great deal of significance. Names—in English grammar we use the word *nouns*—are what we use to identify people, places and/or things. One of the first tasks given to Adam was to assign names to the things that God had created. Until recently, nearly every family in history derived its surname from the father. In the following passage, Paul taught that every family on earth derives its name from fatherhood. "For this reason, I bow my knees before the Father (Pater), from whom every family (Patria) in heaven and on earth derives its name."[1] The original Greek may help us to have a better understanding of what Paul has written. The Greek word for father is **Pater**. The word for family or household in Greek is **Patria**. *Patria* is taken from the word *Pater*. In other words, the root that gives us the word *family* derives from the word *father*. A better translation for *family*, used in this passage, is fatherhood. One might draw the

---

[1] Ephesians 3:14-15

conclusion from Paul's use of these words in the above passage: "No father, no family."

According to Derek Prince, in Old Testament Hebraic culture there was no such thing as a name without a meaning. A person's name gave us a clue to his identity. Historically, one's name would refer to his ancestry, his geographic residence or his vocation. In other words, his name was not simply a noun; it could also function somewhat as a verb or an adjective. As a verb, it would show an action or state of being. As an adjective, it would describe a person, place or thing.

Frequently, too, a male child's surname simply meant the "son of his father." For instance, in the Old Covenant the Hebrew word *ben* means "son of." As Rachel, Jacob's wife, lay dying, she gave birth to a boy whom she called *Benoni*, literally "son of my sorrow." However, Jacob renamed him Benjamin, which translates "son of my right hand." In the New Covenant, the word *bar* before a name means "son of." Therefore, the name Bartimaeus signifies that he was the son of Timaeus (Timothy). Originally, Simon Peter's name was Simon Bar-Jonas, Jonas meaning John. Therefore, he was called Simon the son of John. In English, we would have called him Simon, John's son or, more likely, Simon Johnson. In like manner, Jesus was called the Son of David. Perhaps in English we would have shortened this from David's son to Davidson. A more contemporary and personal example comes from my surname. The prefix "Mc" is a Gaelic form of "son of." Therefore, the name McNally simply means the son of Nally. Unfortunately for me, my first name James is the English derivative of Jacob. Jacob means cheater, liar or supplanter. Like you, I did not have the privilege of selecting my own name. Not being overly fond of the name James (Cheater), I have preferred that people call me Jim.

In times past, surnames could also originate from the father's vocation. Common names found among English speaking people include Miller (one who ground grain), Carpenter (one who works with wood) and Fisher (rather obvious). My wife Kathy's maiden name was Smith (one who works with metals). Her mother had the maiden name Cooper (one who made barrels).

Now let us imagine God, who is the creator and sustainer of the entire universe, selecting a name for Himself. His name would not just be a title and function but a depiction and representation of His own person. Consider the infinite number of possibilities available to him: Captain of Creation; Chairman of the Trinity; Supreme Exalted Ruler; Grand Imperial Majesty; or Chief Executive Officer of the Universe, just to propose a few. Apparently, none of these options struck God's fancy. He wanted a name that would best reflect not only His title but also His function. At some instance in eternity, God said, "I think I'll call Myself Father." God chose to be called Father. From then and forever, that name would be "hallowed" (consecrated, set apart). Using the Law of First Mention, we find that the first word in the Hebrew dictionary is *ab*, which in English translates as father. It also can mean source, originator or generator. I doubt that this is a coincidence.

When referring to the Lord's Prayer, many people quote the following: "Our Father who art in heaven, Hallowed be Your name. Your kingdom come. Your will be done, on earth as it is in heaven. Give us this day our daily bread. And forgive us our debts, as we also have forgiven our debtors. And do not lead us into temptation, but deliver us from evil. For Yours are the kingdom, and the power, and the glory, forever.

Amen."[1] However, I do not see this as the Lord's Prayer, but rather as the Disciples's Prayer, since Jesus was responding to their request that He teach them to pray. Furthermore, Jesus would never need to pray, "Forgive Me My sins or debts!" Therefore, I believe it to be more accurate to refer to Jesus' prayer in John 17 as the Lord's Prayer.

Therefore, one of the most significant revelations of the Bible is that God is a Father and He desires to reveal Himself as such to all humanity. What's more, Jesus told the disciples that when they prayed they were to address God as their Father. Remember that Old Covenant Jewish custom held that the name of God was so revered that the scribes refused to write it down. Even today, I know Messianic Jews who write the word God as "G-D" to avoid spelling it out. One of the Ten Commandments given to Moses was a caution against the careless use of the name of God.[2] God's name was not to be used in some casual or irreverent manner. The fact that Jesus spoke of God as His Father and encouraged His disciples to do the same so enraged the religious leaders of His day that they plotted to kill Him for doing so.[3] In light of this, we can only imagine the shock and horror of the Jewish contemporaries of Jesus, if they had heard Him pray in the Garden of Gethsemane. It was there that He addressed God, not in the formal way as "Father," but rather in the familiar manner in which a child might speak; Jesus calls Him "Abba." The name *Abba* can be loosely translated as *Daddy* or *Papa*.[4] The apostle Paul, as well, would seem to trample upon this sacred ground.[5] He suggests that even you and I might

---

[1] Matthew 6:9-13
[2] Exodus 20:7
[3] John 5:18; John 10:36-39
[4] Mark 14:36
[5] Roman 8:15; Galatians 4:6-7

address God in a more intimate and personal way, as Abba (Daddy). Certainly, to the religious leaders of the day, this would have been considered outright blasphemy. I can remember myself cringing the first time I heard someone refer to our heavenly Father as "Daddy God." An interesting point to mention here is that slaves were forbidden to use the name Abba when speaking to or referring to their masters.

Prior to the beginning, before God was a creator, He was a father. God is not just a father; He is _the Father_. Since God chose the name Father not only to be His title but also His function, we can conclude that there is no higher title, calling or function for men on earth than to be a father. Derek Prince often taught, _"Success in politics, business, athletics or arts will never make up for failure as a father."_ Failure as a father is failure at the highest level. So now, we will look at some of the possible roles and responsibilities of a father.

As mentioned earlier, fatherhood is more than a title or an office; it is also a function. The purpose of a father was to represent God to his family. In fact, a father's authority ultimately derives from and is limited to his representation of God the Father. The manner in which we as fathers are to represent God's Fatherhood is to serve as the priest, the prophet and the king (or ruler) of our home. As the priest of the home, a father is to represent his family before God. The event of the Passover will serve as an illustration for this. The fathers held the exclusive responsibility to select a lamb for each house, to kill the lamb and to spread the blood on the doorposts of the house.[1] In this example, the father as the priest held the power to save his family from the destroying angel. He could not delegate this responsibility to another member of the family. As a prophet, the father was to

---

[1] Exodus 12:3-7

represent God to his family. As mentioned many times in this book, the father in the home is the representative of God. He is to set an example for his children through his words, attitude and conduct.[1] Finally, as the king of his home, the father is to rule by leading his family. Reiterating upon our theme that the pathway to fatherhood is by modeling sonship, his leadership is by way of example. Thus, a father serves by leading and he leads by serving.

Before we continue, I must mention a vital quality that every genuine father possesses. Every father should desire that his children be more successful than he is. Any man who does not desire that his children surpass him should not bear the name "father." As is true in every situation, Jesus and His Father set the example for us. Along this line Jesus said, "For the Father loves the Son, and shows Him all things that He Himself is doing; and greater works than these will He show Him, that you may marvel."[2] Later Jesus said to His disciples, "Truly, I say to you, he who believes in Me, the works that I do shall he do also; and greater works than these shall he do; because I go to the Father."[3] Simply analyzing these two passages makes it clear that the Father wanted Jesus to do "great works." In like manner, Jesus desired for us to excel and do even "greater works than these."

---

[1] Deuteronomy 6:4-9
[2] John 5:20
[3] John 14:12

10

A Kingdom of Fathers and Sons

So what does our understanding of the Kingdom of God have to do with fatherhood and sonship? It has everything to do with sonship, because kingdoms are perpetuated through sons. One distinguishing feature of a kingdom or a monarchy is nepotism. The definition of *nepotism* is "favoritism shown to relatives or bestowal of patronage by reason of relationship rather than merit." In a kingdom (or monarchy), rulership is passed down through hereditary lines. Normally, the firstborn son of the king would be in line to be the next monarch. For this reason, genealogy played a significant role in who was to rule. According to the genealogical record in Matthew's gospel, Joseph, the foster father of Jesus, was of the royal line of David. With this in mind, I suggest that, had it not been for the sin of Jeconiah, Joseph, the foster father of Jesus, might have been in line to become the king of Israel.[1]

Jesus received the Kingdom from His Father. He inherited the Kingdom, because He was the only Son. One might call this an act of nepotism. Luke recorded that Mary asked Jesus why He had stayed behind after the Passover in Jerusalem. Jesus' response gives us insight into His life's purpose. Clearly, Jesus understood that the Kingdom was His

---

[1] Jeremiah 22:28-30; Matthew 1:11

Father's business.[1] Jesus assumed that Joseph and Mary would understand His priorities. As a son, Jesus considered His Father's business His primary concern. God's vocation is running His kingdom. Jesus was and is the co-ruler of that kingdom.[2] In our search for relevance, purpose and destiny, the Kingdom message must be paramount. Jesus said, "Seek ye first the kingdom of God..."[3] First means first. Just as the relationship between Father and Son forms the DNA of all that exists, so also does this relationship set the pattern for how it is to be governed. Side by side with His Son on the throne of heaven sits the Father, ruling the visible and invisible cosmos.

Historically, it may be argued that religion has created far more problems than it has solved. In fact, religious zealots continue to perpetrate one of the greatest threats facing society today. So how can the Christian gospel be a part of the solution, instead of a part of the problem? Essentially, the message of the New Covenant is not so much about a religion as it is about a governmental order. The word *gospel* is simply defined as good news. Many of us have heard the "good news of salvation," the "good news of the church," or the good news of some particular aspect of God's grace, such as healing or prosperity. When we speak of the gospel of the kingdom of God, we are talking about the good news of God's governmental order that exists in heaven, extending into the earth. Another way to refer to the gospel of the kingdom of God is to call it "the good news of the monarchy of Jesus Christ, who is the absolute monarch." *Monarch* is formed from the prefix *mono*, meaning *one*, and *arch*, meaning

---

[1] Luke 2:49 (KJV)
[2] John 5:36
[3] Matthew 6:33

eminent; that is, one who is distinguished as being above all others, whether by birth, high station, merit, talent or virtue. While the individual, the family, and the church are very important themes of the Bible, we best understand each of these in the context of God's kingdom.

In the Old Covenant, the prophet Daniel spoke of a succession of worldly kingdoms destined to be destroyed by a kingdom set in place by God.[1] This kingdom, which will last forever, will be ruled by the Son of Man.[2] These passages reveal God's intention that Israel was to be governed by laws that were derived directly from heaven. When the people of Israel demanded a king like every other nation, Samuel rebuked them for desiring any king but God Himself.[3] The monarchies of Israel were at best a compromise, allowing the reigning monarch to pass for God's representative on the earth. Samuel warned the people that earthly kings would take from them. Notice that the first two things these monarchs would take for themselves were "their sons and daughters."[4] That is exactly what King Saul began to do, even taking David from the house of Jesse his father. With the majority of the kings of both Judah and Israel, their reigns were dismal and disastrous failures. Little wonder that the Old Covenant saints cried out that God would take back for Himself His great power and reign. The prophets predicted the coming of a ruler who would overcome all earthly rulers. Messianic hopes and language fueled the lives of these saints.

The first of the New Covenant prophets broke onto the scene in the person of John the Baptist. His message reiterated this Messianic hope: "Repent, for the kingdom of

---

[1] Daniel 2:44
[2] Daniel 7:13-14
[3] 1 Samuel 8:5-7
[4] 1 Samuel 8:11&13

heaven is at hand."[1] The commencement of Jesus' ministry is described in these words, "And Jesus went about in all Galilee, teaching in their synagogues, and preaching the gospel of the kingdom..."[2] Note that the gospels use the terms "kingdom of heaven" and "kingdom of God" interchangeably. Luke recorded, "...soon afterwards, He went about through cities and villages, preaching and bringing the good news of the kingdom of God, and with Him were the twelve."[3] When the twelve were sent forth, their mission is given in these words, "And He sent them forth to preach the kingdom of God..."[4] The parables of Jesus, which formed a large and dominant portion of His teaching, are collectively referred to as "the mysteries of the kingdom of heaven."[5] In fact, many of these parables commence with the phrase, "The kingdom of heaven [or kingdom of God] is like..."[6] The gospel preached by John the Baptist, Jesus, Peter and Paul is the gospel of the monarchial order of God. Therefore, the gospel of the New Covenant is as much a governmental message as it is a religious message.

Concerning our salvation Paul wrote, "For He delivered us from the domain of darkness, and transferred us to the kingdom of His beloved Son, in whom we have redemption, the forgiveness of sins."[7] He continues, "For by Him all things were created, both in the heavens and on earth, visible and invisible, whether thrones or dominions or rulers or authorities, all things have been created by Him and for

---

[1] Matthew 3:2
[2] Matthew 4:23
[3] Luke 8:1
[4] Luke 9:2
[5] Matthew 13:11
[6] Matthew 13:31-52; 20:1
[7] Colossians 1:13-14

Him."[1] Words in these passages such as *domain* and *dominions, kingdoms* and *thrones, rulers* and *authorities* are terms that are more governmental than they are religious. In addition, these verses use the analogy of citizenship not membership. The gospel message is not primarily about the birth of a religious leader named Jesus, but rather of a King and His kingdom. In truth, reducing Christianity to being simply another religion makes it less potent and relevant. It allows Christianity to be marginalized and therefore compared to such religions as Islam, Buddhism, and Hinduism, which is a travesty of the highest order.

The gospel of the kingdom of God is about a king— actually The King—who came to earth to redeem, reclaim, restore and extend His domain, His legitimate authority to rule and reign over His creation. God's answer to the chaos of the world system was not to spread a religion but to reorder the governmental structure that rules it. **The focus of the gospel was not primarily to get us to heaven when we die, but rather to get heaven into us while we live.** Jesus taught His disciples to pray, "Your kingdom come on earth!"[2]

A major difficulty in the United States is that our nation was founded in outright hostility toward kingdom government. Even if we believe that the republican (*i.e.*, representative democracy) form of government is the best of earthly choices, we must not consider it the Biblical model. In fact, to intermingle or replace Kingdom understanding with classical Hellenistic thinking can cause us to do great violence to the Scriptures. The Greek word *demo* means people. It is the root word for *demographics*, as well as *democracy*. The Greek word *crasis* means rule. Democratic

---

[1] Colossians 1:16
[2] Matthew 6:9-10; Luke 11:2

government, the rule of the people, is rooted in Hellenistic philosophy. Theocracy or Christocracy, the rulership of God, is the Biblical model. To be certain, earthly kingdoms fail miserably in any effort to use them as analogies for God's kingdom. However, if Israel had been a democracy, the popular vote in the wilderness campaign would have been several million against three to go back to Egypt.

As incredible as it might seem, our God is our Father, and our Father is our King. Amazingly, our King has chosen to rule through delegated authority. Let us once again apply the law of first mention. "God said, 'Let Us make man in Our image, according to Our likeness; and let them rule over the fish of the sea, over the birds of the sky, over the cattle, over all the earth, and over every creeping thing that creeps on the earth.' And God created man in His own image, in the image of God He created him; male and female He created them. And God blessed them; and God said to them, 'Be fruitful and multiply, and fill the earth, and subdue it; and rule over the fish of the sea, over the birds of the sky, over every living thing that moves on the earth.' "[1] It is important to note that the name *Adam* can be translated as *man, humanity* or *mankind*. We have here the first mention of humankind (male and female). God created humanity in His image and likeness, and then He blessed _them,_ and told _them_ to "...be fruitful and multiply." This is an obvious reference to male and female reproduction. Then God said, "Let them rule..."[2] He did not say, "Let him rule." Those He told to reproduce, He also told to rule. Neither did He say, "Let Us rule" but "Let them rule." This passage alone has tremendous ramifications and implications. Since God said, "Let them rule...," God

---

[1] Genesis 1:26-28
[2] Genesis 1:26

designated and delegated the rule of earth to humankind, flesh and blood. This we know as the "dominion mandate." The purpose and destiny of humanity was to rule over the visible world that God had created. The Psalmist writes, "The heavens are the heavens of the Lord; But the earth He has given to the sons of men."[1]

In the above passages from Genesis God lists four things over which man is to rule: 1) the fish, 2) the birds, 3) the cattle or beasts and 4) the creeping things. Notice here that there is no reference to humanity subduing and ruling over humanity. Furthermore, God repeats this dominion mandate to Noah after the flood. "And God blessed Noah and his sons and said to them, 'Be fruitful and multiply, and fill the earth. And the fear of you and the terror of you shall be on every beast of the earth and on every bird of the sky; with everything that creeps on the ground, and all the fish of the sea, into your hand they are given.' "[2] The four identical biological groups are mentioned to Noah as they were to Adam.

God chose to rule the earth using flesh and blood, and Adam (mankind) was His delegated ruler. When Adam sinned, he did not lose a religion; he lost his legal right to represent God's government on the earth. Adam had committed high treason, punishable by death. Since God had committed rulership of the earth to flesh and blood, He needed a Second Adam. "And the Word became flesh, and dwelt among us, and we beheld His glory, glory as of the only begotten from the Father, full of grace and truth."[3] He who eternally is the Son of God became the Son of Man. What was

---

[1] Psalm 115:16
[2] Genesis 9:1
[3] John 1:14-15

lost by flesh and blood would be redeemed by flesh and blood.

More than seven hundred years before the birth of Christ, Isaiah wrote, "For a child will be born to us, a son will be given to us; And the government will rest on His shoulders; And His name will be called Wonderful Counselor, Mighty God, Everlasting Father, Prince of Peace. There will be no end to the increase of His government or of peace, On the throne of David and over his kingdom..."[1] Reiterating and reinforcing our theme that the gospel is primarily a message regarding governmental reorder, the verses above mention *government* twice, *prince* once, *throne* once, and *kingdom* twice. These are governmental words, not religious words.

---

[1] Isaiah 9:6-7

11

Kingdom Authority

*T*he gospel preached in the New Covenant is a governmental message. It is about the reign of a King and His kingdom. One cannot speak of governments, whether they are a democracy, a republic, a dictatorship or a kingdom, without addressing the issue of authority. In a republic or a democracy, ultimate authority lies with the people. The Constitution of the United States uses the separation of powers to protect the people from authoritarianism. Ideally, the congress was to make the laws, the courts were to judge or interpret the laws, and the executive branch, the president, was to enforce the laws. However, in a kingdom ultimate authority rests exclusively with the king. "For the Lord is our judge, the Lord is our lawgiver, the Lord is our king; He will save us."[1] As citizens of the Kingdom, we are called to understand and embrace Kingdom authority. Jesus has been given all authority.[2] As I have mentioned, first means first; then too, all means all. Yet, He has chosen to rule through delegated authority. He has all authority, and he can delegate it to whomever He chooses.

Perhaps the single greatest effect of being a citizen of the kingdom of God is the loss of our autonomy. We may define

---

[1] Isaiah 33:22
[2] Matthew 28:18

autonomy as the right, the ability and the capacity to make personal independent moral decisions and then to act upon them. The Bible teaches that God alone is autonomous, sovereign, self-sufficient and independent. He created everything, He owns everything and He rules over everything. He answers to no one, nor is He accountable to anyone, except within the Trinity itself. God has reserved for Himself the authority to have the final say on what is right and wrong, what is good and evil, what is holy, what is defiled, and what is acceptable and unacceptable. Man's original sin was to challenge the legitimate right of God to place restrictions upon our liberty. Satan deviously suggested to Eve that if she would disobey a clear command of God, she would thereby become like Him, determining good and evil, and thus becoming autonomous. The following may help us see where this devious obsession for autonomy leads us.

The Old Covenant is filled with detailed instructions from the Lord. For example, King David wanted the Ark moved from the house of Abinadab to the Temple in Jerusalem. In clear violation of God's instructions, the priests placed the Ark on a cart instead of carrying it on poles.[1] When the cart tottered and tipped, Uzzah took hold of it to steady it. God had warned Aaron that if anyone touched the Ark, he would die. God struck and killed Uzzah. We hear people rationalize, "God is not concerned with the details, but only with the spirit in which it is done." Tell that to Uzzah! Still, it seems today, the greater the details, the more apt we are to modify the instructions.

Paradoxically, for the most part the New Covenant does not give as many detailed instructions. For example, we find few specifics regarding the order of a church service, the

---

[1] Numbers 4:1-15

exact method of baptism or the manner in which we should serve the Lord's Supper. We have the freedom to improvise. However, rather than enjoy this liberty, we use it as occasion to divide and fragment. When God gives us details, we want freedom; but when He gives us freedom to improvise, we want to impose restrictions. The essence of this is our diabolical lust for autonomy. In simple terms, we humans say, "Nobody can tell me what to do."

Jesus Christ is not only the King of heaven; He is the King of earth, not simply in the past or in the future, but today. He received that authority from His Father. Still, Jesus is also under authority. In His own ministry, Jesus primarily focused upward. His Father was the One who had sent Him. He positioned and postured Himself under and toward His Father. Jesus stated clearly that He did nothing of His own initiative.[1] He always took his prompts and cues from His Father. He spoke what He heard his Father speak, and He did what He saw his Father do. Jesus understood that His authority was related to His mission. Because of this, let us look at some of the ramifications related to the authority of Jesus.

The first principle: whenever and wherever we encounter God, we will meet His authority. Humble submission is the only appropriate attitude and the sole sane and legitimate response to encountering God. The Greek word for *to submit one's self* (also, *to be in obedience*) is *hupotasso,* which translates as "to arrange under." It is primarily a military term. Let me distinguish between submission and obedience. Submission is an attitude or posture of heart, while obedience is an action. It is possible for one to obey without being submitted. What's more, one

---

[1] John 8:28

can be submitted, and not obey. Certainly, if one is asked by an authority to do that which is unethical, illegal, immoral or unscriptural, that person should humbly decline to do so.

A second principle to consider is that God has chosen to rule through delegated authority. God chose Paul to be the apostle to the Gentiles. His task included helping the gentile society, heavily influenced by Hellenistic philosophy, to restructure its thinking from democracy to a Kingdom mentality. To do this Paul taught Kingdom order in the marriage, the family and the workplace. In his letter to the Ephesians, Paul addressed the issue of authority in relationships at every level. His desire was for people to have a functional understanding of Kingdom authority. Paul gave us insight into where we as people under authority should look to take our cues. Since God rules through delegated authority, our submission to delegated authority is equivalent to our submission to God. I contend that whenever there are two or more people together, one of them is in authority; *e.g.*, by age, by maturity, by rank, by anointing or by consent. There is always a first among equals. God is a God of order, of rank and therefore of authority. Having this in mind there are at least four arenas where we are regularly apt to encounter God's delegated authority.

First, God's authority is expressed in civil government. Paul wrote, "Let every person be in subjection to the governing authorities. For there is no authority except from God, and God establishes those which exist. Therefore he who resists authority has opposed the ordinance of God; and they who have opposed will receive condemnation upon themselves."[1] Peter added, "Submit yourselves for the Lord's sake to every human institution, whether to a king as the one

---

[1] Romans 13:1-2

in authority, or to governors as sent by him for the punishment of evildoers and the praise of those who do right."[1] However, what should our posture be if the civil officials are corrupt and unjust? Peter wrote, "Servants, be submissive to your masters with all respect, not only to those who are good and gentle, but also to those who are unreasonable. For this finds favor, if for the sake of conscience toward God a man bears up under sorrows when suffering unjustly."[2] The Greek word for *unreasonable* is *skolios*, meaning crooked, from which we get the term *scoliosis*. Remember, however, submission is a posture of humility of heart.

Second, God's authority is present in the home. Since God has ordained family to be the building block for society, it is important that each family understands the rule of God in the home. Paul taught the following order for family life: "Wives, be subject to your own husbands, as to the Lord."[3] He then required that "Husbands, love your wives, just as Christ also loved the church and gave Himself up for her..."[4] To the children he wrote, "Children, obey your parents in the Lord, for this is right."[5] As I mentioned earlier, Christianity is rooted in Judaism. The Judaic model is patriarchal, which means the father is to lead the family. Referring to this, I quoted Paul regarding the centricity of fathers in families. "For this reason, I bow my knees before the Father, from whom every family in heaven and on earth derives its name..."[6] It was assumed that as the father went the family

---

[1] 1 Peter 2:13-14
[2] 1 Peter 2:18-19
[3] Ephesians 5:22; Colossians 3:18
[4] Ephesians 5:25; Colossians 3:19
[5] Ephesians 6:1; Colossians 3:20
[6] Ephesians 3:14-15

would go also. In fact, the original promise made to Abram in Genesis was not simply to bless individuals, but rather to "bless all the families of the earth."[1] Joshua spoke for his family when he said, "... as for me and my house (or family), we will serve the Lord."[2] Historically, the responsibility of the father to lead the family was recognized, understood and generally accepted. When the Philippian jailer asked what he must do to be saved, Paul and Silas said, "Believe in the Lord Jesus, and you shall be saved, you and your household."[3] The word *household* is translated from the Greek word *oikus*, which also means *family*.

   Third, God's authority is found in the workplace. Let me mention a few facts about the importance of the workplace in the Bible. The Hebrew word for work is *avodah*, which is the root word for *work, worship* and *worth*. This Hebrew word is mentioned more than 800 times in the Bible, more often than all the words used to express worship, music, praise and singing combined. Of the 132 public appearances of Jesus mentioned in the New Covenant, 122 were in the market-place. Of the 52 parables told by Jesus, 45 referred to business or work. Of the 40 divine interventions in the book of Acts, 39 took place in the market arena. Not one of the twelve disciples called by Jesus was a religious leader. The Bible indicates that Jesus spent the first thirty years of His life as a carpenter. Paul wrote, "Slaves [employees], in all things obey those who are your masters [employers] on earth, not with external service, as those who merely please men, but with sincerity of heart, fearing the Lord. Whatever you do, do your work heartily, as for the Lord rather than for men; knowing

---

[1] Genesis 12:3
[2] Joshua 24:15
[3] Acts 16:31

that from the Lord, you will receive the reward of the inheritance. It is the Lord Christ whom you serve. For he who does wrong will receive the consequences of the wrong which he has done, and that without partiality."[1] Since God ordained work even before the fall, He wants His kingdom to be reflected in the workplace.

Fourth (but not listed by importance) we meet God's authority in the Church. Spiritual authority is one of the ultimate issues of the universe. "Jesus Christ is Lord" is a statement regarding spiritual authority. Although the Church is not the Kingdom, it contains one of the most important analogies to God's rulership on the earth. Jesus Himself linked the understanding of authority with faith. When Jesus offered to come and heal the centurion's servant, the centurion said it was not necessary for Him to come, "...but just say the word."[2] The centurion understood how authority functioned. Jesus heard this and was amazed. It is extremely important to note that Jesus equated the centurion's understanding of authority with great faith.[3] Our understanding of authority, and our attitude toward it, is an essential element of our desire and ability to walk by faith.

---

[1] Colossians 3:22-25; Ephesians 6:5 and 9
[2] Matthew 8:8
[3] Matthew 8:5-10

12

Spiritual Authority vs. Authoritarianism

A prerequisite to addressing the subject of sonship and fatherhood is that we come face to face with the issue of authority. As we explore the realm of spiritual authority, we benefit greatly if we can identify and avoid certain pitfalls. I am sure that you will agree that there is a distinct difference between spiritual authority and an authoritarian spirit. **To avoid authoritarianism in any given situation, we will be forced to undergo a critical and massive paradigm shift.** Failure to make this shift will nearly always bring about abuse. To help you to understand what I mean by this paradigm shift, let us take a fresh look at the conversation between Jesus and the Centurion mentioned earlier and recorded by both Matthew and Luke. Since both of these are nearly identical in content, for our purpose, we will simply refer to Matthew's account.

"And when He had entered Capernaum, a centurion came to Him, entreating Him, and saying, 'Lord, my servant is lying paralyzed at home, suffering great pain.' And He said to him, 'I will come and heal him.' But the centurion answered and said, 'Lord, I am not worthy for You to come under my roof, but just say the word, and my servant will be healed. For I, too, am a man under authority, with soldiers under me; and I say to this one, 'Go!' and he goes, and to another, 'Come!'

and he comes, and to my slave, 'Do this!' and he does it.' Now when Jesus heard this, He marveled, and said to those who were following, 'Truly I say to you, I have not found such great faith with anyone in Israel.' "[1]

Essentially, the emphasis of true spiritual authority must be upward, not downward. That is to say, our primary focus of attention must be upon who is over us, as opposed to whom we are over. Take careful note of the Centurion's statement. "I, too, am a man under authority." And this is what qualified him to exercise authority over others. When speaking about submission to spiritual authority, I try always to warn my listener to be cautious about coming under the authority of someone who is himself unwilling to come under authority.

Secondly, authentic spiritual authority is rarely imposed. It is most effective only when it is recognized and submitted to voluntarily. Wherever true spiritual authority exists, it functions most justly and effectively by being dominant without being domineering. I contend that those of us in leadership should never be overly preoccupied with how our followers view us. Spiritual leaders should never demand such things as admiration, honor, respect and service. For us to insist on these attitudes from others are at best futile and at worst dangerous. A more effective approach is for each of us to make certain that we guard our own hearts and properly posture ourselves toward the one God has sent and set over us. The life of our Lord Jesus Christ best illustrates this concept. When we conduct ourselves in this manner, we may say, "If you desire to know how a son should relate to his father, watch me."

Unfortunately, when I ask religious leaders about their

---

[1] Matthew 8:5 - 10

ministry, they nearly always refer to whom or for what they give oversight, never mentioning to whom they are accountable. It is expressed like this: I am over the nursery, over the worship team or I have a congregation of so many, whatever the number. Experience has shown me that many in the church—including pastors and leaders—do not want and/or choose to submit to authority because they fear its abuses. Obviously, they trust themselves not to abuse power more than they trust any others. In such a scenario, a leader lacks accountability and is immune to correction, modification or adjustment.

Therefore, what can we say or do about this fear of abuse? First, let us concur that authority in any realm carries with it the susceptibility and even the propensity for abuse and misuse. It would be ridiculous to suggest that in the home, in the church and in society, there have not been abuses of authority. Whether this abuse or misuse of authority comes from fathers, church leaders, police officers or presidents, the effects are often devastating and long-lasting. On the other hand, when people refuse to submit to authority, there can be a second and much more surreptitious reason.

Ironically, one of the major sources for the exploitive misuse of authority comes from those in leadership who refuse to be under authority. This is probably no more prevalent than in the relationship found in the home, especially between fathers and children. Rarely have I known men who would allow someone to speak to them in the manner that they speak to their children.

I propose as well that there are some who fear the abuse of authority because they are subconsciously aware of how they would use authority, if authority were granted them. In fact, it has been my experience that the vast majority of those who abuse authority are extremely insecure. Micromanagement of insecure fathers and leaders arises out of the need to control all variables, which is a breeding ground for authoritarianism.

Earlier I wrote that, unlike nearly all earthly kingdoms, the kingdom of God allows tremendous freedom. God in His great generosity and love gives us almost boundless resources and opportunities. The trouble begins with the word "almost." God does set parameters. **The manner in which God demonstrates His ownership, and consequently His rulership, is to set aside or designate a portion of something for Himself.** Using the Law of Pattern, let us look at this more closely. Remember, earlier in this book I said that God delegated authority to mankind to rule over the fish, the birds, the cattle and the creeping things, and I suggested that God reserved for Himself the right to rule over mankind. Now let me suggest that God created the Garden of Eden and said to Adam, "You are free to eat from all the trees except one." That tree belonged to God, so they were to leave it alone. God said there are seven days in a week and you are free to use six of them. However, the seventh is His, so we are not to touch it. All the nations are there for us to enjoy, but Israel is His; therefore, do not touch it. The wealth of the world is ours, but the tithe is His; do not touch it. I trust that you see a definite pattern in this list.

Now allow me to illustrate what I shall refer to as the Adam and Eve Principle. I have four pockets in the jeans that I am wearing. You can have whatever you find in three of them, but this right front pocket is mine. Without knowing what is in the other three pockets, immediately, which pocket do you want? Those of you who have children may consider this question. How often did you say, "No! Don't touch that!" followed up shortly thereafter with, "What part of 'no' do you not understand?" It is probably ludicrous for me to say that numerous adults still have not grasped this simple command.

Summing up our look at spiritual authority, I believe that "God anoints whom He appoints."

The word "anti-Christ" [*anti* (against); *Christ*, (the anointed)] can be broken down to mean, "Against the anointing of God." The current trend in our Western culture to rebel against appointed authority is an ungodly trend. One will never understand sonship until he has dealt with the issue of authority.

Finally, we must be reminded that the freedom to use a thing should not be confused with ownership. Borrowing my car does not give you title to it. In the Kingdom, God owns everything. We are merely stewards of what he gives us to use. For example, the Biblical principle and goal of leadership is to serve. Essentially, one leads by serving, and one serves by leading. This is not double talk. **The question is not whether we choose to recognize, honor and serve, but rather whom we choose to recognize, honor and serve.**

13

Spiritual Fatherhood

I have been told, "I can't find spiritual fatherhood in my concordance, and I don't believe it is biblical." My response was simply in the form of a question: "Do you mean to tell me that Abraham was your 'natural father' and not your 'spiritual father'?" One of Christianity's fundamental tenets is that we are called the children of Abraham.[1] We are not the biological children of Abraham, but through faith in Christ we are his spiritual children. A question regarding calling a person a father has arisen from this passage: "And call no man your father upon the earth: for one is your Father, which is in heaven."[2] Careful exegesis of this passage reveals an entirely different understanding. Jesus was addressing religious leaders who loved title and position. They loved to be noticed; hence, they loved places of honor, chief seats in the synagogues and respectful greetings in the marketplace. The issue Jesus addressed here was the use of titles as a means for one to exalt oneself. Obviously, if our desire and purpose for titles is to exalt ourselves, it matters little what titles we use. As an example of this, numerous ministers today aspire to put the title of Apostle on their business card. It is neither my desire nor purpose to question the

---

[1] Galatians 3:7 & 29
[2] Matthew 23:9

authenticity of this designation. *However, I do believe it might be healthy to consider referring to the five-fold ministries found in Paul's letter to the Ephesians as verbs instead of nouns.* Moreover, it would do violence to the Scriptures to suggest that Jesus' purpose was to ban the use of the title of father, since one of the Ten Commandments require us to "honor your father."

Perhaps it has always been God's desire that each natural or biological father would be a spiritual father to his children, as well. This would always be the preferable scenario. Regrettably, one result of the entrance of sin into the world is the frequent failure of our natural fathers, especially as the spiritual leaders of the family. Thankfully, God has provided a plan for those whose fathers have failed. The failure of our natural fathers need not be perpetuated nor be used as a rationalization for our own behavior. God rebuked Israel for using this proverb: "The fathers eat the sour grapes, but the children's teeth are set on edge."[1]

In addition, I have heard a number of people say, "I don't follow any man; I only follow Jesus." This may sound spiritual, but the Bible does not support it. I believe that the majority of the people who say this have been hurt by their fathers, pastors, or some other authority figures. However, for others it is an effort to avoid being accountable to anyone. To be certain, our ultimate allegiance is not to men. We are to follow the Lord. Nevertheless, even after the ascension of Jesus Christ and Pentecost, God continued to send men. Referring back to the law of pattern let us consider the manner in which God has intervened in the affairs of man. As a rule throughout the Old and New Covenants when God got involved in human affairs, He did not send a syllabus, a

---

[1] Ezekiel 18:2

curriculum or a program. On rare occasions, He did send angels, but most often, the manner in which God intervenes is to select and send a man. In fact, even after He sent His only begotten Son, God did not cease from the pattern of sending men. The word *apostle* comes from the Greek word *apostellos* [*apo* (from); *stellos* (to send)]. It means, "one sent forth." Since so many people say, "God sent me!" one of the greatest challenges for believers is to identify, acknowledge and appreciate the person God genuinely sends.

Paul wrote, "God has sent apostles, prophets, evangelists, pastors, and teachers."[1] He refers to these men as gifts from God to the church, and Paul was one of these gifts of men sent by God. He boldly challenged men to imitate his faith and to follow him as he followed Christ. Paul did not say, "Don't look at me, just look at Jesus." He said, "Follow me and be imitators of me, as I follow Christ."[2] Furthermore, Paul urged the Thessalonians to "Recognize (to know in the King James Version) or (to respect, New International Version) those who are over you in the Lord," and "to esteem them very highly."[3] Paul also urged Titus, who was his spiritual son, to encourage young men to "walk as examples."[4] The writer of Hebrews exhorts us "to imitate, obey, and submit to men of faith."[5]

The manner in which we receive and honor the "man of God" can greatly affect God's ability to influence and affect our lives. Jesus said, "He who receives you receives Me, and he who receives Me receives Him who sent Me. He who receives a prophet in the name of a prophet shall receive a

---

[1] Ephesians 4:7-11
[2] 1 Corinthians 4:16; 1 Corinthians 11:1; Philippians 3:17
[3] 1 Thessalonians 5:12-13
[4] Titus 2:6-8
[5] Hebrews 6:11-12; Hebrews 13:17

prophet's reward; and he who receives a righteous man in the name of a righteous man shall receive a righteous man's reward. And whoever in the name of a disciple gives to one of these little ones even a cup of cold water to drink; truly I say to you he shall not lose his reward."[1] John quotes Jesus, saying, "Truly, truly, I say to you, he who receives whomever I send receives Me; and he who receives Me receives Him who sent Me."[2] Clearly, Jesus asserts that receiving the one whom God sends is directly related to receiving the Son and the Father. When God sends a "man of God," we must be careful to recognize, welcome and accept the messenger as well as the message. Today, as in every era, God continues to send men. Therefore, I maintain that when natural fathers fail, God's solution is to send men, not limited to but including "spiritual fathers." Clearly, these men are not the exact image of the Father, but God sends them. With the exception of Jesus, all those whom God sends are at best feeble and frail, perhaps even pathetic representations. However, God still uses them in an attempt to demonstrate His Fatherhood.

Another factor to consider—a consequence of the pollution of sin—is the introduction of wars, disease, death and disaster into the human arena. Still, for every problem confronting man God has a solution. For example, historically, men have been the primary source for soldiers, the results of which are widows and orphans. It would be difficult to miss the emphasis throughout the Bible of God's interest in caring for widows and orphans. James the brother of Jesus wrote, "Pure religion and undefiled before God and the Father is this, to visit the fatherless and widows in their affliction."[3] So

---

[1] Matthew 10:40-42
[2] John 13:20
[3] James 1:27

even when fathers fall short, desert or die prematurely, God still has a plan.

To illustrate this point, let us look at the example of Paul and Timothy. We are not told what happened to Timothy's natural father. We only know that a godly mother and grandmother raised him. Paul attributes the faith Timothy possessed to these two women. Nevertheless, God did not leave Timothy in this position. He sent Paul, who embraced Timothy as a spiritual son.[1] Although he was not their biological father, Paul referred to Timothy, Titus and Onesimus as his children instead of as his students or disciples.

The most obvious question from all that I have written above is this: _Must everyone have a spiritual father?_ Adam had no spiritual father. God Himself was his father. Abraham had no spiritual father, but he became a spiritual father to all who believe. Like Abraham, there are patriarchal men who have no spiritual father. Therefore, the answer to the question is "No, you are not required to have a spiritual father." It is a privilege, not an obligation, to have a spiritual father.

Dan Wolfe has been a spiritual father to me for nearly four decades. Dan's earthly father was a spiritual pioneer, but he died when Dan was only eight years old. From that point on, a godly mother raised him. From the age of eight, Dan had neither a natural nor a spiritual father. At age thirteen, Dan received Jesus Christ as his Lord and Savior. Later, as a teenager growing up in the city of Detroit, he asked God to be a Father to him. God answered this prayer. Like Abraham, Dan's natural father died during the journey. I refer to men like Dan, who have fathered others without having the advantage of being fathered themselves, as patriarchal. I want to point out here, that although Dan did not have a

---

[1] 2 Timothy 1:2-5; Philippians 2:21-22

spiritual father, he has always submitted to someone for pastoral oversight. For most of the 1970's Dan looked to Derek Prince for oversight. For the past two decades, Dan has looked to Charles Simpson. I would define both Derek and Charles as pastors and not spiritual fathers to Dan. The point I am making is that Dan is a man under authority.

More recently in my journey to walk as a son, God has brought Tony Fitzgerald into my life. Tony is the founder of Church of the Nations, a worldwide network of churches and ministries. Tony has been a real source of inspiration and encouragement to me. His teachings on the kingdom of God have greatly influenced my pursuit of understanding of this theme. The combined influence and example of spiritual fathers like Dan Wolfe, Tony Fitzgerald, Charles Simpson and John Beckett have played a major role in forming all that I am writing. The example set by the relationship between Charles Simpson, his late father Vernon, and his own sons and daughter are prime examples of what I am endeavoring to communicate. The business example of John Beckett, his late father and John's son Kevin demonstrate the father/son model in the corporate world.

Having spiritual fatherhood has been one of the many great blessings that God has given me on the earth. However, I must make this one thing clear. If or when God sends a spiritual father to us, the choice to receive him remains with each of us. Genuine spiritual authority is rarely imposed; we are asked to simply recognize, receive, and voluntarily submit to it. Finally, let me make this very clear. **A spiritual father is not a mediator between oneself and God.** Jesus Christ alone is our only mediator.[1] As I often say, a spiritual father is simply like the sight on a gun. He is one who can help us to

---

[1] 1 Timothy 2:5

focus upon or aim toward our Heavenly Father. The sight on the gun is not the target! Following the example of Jesus is the target.

A major dilemma that people have faced throughout history is to recognize and receive those whom God has anointed and sent to them. I believe that this is still a problem today. Each of us faces the task of recognizing and receiving spiritual fatherhood, if or when God sends it to us. I suggest that if one is searching for spiritual fatherhood, he would be wise to consider looking for someone who is demonstrating sonship. I am fully aware that we are not to idolize or worship any man except Jesus Christ. However, God can and does give us fathers in the faith (patriarchal men of proven integrity), who can set examples for us to imitate. In addition, having a spiritual father does not absolve us from the responsibility to honor our natural or biological fathers. Spiritual fathers are not meant to replace our natural fathers, but they can certainly fill in the gaps that were created by their failure. In my experience, the majority of those who have related to me as a spiritual father have found restoration and/or renewal in their relationship with their natural fathers. Witnessing this has always been a great blessing for me.

Adding further to this line of thinking, the Scriptures seem to indicate that Israel will not "see Jesus" unless it will recognize and bless "those" whom He sends.[1] If this is the case, along with Israel we may not be able to see Him either, until we recognize and welcome those whom He sends.

The entire world is in great need of leaders who are role models. **More than likely, what does not work at home will probably not work in the church or in society.** Once

---

[1] Matthew 23:37-39; Luke 13:34-35

again, to be an example means this: "We are the sight on the rifle, not the target." Jesus alone is our target. We are in desperate need of those who practice what they preach, especially in their homes. It is good to remember—a leader is simply the first one to walk through a field filled with land mines. If the leader does not blow up, his followers can be confident to step where he stepped.

14

Mentors and Fathers

A s I have suggested, being a follower of Jesus Christ is as much a governmental decision as it is a religious decision. When we accept Jesus Christ as both our Lord and our Savior, we become citizens of the Kingdom, not simply members of a church or an institution. We acknowledge God's absolute and indisputable right to rule and reign over us. Citizens of God's kingdom are to be distinguished and differentiated by their lifestyle. Early Christians were identified and referred to as "people of the Way." This would suggest that Christians were recognized, not so much by what they believed and taught, but for the way or manner in which they lived. The lifestyle of the Christian was to be the authentication of his testimony. Paul confessed, "I admit to you, that according to the Way which they call a sect I do serve the God of our fathers, believing everything that is in accordance with the Law, and that is written in the Prophets."[1] **As mentioned earlier, one's ministry should not be one's life, as much as one's life should be one's ministry.**

God's aspiration, His goal and His purpose are to have His government functioning within each of us. The kingdom of God uses external government to help us to internalize His

---

[1] Acts 24:14

Kingdom rule. Discipleship is the practical way in which His Kingdom rule is learned. Michael Puffett from Maidstone, England, a friend and contributor to this book, has this simple definition of discipleship: _"I do, you watch; you do, I watch; you go and do."_ Each of us must repeat this process. In the book of Acts, Luke tells us that the first time the disciples of Jesus Christ were called Christians was in Antioch.[1] The words _disciple_ and _discipline_ have the same root. Derek Prince once said that a very strict interpretation of this passage would imply that if you were not being discipled, you were not considered a Christian, at least in Antioch. If you were a Christian, you were a disciple. That is where mentoring comes in.

In January of 2003, I was invited by Dr. Bradley Stuart, a spiritual son from South Africa, to minister with him in Belize. We were teaching from my manual, _Sonship: The Path to Fatherhood_. During our time of sharing, a question arose about the difference between fathers and mentors. Since then both Bradley and I have discussed this issue in detail. In his first letter to the Corinthians Paul implies that there is a distinction between the role of a mentor and the role of a father. He wrote, "For if you were to have countless tutors (or mentors) in Christ, yet you would not have many fathers; for in Christ Jesus I became your father through the gospel. I exhort you therefore, be imitators of me. For this reason I have sent to you Timothy, who is my beloved and faithful child in the Lord, and he will remind you of my ways which are in Christ, just as I teach everywhere in every church."[2]

For our purpose, I will use the words _tutor_ and _mentor_ interchangeably. All too often, what people call fathering

---

[1] Acts 11:26
[2] 1 Corinthians 4:15-17

would be better termed mentoring. Fathering and mentoring have certain fundamental differences. The word translated as *tutor* in our passage above comes from the Greek word *paidagogos*. It literally means "child leader" and refers to a person who would function similarly to an *au pair*. The Greeks referred to a *paidagogos* as the person or servant who attended a child, had the general care of him, and who led him to school for the purpose of being instructed by the *didaskalos*, the teacher. Paul wrote that there were countless mentors. Apparently, there were numerous persons in Corinth who offered their services to instruct people, and some of them were not overly fond of the Apostle Paul. The word "countless" in the above passage comes from the Greek word for *myriads*. Implied here is the fact that many (myriads) may offer to instruct you without any parental feeling toward you, since you are not their spiritual child. Some of those whom God sends are merely meant to be mentors, while others are meant to be fathers.

Using some of what Bradley and I concluded, I believe it will benefit us to differentiate between fathers and mentors. Even if the contrasts between mentoring and fathering are not always black and white, it is important for us that we can make a distinction between the two. Certainly, there is some measure of overlap, but for the most part the relationship between students and teachers is not the same as the relationship between a father and his children. Let us look at some differences.

❖ We may have many mentors but not many fathers.

❖ Fatherhood is for a lifetime, mentoring for a season.

❖ A father is a source of life, while a mentor is primarily a source of knowledge. The Hebrew word *ab* means *father* or *source*.

❖ Probably the major difference between a father and a mentor is the issue of relationship. Fatherhood depends on a relationship being organic, while mentoring can function in a programmatic and organizational setting.

❖ A genuine father is primarily concerned with who the child is to become, a mentor more likely to deal with what a student does.

❖ A father will focus on a child's heritage and legacy, whereas a mentor is more likely to concentrate on developing a person's talents, abilities and ministry.

❖ A father does not recruit sons. They are his by birth or adoption.

❖ One may resign as a mentor, but one cannot resign as a father. A man who quits as a father does not relinquish his responsibility.

❖ Fatherhood cannot be franchised. Mentoring can.

❖ A father desires sons and daughters; a mentor is satisfied to have students or pupils.

❖ Fathers want to build families; mentors, organizations.

❖ Fathers understand that it takes time to build a family, while mentors press for immediate results.

❖ Genuine fathers desire their children to be more successful than themselves; a mentor might be content to focus on a student's self-achievement or self-realization.

❖ Fathers long for their children to be "father pleasers," mentors for their students simply to follow a set of rules and regulations.

❖ Fathers lead and demonstrate; mentors direct and explain.

Of course, this list is far from exhaustive, but it is sufficient to make my point. The manner in which the kingdom of God will advance is through sons who are prepared, equipped, trained and sent forth. I contend that a vital focus and intention of a mentor must be to teach children _sonship_. Programs, ministries and ministers have an obligation"...to restore the hearts of the fathers back to the children, and the hearts of the children back to the fathers."[1] In so doing, they are recovering their scriptural DNA. Taking the respect, honor and allegiance of children from the fathers and giving it to or replacing it with a program, organization, institution or denomination is a serious misuse of influence. A key to understanding the kingdom of God is the centricity of fatherhood and sonship in the message. We must not forget that our Father is a King, and our King is our Father. Kingdoms are perpetuated through sons, not students. It is the message of the kingdom of God that must go forth to the nations. Jesus said, "And this gospel of the kingdom shall be preached in the whole world for a witness to all the nations, and then the end shall come."[2]

---

[1] Malachi 4:5-6
[2] Matthew 24:14

15

Father and Son as One

*M*any religions are willing to acknowledge Jesus as a great teacher or mentor; however, the revelation of Scripture is that He is a son. As a son, Jesus prayed, "...that they [*i.e.*, you and I] may all be one; even as You, Father, art in Me, and I in Thee, that they also may be in Us; that the world may believe that You did send Me."[1] In this great intercessory prayer recorded by John, Jesus prayed for the unity of all believers. The root word for *unity* is *unit*, meaning one. So how do two (or more) become as one? Through covenant commitment. A blood covenant is not a partnership; it is a merger. Aristotle described covenant as two souls in one body. Like scrambling two eggs, the two become as one; each loses its identity in the other. **We should notice that the great archetype of unity in the Scriptures is revealed in the blood covenant relationship between Father and Son.** Furthermore, it is implied by the passage that modeling this unity is a key to world evangelism. Walking out covenant relationships is the way unity is displayed.

The phrase "cutting covenant" is rooted in the practice of ratifying an agreement or contract through the shedding, the exchange, and at times the drinking of blood. From time

---

[1] John 17:21

immemorial to present day, the blood covenant is the strongest legal contract and most sacred binding agreement known to man. It is a permanent, unalterable and indissoluble contract. It is comparable to a last will, which can only be validated by the shedding of blood or death.[1] Deriving from the origin of sealing a deal by bloodshed, Americans use the phrase "to cut a deal." The Jewish Passover meal and the celebration of the Lord's Supper are meant to reenact, remember and reinforce the covenant that God made with Israel and with His church.

Judaism and Christianity do not stand alone in the recognition and practice of a blood covenant. Nearly every primitive religion—and most heathen tribes—has operated and is based upon a blood covenant. In the Arabic language, the words for *blood, friendship* and *affection* share the same root. David Livingstone and Henry Stanley, famed missionaries to Central Africa, allegedly cut covenant over fifty times, and wrote that they never once saw it broken. E. W. Kenyon, a noted authority on the blood covenant, believed that the key to the gospel in Africa is for missionaries to explain it in terms of covenant.

Covenant relationships are essential elements of the Kingdom, the church, the family, especially as they relate to fathers and sons. The Holy Bible consists of two distinct and clearly defined Covenants, the Old and the New. The King James Version translated the word *Covenant* as *Testament*, but I shall prefer to use the word *covenant*. It would be impossible in one chapter to do justice to the subject of covenant, since volumes of books and articles have been published on it. However, I will attempt briefly to interweave the subject of covenant with our theme as it relates to fathers

---

[1] Hebrews 9:16-17

and sons.

Adam and Eve were uniquely blessed with an intimate relationship with God and were able to enjoy uninterrupted fellowship with their Creator. However, when sin entered into the world through Adam and Eve, their relationship with God was broken. The consequence of their sin was guilt and shame resulting in the awareness of their nakedness. Since the Bible teaches, "Without the shedding of blood, there is no remission of sin..."[1] only a blood sacrifice could restore this relationship. After a futile attempt to cover themselves with fig leaves, Adam and Eve were restored only after the shedding of blood.[2] Conceivably, the first death ever recorded may have occurred by the hand of God. A living creature had to die in order for its skins to cover Adam and Eve. We then read that Adam and Eve's firstborn son Cain offered a bloodless sacrifice to God, which God rejected. Cain's sacrifice was made up of grain that grew from the ground that God had cursed. Cain's brother Abel offered a blood sacrifice, which God accepted. God's rejection of Cain's bloodless sacrifice and His acceptance of Abel's bloody sacrifice alienated Cain from his brother. This enmity resulted in the first recorded death of a human. In fact, this first death of a human was fratricide; Cain murdered his brother Abel, and the issue was linked to a blood covenant offering.

Numerous references throughout the Scriptures to the Biblical pattern of flesh and blood (*i.e.*, bread, wheat or flour coupled with grapes or wine) are continual reminders of God's unalterable commitment to His Covenant. Remember, Joseph was unjustly imprisoned due to the false accusations of Potiphar's wife. Joseph's prison cellmates, a baker (bread)

---

[1] Hebrews 9:22
[2] Genesis 3:21

and a cupbearer (wine) each had a dream. In the actualization of the dream, the baker (bread representing the body) would die; the cupbearer (wine representing the blood) would live.[1] I propose to you that Joseph possessed a unique and profound understanding of covenant. His interpretation of his cellmates's dreams became the vehicle that eventually led him into the presence of Pharaoh. Simply put, Joseph's revelation of covenant took him from prisoner to prime minister.

Later, we learn that Joseph put a cup (used for wine) into the sack of grain (ingredient for bread) that the brothers took back to Jacob (also known as Israel). Once again, we observe that these symbols of covenant illustrate his deep understanding of God's covenant faithfulness. In his position at Pharaoh's right hand, Joseph was restored back to his father and his family. Furthermore, he used his influence to save not only his brothers but also an entire nation. God is a covenant keeper. Joseph understood this, and so must we.

In order to become a citizen of the Kingdom, as well as a son in the house, one is well served to have at least a basic understanding of a blood covenant. The Bible mentions the word *covenant* over three hundred times. The Hebrew word for covenant, *b'rith*, literally means "a cut where blood flows." It seems God does nothing of significance except through the process of entering into a covenant. As if He Himself could not be trusted, God has consented to bind Himself relationally by sealing His promises with blood.[2] The entire redemptive plan of God hinges upon our understanding of His Covenants, because they bind up God's relationships with humanity. Nearly 2,000 years ago the most solemn, supreme

---

[1] Genesis 40
[2] Deuteronomy 7:9

and sensational blood covenant ceremony the world has ever seen was performed on a hill called Calvary. **As I am sure you know, our personal salvation is crucially linked to this covenant, the sacrifice of obedience a son made for a father.**

People enter into covenant for numerous reasons. Let me mention three examples. First, a weak tribe living by the side of a stronger tribe is in danger of destruction or extinction. A blood covenant assures both parties the security of being preserved. Suspicion and enmity would immediately cease. Secondly, suppose two businesspersons want to insure that one will not take advantage of the other. Instead of forming a partnership, they merge. The welfare of each depends upon the keeping of the covenant by the other. Thirdly, cutting a covenant can be for the sake of love. A man and a woman make a covenant when they marry in order to secure and assure the absolute fidelity of each spouse in this union.

Within the ceremony of a blood covenant there exist some common ritualistic practices. Normally, if two people or tribes desire to make covenant, they bring witnesses and a priest. They exchange significant gifts to indicate that each one's possessions belong to the other. The priest makes incisions, usually in the wrists of the participants or their representatives. Normally, drops of blood are mixed with wine in a cup. The participants or substitutes then sip from the cup. Sometimes they put their bleeding wrists together to allow their blood to mingle, or they touch their tongues to the wound. In so doing, they become "blood brothers." As soon as the blood ritual is over, each pronounces blessings and curses. The blessings are for those who honor and keep the covenant, while the curses are to afflict those who might dare to break it. This practice of blessing and cursing is clearly demonstrated by the example of Moses in the book of Deuteronomy.[1] Often a substance would be put into the fresh wound to make a visible scar. Finally, the participants would share a meal and plant a tree or erect a pile of stones as a visible memorial for generations that followed.[2] The moment a covenant is solemnized, everything in the world that a blood covenant man owns is at the disposal of his blood brother. Yet, his brother would never ask for anything unless he was desperately in need.

Although in Western society, we associate blood with death (*e.g.*, bloodbath, bloodthirsty) the Bible teaches us that "the life is in the blood."[3] For this reason, the Scriptures refer to the heart as the fountain of life.[4] Since the blood of an animal or a person was synonymous with his life, by the drinking of blood two lives were intermingled. It is no longer *I* but *we*, and not *mine* but *ours*. Since the life is in the blood, both the Old and New Covenant prohibited the drinking of animal blood. Sometimes the cutting of covenant has degenerated into a grotesque rite. Deviant forms of blood covenants have arisen in practice as well as legend. A number of serial killers have practiced the custom of cannibalism and drinking blood, hence the term "bloodthirsty." The superstitious stories of vampires have their origins in the life being transmitted via blood.

---

[1] Deuteronomy 11:26-28; Deuteronomy 28:1-68
[2] Genesis 31:46-53
[3] Leviticus 17:11
[4] Proverbs 4:23

16

Cutting Covenant

*I*t will benefit us to consider some of the ramifications of making a covenant with our God, since the only manner in which people can share the life of God is by entering into a blood covenant with Him.[1] The relationship between Abram (renamed Abraham) and God was based on a blood covenant.[2] It would be important to note that God said, "As for me," not "I will if you will." The phrase, "as for me" is essential to our understanding of covenant. Covenant depends upon a unilateral decision made by each party. The fifteenth chapter of Genesis provides a vivid description of this covenant rite. Animals were cut into pieces, and God passed between the parts of the severed animals like a smoking oven and flaming torch. The symbolism is clear: *Break this covenant and you'll be butchered like these animals.* Violating or breaking covenant carries grave and grim consequences. In every ancient civilization, to break a covenant was equivalent to cursing your own life and the very ground that you walked upon. Ancient documents indicate that if one were to break a covenant, he could expect to be hunted down and slain by his own family. The shedding of animal blood was a token and assurance that the death of

---

[1] John 6:53
[2] Genesis 15:18

the real testator Jesus Christ would occur in due season. Later, in Genesis 17, God required that the covenant be ratified by circumcision. Now, added to the phrase "as for me," would come the condition "as for you."[1] Therefore, some of God's promises are unconditional, while others carry qualifying conditions.

There are numerous examples of covenant throughout the Bible, but it is not the purpose of this book to explore all of them. However, I would like to suggest some of the essential characteristics of covenant life:

The decision to make covenant is personal. Each person who enters covenant should do so with these words—"As for me." It is not a fifty-fifty agreement; it is a one hundred percent commitment on the part of each party. Before God put the condition of circumcision upon Abraham and the adult males of Israel, He made distinct promises and committed Himself to be their God.[2] God said, "As for Me," prior to saying, "As for you."

The life force of covenant is love. That which would distinguish the citizens of the Kingdom and the sons of God was love. "By this all men will know that you are My disciples, if you have love for one another."[3] Biblical love is not a feeling, but rather a decision to remain loyal no matter what happens. It can be best expressed in these words: "I will never ever leave you, nor will I ever forsake you."

The requirement of covenant is sacrifice. The Psalmist wrote, "The Mighty One, God, the Lord, has spoken, and summoned the earth from the rising of the sun to its setting. Gather My godly ones to Me, those who have made a

---

[1] Genesis 17:9
[2] Genesis 17:4-7
[3] John 13:35

covenant with Me by sacrifice."[1] The blood sacrifice symbolized the death of each party to honor the covenant. For example, as they made the incision, or as they walked between the parts of the animal, each party was saying in effect, "This is my death. The shed blood was representative of my life. As I enter this covenant, I enter by death. Now that I am in a covenant, I have no more right to live outside of it, nor do I have the right to live for myself." Of course, we do not speak simply of physical death, but rather a death to self. Dan Wolfe once opened a marriage ceremony with these words: "You have come to this altar to die!" As long as a person refuses to die to self, he is not in covenant.

The evidence of covenant is absolute trust. God said to Abraham, "And I will establish My covenant between Me and you and your descendants after you throughout their generations for an everlasting covenant, to be God to you and to your descendants after you."[2] Abraham understood covenant. Abraham was told, "Take now your son, your only son, whom you love, Isaac, and go to the land of Moriah; and offer him there as a burnt offering on one of the mountains of which I will tell you."[3] Abraham did not hesitate, but got up early the next morning, took a three-day journey, and made all the preparations to sacrifice his son Isaac. At the base of the mountain, Abraham said to the young men who had accompanied them, "Stay here with the donkey, and I and the lad will go yonder; and we will worship and return to you."[4] The writer of Hebrews explains, "By faith Abraham, when he was tested, offered up Isaac; and he who had received the promises was offering up his only begotten son; it was he to

---

[1] Psalm 50:1&5
[2] Genesis 17:7
[3] Genesis 22:2
[4] Genesis 22:5

whom it was said, 'In Isaac your descendants shall be called.' He considered that God is able to raise men even from the dead; from which he also received him back as a type." [1]

The blessing of covenant is intimacy. Among those whom we call unbelievers, we see the desire for and the practice of intimacy and physical union apart from covenant commitment. In natural relationships, we refer to this as fornication. Yet, among the fellowship of believers, we see a desire for intimacy and physical union apart from covenant. The restrictions of covenant allow for transparency and vulnerability, because it assures us that even in the midst of failures and weaknesses, we will not be abandoned or disgraced. The Psalmist expresses it like this: "The secret of the Lord is for those who fear Him, and He will make them know His covenant." [2]

The grace to keep covenant comes from God's faithfulness. Since souls and life are conveyed and transferred via blood, imagine the ramifications of being in covenant with God Himself. That is exactly what transpired on Calvary. Jesus was both the priest and the sacrifice of this ritual. Essential to our understanding of sonship and fatherhood, this was the Son laying down His life for the Father. As a prototype illustrated by the story of Abraham and Isaac on Mount Moriah, the archetype is herein displayed. Notice, it involves the relationship between fathers and sons.

Through the New Covenant in His blood, we became "blood brothers" with Jesus Christ. The results of that are unfathomable. When one is born again, his heart is circumcised, which is the entrance into the New Covenant.

---

[1] Hebrews 11:17-20
[2] Psalm 25:14

Through covenant, we become a part of the family of God. God initiated the covenant with us. Because the character of God is unchangeable, God will never break this covenant. Paul writes, "If we are faithless, He remains faithful; for He cannot deny Himself."[1] Holy Communion (the Lord's Supper) is the reaffirmation of this relationship. As I mentioned earlier, covenant is the bond that God chose to hold people together in relationships. It remains the most sacred of all agreements.

The Kingdom, the church and the family therefore is a collection of individuals bound together in the Blood Covenant of Jesus Christ. In the early church believers shared communion from house to house. Like the Passover, it was a "family event." We, as a family, regularly take communion together in our home, and I have encouraged other families to do the same. As I have mentioned, tragically, in much of Western society, we have totally lost the understanding of the sanctity of covenant. Perhaps, the sole remaining example of covenant is marriage, but the very definition of marriage suffers under severe attack in our day. Sadly, in recent years this institution has undergone radical disintegration. Today, the plague of divorce, which is the breaking of the marriage covenant, has reached epidemic proportions even in evangelical circles.

In light of the above, let us look further at the writings of John to understand Jesus' discourse regarding covenant and the response of his disciples. In John 6, it is clear that Jesus was referring to the covenant practice of drinking blood. "Jesus therefore said to them, 'Truly, truly, I say to you, unless you eat the flesh of the Son of Man and drink His blood, you have no life in yourselves. He who eats My flesh and drinks

[1] 2 Timothy 2:13

My blood has eternal life, and I will raise him up on the last day. For My flesh is true food, and My blood is true drink. He who eats My flesh and drinks My blood abides in Me, and I in him.' "[1]

Like many today, even his disciples did not comprehend spiritual things in their natural minds. "Many therefore of His disciples, when they heard this said, 'This is a difficult statement; who can listen to it?' "[2] Jesus explained that spiritual concepts need spiritual revelation. " 'It is the Spirit who gives life; the flesh profits nothing; the words that I have spoken to you are spirit and are life. But there are some of you who do not believe.' For Jesus knew from the beginning who they were who did not believe, and who it was that would betray Him. And He was saying, 'For this reason I have said to you, that no one can come to Me, unless it has been granted him from the Father.' "[3]

Although I am aware that the numbers for the chapters and verses were not in the original manuscripts, observe the number of the passage that follows the above. **John 6:66 (Six-sixty-six) should sober us!** "As a result of this (e.g., His teaching of covenant) many of His disciples withdrew, and were not walking with Him anymore."[4] Could this be a coincidence? Perhaps, but I doubt it. The Greek word for *stumbling block* is **skandalon**, from which we derive the word *scandalize*. Teaching on covenant still has the potential to scandalize people. Look now at Jesus' question, "Jesus said therefore to the twelve, 'You do not want to go away also, do you?' "[5] To His own disciples He asked, "Will you leave also?"

---

[1] John 6:53-56
[2] John 6:60
[3] John 6:63-65
[4] John 6:66
[5] John 6:67

This does not sound like the one who taught on leaving the ninety-nine to retrieve the one who left.

Finally, look at Peter's response. "Simon Peter answered Him, 'Lord, to whom shall we go? You have words of eternal life. And we have believed and have come to know that You are the Holy One of God.' "[1] It appears to me that Peter and the disciples had considered and weighed their alternatives and arrived at the conclusion that Jesus was their "life source." They had concluded that there was no place else to go.

One should note that Judas Iscariot never referred to Jesus as Lord but always called Him Rabbi, the Hebrew title for a teacher or mentor. By stealing money, Judas Iscariot had been disloyal to Jesus and the disciples before the Passover. However, not until Judas shared in that covenant meal was he exposed as a traitor.

---

[1] John 6:67-69

17

A Father's Rejection

*F*or decades, I have heard people and especially men say, "I know my father loved me, but he didn't know how to demonstrate it." A couple of years ago a friend of mine named Harry shared a dream. The dream went something like this: Harry, in the presence of his father, was sitting and sobbing in a room. His father asked him, "Why are you crying?" Harry responded tearfully, "Dad, all I ever wanted was for you to put your arms around me and tell me that you loved me." At that moment, his father stood up and walked toward him. As Harry prepared to receive his embrace, he looked and saw that his father had no arms! I believe that the cultural predispositions and the biases of Western stoicism have amputated the emotional arms of many of our fathers.

I never knew personally my Grandpa McNally, because he died when I was an infant. He was a fire chief in an Irish neighborhood of Saginaw, Michigan. I cannot remember my dad ever speaking to me about him. The only story that I have ever heard regarding Grandpa McNally and my dad is one that my oldest brother Dick shared. In Grandpa's era, horses pulled the fire wagons. Somehow, one day my dad had angered my grandpa at the fire station. Grandpa took the horsewhip and began to beat my dad with it. My grandpa did not stop beating my dad until the other firefighters pulled him off and threatened him. I am telling you the absolute truth; this is the only story I have ever heard regarding my father and grandfather's relationship.

My natural father was a product of that culture. The final years of both my mom and dad's lives were spent as members of our congregation in Marcellus and Benton Harbor, Michigan. For me, Harry's dream described my relationship with my dad. Tragically, my dad followed the example of his father. No, he did not work for the fire department but rather spent his life as a Methodist minister. He did not possess a horsewhip, but he did have an electrical extension cord available. Since I was frail and sickly as a child, I was spared some of his unpredictable and violent outbursts. My two older brothers did not fare so well. Even after I became a Christian, it took me nearly a decade before I truly forgave my father, and by that time he had become quite senile.

For many of us, healing can come simply through realizing that our fathers did not have the ability, the capacity or the understanding needed to reproduce wholesome sons and daughters. Yet to blame our own delinquency on the dysfunctional parents does nothing to solve the problem. We all have come from a dysfunctional family; Adam and Eve were dysfunctional! We must resolve that the curse stop here.

So the fact that God chose the name *Father* for Himself presents many of us with a quandary. Every human being has a biological father. The result is that the word *father* triggers certain images in everyone's mind. Psychologists have suggested that our concept of God forms in early childhood. Since our concept of God is significantly impacted and influenced by our view of our natural fathers, it is essential that we correct any wrong views we have. If we have a wrong view of our father, we can have a wrong view of God, since He is The Father. Now consider this: when we worship our heavenly Father, any wrong concepts or false images we have of fatherhood can lead us into a form of idolatry. In order to worship in spirit and in truth, we must have an accurate and truthful image of God. Using the law of first mention, God described Himself to Moses in this manner: "Then the LORD passed by in front of him and proclaimed, 'The Lord, the Lord God, compassionate and gracious, slow to anger, and abounding in lovingkindness and truth.' "[1] Are these the character traits that describe our biological parents?

As previously cited, our perception of the Father often arises out of the relationship we have with our natural or biological fathers. Children whose fathers have rejected and abandoned the family may have difficulty believing that their Heavenly Father will be available whenever they need Him. Obviously, children whose fathers are cold, rigid and severe have a picture of God that is much different from the children whose fathers are warm and approachable. Simply by listening carefully to a person's prayers, one can often detect the type of relationship that person has had with his or her father. If a person's prayers are general, ritualistic and repetitive, the relationship with the natural father was probably austere, cool and formal. If the prayers are guarded and filled with guilt and penitence, we might surmise the father-child relationship was tainted with cruelty, violence and fear. If a father, however, was warm, gracious and involved, the prayers of the children are likely to be honest, bold and natural. Transferring our love and respect for the invisible Father God is clearly simpler if our natural father attempted to reflect His nature. Many people, including me, have thought, "If God is like my father, I don't need Him."

---

[1] Exodus 34:6

Finally and perhaps most importantly, children whose fathers were passive in their role as the spiritual leaders of their home will find it difficult to see the need for a vital and intimate relationship with God.

The Bible records numerous examples of fathers who failed and of the disastrous consequences of these failures. For the sake of efficiency, I will mention just two examples from the life of King David. Yes, even the great King David must be included among biblical fathers who experienced failure. Absalom was one of David's wicked sons, but David loved him to the end. Absalom manipulated, seduced and stole the hearts of the men of Israel away from his father, King David.[1] Another of David's sons was Adonijah. "Adonijah, exalted himself, saying, 'I will be king.' So he prepared for himself chariots and horsemen with fifty men to run before him. His father had never crossed him at any time by asking, 'Why have you done so?' He was also a very handsome man; and he was born after Absalom."[2] These sons of David instigated and led mutinous insurrections against their own father. Notice that the passage referring to Adonijah says that his father "never crossed him." He never challenged him nor held him accountable by asking him, "Why have you done such and such a thing?" These two examples illustrate that when the hearts of children rise up and turn against their fathers, curses and calamities are imminent.

One tragic consequence of our current culture in America is that many fathers and mothers do not see nor experience their children as a blessing. Derek Prince taught extensively on the blessings and curses of the Bible. One of the curses mentioned in Deuteronomy is "You shall beget

---

[1] 2 Samuel 15:6 & 13
[2] 1 Kings 1:5-6

sons and daughters, but you shall not enjoy them; for they shall go into captivity."[1] Renegade fathers reproduce renegade kids. The result is that hordes of kids have been seduced into the captivity of alcohol abuse, drug addictions, illicit sex, violent street gangs, abusive cults, witchcraft and Satanism.

To illustrate this, let us consider the damaging effect on the course of history caused by the children of renegade, absentee, viciously cruel and/or dysfunctional fathers. Paul C. Vitz, in his book *Faith of the Fatherless: The Psychology of Atheism*—a book I highly recommend for those who would like to study this subject more thoroughly—documents this for us. The horrendous consequences resulting from the behavior of these few examples is impossible to calculate or comprehend. Not only the names of the following persons, but also the names of their fathers, should appear in a "Hall of Infamy." Not surprisingly, each of those listed below had at least one common denominator—a repulsive, horrible or nonexistent relationship with his or her father.

Voltaire: (French philosopher who believed that Christianity was a good thing for chambermaids and tailors to believe in but for the use of the elite advocated a simple deism) "A recent biographer, A. D. Aldridge, has noted that Voltaire demonstrated neither affection for his parents nor attachment to family traditions: 'Although Voltaire wrote extensively about his father, he said virtually nothing in his favor.' "[2]

Sigmund Freud: (Atheist Philosopher) "That Sigmund

---

[1] Deuteronomy 28:41

[2] *Faith of the Fatherless* by Paul C. Vitz. Spence Publishing Company. Dallas, Texas. 1999, p. 39

Freud's father, Jacob, was a disappointment or worse to his son is generally agreed upon by his biographers.... Specifically, in two of his letters as an adult, Freud writes that his father was a sexual pervert and that Jacob's children [which included Sigmund] suffered as a result."[1]

Josef Stalin: "Perhaps the simplest summary of Stalin's relationship to his father is the following comment made by a friend who knew Stalin during his early years: 'Undeserved and severe beatings made the boy [Stalin] as hard and heartless as the father was.' "[2]

Adolf Hitler: "Like Stalin, young Adolf received severe and regular beatings from his father.... His older half-sister, Paula, reported that Adolf 'got his sound thrashing every day.' "[3]

Madalyn Murray O'Hair: (Founder of American Atheists, she campaigned for the separation of church and state and was instrumental in banning school prayer.) "Whatever the cause of O'Hair's intense hatred of her father, it is clear from her son's book that it was deep, and that it went back into her childhood; abuse—psychological and possibly physical—is a likely cause."[4]

Mao Zedong: "Mao's father is described as a family tyrant, and from childhood young Mao sided with his mother and other members of the family in implicit rebellions. He clearly hated his father and learned his first appreciation of revolution and rebellion in his own family setting."[5]

---

[1] Ibid., pp. 47-48
[2] Ibid., p.104
[3] Ibid., pp. 105-106
[4] Ibid., p. 55
[5] Ibid., p. 107

It is impossible to calculate the devastation caused by these few people. Imagine how the entire course of history might have changed if one or all of them had been properly fathered. The power and effect of a father's influence, or lack thereof, cannot be overstated. In fact, I believe that a father's rejection is perhaps the most powerful and devastating force on earth. I submit to you that when Jesus Christ died on the cross, He did not simply die of physical wounds. The beatings did not kill Him. The nails used to hold Him on the cross did not kill Him. The bleeding from the crown of thorns pressed onto His head did not kill Him. When the Roman soldiers came to break His legs, they found that He was already dead. A spear was thrust into the side of His corpse. I have no reason to believe, as some scholars say, that He died due to suffocation from hanging.

So, what caused the death of Jesus? The Scriptures unveil these moments, and record the final words of Jesus before He died. Matthew wrote, "About 3:00 PM Jesus cried out with a loud voice saying, 'Eloi, Eloi, lama sabachthani?' that is, 'My God, My God, why have you forsaken me?' ...And Jesus cried out again with a loud voice and gave up His spirit."[1] Mark recorded it this way. "At the ninth hour (3:00 PM) Jesus cried out with a loud voice, 'Eloi, Eloi, lama sabachthani?' which translates, 'My God, My God, why have You forsaken Me?' "[2] "And Jesus uttered a loud cry, and breathed His last."[3]

Not one of us can imagine or envision the horror of this moment. Sin separates us from the Father, but Jesus was sinless. Therefore, He had never before experienced separation from His Father. Paul taught, "He [God the Father]

---

[1] Matthew 27:46 & 50
[2] Mark 15:34
[3] Mark 15:37

made Him [Jesus] who knew no sin to be sin on our behalf, so that we might become the righteousness of God in Him [Jesus]."[1] As Jesus Christ became sin for us, the holiness of God required that He turn away from His dying Son. For the first and only instance in all of time and eternity, Jesus experienced the separation and rejection of His Father. From the pain of a broken heart, Jesus cried out, and breathed His last. I believe that the cause of the death of Jesus Christ was a broken heart, which was a result of the rejection of His Father. If the Father's rejection of Jesus for that brief moment killed Him, then a father's rejection could be the most powerful and destructive force in the world. With this in mind, imagine the epidemic of devastation, death and destruction caused by the rejection of fathers upon our youth of today.

---

[1] 2 Corinthians 5:21

18

Preparation for Restoration

Malachi is the final book of the Old Covenant. The words of the prophet Malachi were recorded over two thousand years ago, yet they remain as relevant today as the day in which they were penned. Let us now look at the concluding two verses of Malachi. "Behold, I will send you Elijah the prophet before the coming of the great and dreadful day of the Lord. And he will turn the hearts of the fathers to the children, and the hearts of the children to their fathers, lest I come and strike the earth with a curse."[1]

It is generally accepted that Malachi is not only a name but also a Hebrew word meaning "my messenger." In all probability, it derives from the following passage of Scripture: "Behold, I will send my messenger, and he shall prepare the way before Me: and the Lord, whom you seek, shall suddenly come to his temple, even the messenger of the covenant, whom you delight in: Behold, he shall come, says the Lord of hosts."[2] This passage informs us that God would send two messengers. The first messenger would come in the likeness of the Old Covenant prophet Elijah. The mission of this first messenger would be to prepare the way for the second messenger. The second messenger would be the

---

[1] Malachi 4:5-6
[2] Malachi 3:1

Messiah, spoken of here as the "messenger of the covenant." The manner in which the first messenger would prepare the way for the second is by turning the hearts of the fathers to the children and the hearts of the children to the fathers. Justifiably we could assume from this that a relational breakdown existed between fathers and children that needed restoration. Now notice that the final word written in the Old Covenant is the word "curse."[1] This curse is associated with the relational breakdown between fathers and children. If the Bible had ended with the Old Covenant, it would have ended with a curse.

Nearly all scholars agree that Malachi wrote his prophecy during the Persian period. Although no one assigns an exact date, several scholars place the book of Malachi between 445 and 432 B.C. From Malachi, the final book of the Old Covenant, to Matthew, the first book of the New Covenant, Israel experienced over four hundred years without a prophetic voice. It is widely accepted that a generation lasts forty years, so four centuries represents ten generations. With this in mind, we note the warning that God gave through Moses that no bastard (one of illegitimate birth), neither "any of his descendants, even to the tenth generation, shall enter the assembly of the Lord."[2] The writer of Hebrews calls those who do not receive discipline "illegitimate children and not sons."[3] In Malachi's time, the nation of Israel had continued to refuse the correction and discipline of the Lord. Through continual disobedience, Israel certainly had fit this description of an illegitimate child described in the book of Hebrews. The result was God's

---

[1] Malachi 4:6
[2] Deuteronomy 23:2
[3] Hebrews 12:6-8

silence!

After four hundred years without a prophetic voice, a peculiar desert dweller reminiscent of Elijah of old comes out of nowhere. His diet and dress alone make him distinct among the multitude. We have come to know this eccentric prophet as John the Baptist. As the gospels open the New Covenant, we see that John the Baptist fulfilled the prophecy of Malachi. In Matthew's gospel, Jesus confirmed that John the Baptist was "Elijah, who was to come."[1] Assuredly, John the Baptist was not a reincarnation of Elijah, he simply came "...in the spirit and power of Elijah."[2] I consider John to be the last of the Old Covenant prophets and the first of the New Covenant prophets.

Malachi prophesied that God would send Elijah before the "great and dreadful day of the Lord."[3] I suggest to you that this passage speaks of two days, rather than one. I believe, and hope you will agree, that the "great day" refers to the coming of Christ as a babe in a Bethlehem stable. I do not believe that this reference to the coming of Christ could be described as a dreadful day. The "dreadful day" refers to His long awaited and final physical return at the end of the age. Speaking of the messenger of the covenant, the text of the third chapter of Malachi could be applied easily to that dreadful coming of Christ. It says, "...who can endure the day of His coming, and who can stand when He appears." It goes on to speak almost exclusively of judgment, and not of redemption.[4] We know Jesus came as the sacrificial Lamb of God who takes away the sin of the world.[5] At the end of the

---

[1] Matthew 11:13-14; Matthew 17:10-13
[2] Luke 1:17
[3] Malachi 4:5
[4] Malachi 3:1-5
[5] John 1:29 & 36

age, He will come again as the Captain of the Lord of Hosts and "...the Lion of the tribe of Judah."[1]

According to Malachi, the spirit of Elijah would turn the hearts of the fathers back to the children and the hearts of the children back to the fathers. From these Scriptures we can see that the restoration of father and child relationships prepares the way for Jesus to come. Anyone who does not acknowledge the worldwide need for the restoration of fathers and children is in unreality. Perhaps more than at any other period of history we are in need of a fresh visitation of the spirit and power of Elijah. I cling to the hope that God's promise to send the "spirit of Elijah" will be repeated before the dreadful day, Christ's final and ultimate return. The restoration of the relationship between fathers and their children laid the preparatory path for the Lord's advent that we refer to as the "great day." I contend that it will also lay the path for His final return, which I believe is the "dreadful day." This fact alone makes Malachi's message as pertinent for today as it was for the coming of Jesus Christ at His miraculous birth.

Let us now look at how this restoration played itself out in the life of the Lord Jesus. Jesus Christ, as we noted earlier, was and always will be the eternal Son of God. However, before coming to earth He emptied Himself of that position and title. Paul tells us, "Although He existed in the form of God, did not regard equality with God a thing to be grasped, but emptied Himself, taking the form of a bond-servant, and being made in the likeness of men. And being found in appearance as a man..."[2] He who was eternally the Son of God now entered into a time-space world to become the Son of

---

[1] Revelation 5:5
[2] Philippians 2:6-8

Man. His purpose would be to restore us to His Father by walking out sonship in the flesh. John paints a beautiful picture of this as he recounts the final days of Jesus on the earth.

19

A Place Prepared For Us

*O*ftentimes in my life I have read familiar passages of Scripture and interpreted them based on what I had been taught. Then someone would come and share an insight that totally unraveled my understanding of these passages. I refer to these as keys that unlock the hidden mysteries of Scripture. Recently, Tony Fitzgerald shared some insight with me from the book of John that revolutionized my thinking in regards to what transpired in the final events of Jesus' journey. The most disastrous and devastating outcome of the sin of Adam was that his sin closed the door to fellowship with the Father in heaven. Sin severed the relationship between man and his Father creator. Adam and Eve's desire for autonomy and independence introduced division between a father and his earthborn son. Under the Old Covenant, access into this fellowship was strictly limited. In fact, by law, only once a year could come one priest into the Holy of Holies. The awesome message of the New Covenant is that through the work of Jesus Christ a way has been prepared for humanity to have open access and fellowship with the heavenly Father once again. This is the heart of the good news. Since the restoration of sonship and fatherhood has been an underlying theme of this book, let us look again at the manner in which this restoration took place.

I will take up the account in John 13. John wrote, "Now before the Feast of the Passover, Jesus knowing that His hour had come that He should depart out of this world to the Father, having loved His own who were in the world, He loved them to the end."[1] This was an extremely serious moment. The disciples are with Jesus for the final meal together. He is about to depart from this world to go to His Father. Please take note of where He was going; this will be essential for what I have to write. Jesus was about to go to His Father. Continuing, He said, " 'Little children, I am with you a little while longer. You will seek Me; and as I said to the Jews, now I also say to you, 'Where I am going, you cannot come.' ... 'Where I go, you cannot follow Me now; but you will follow later.' "[2] As He had said to the Jews, He now says to His disciples—I will be leaving very soon. Then He said that where He was going, His disciples would be unable to come but would follow later.

Simon Peter had asked Him (midway in the conversation cited above), "Lord, where are you going?"[3] Remember, Peter is the person with the keys. If Jesus leaves, Peter is the one in charge. Peter does not know where He is going, but he is going to have to follow Him later. Peter responded, "Lord, why can I not follow You right now? I will lay down my life for You."[4] Obviously, Peter questioned the Lord's understanding of his commitment. Peter assumed the Lord was speaking about death, and essentially said to Jesus, If there is going to be a fight, I am ready for it. In fact, I am ready to die. I am not sure about these other eleven men, but I am "in for a penny, in for a pound."

Jesus responded with a question, "Will you lay down

---

[1] John 13:1
[2] John 13:33, 36b
[3] John:13:36a
[4] John 13:37

your life for me? Truly, truly, I say to you, a rooster will not crow until you deny Me three times."[1] In other words, Jesus asked Peter, Do you really understand what you are saying?

Perhaps if we apply this question to our own lives, we would say we are ready to die for the Lord. Repeating the word "truly," Jesus suggested to Peter that he was in unreality. Since the Jewish day begins at dusk, and this conversation was taking place on the evening of the Passover, Jesus was saying that before the day is half over you will deny not once, but three times. This seems a rather harsh statement to the man who would be the lead disciple.

Now we arrive at the crux of the issue. There are no chapter and verse division in the original texts of the Old and New Covenant. The numbers of chapters and verses were inserted centuries later. Therefore, there is no chapter division between the end of chapter 13 and the beginning of chapter 14. We must conclude from this that what follows is simply a continuation of the conversation between Jesus and Peter. Therefore, we can read it like this, "...you will deny Me three times, but let not your heart be troubled!"[2] What a great comfort! In essence Jesus was saying, Well, Peter, you're delusional about your commitment, but don't worry, Peter; don't allow anything that is about to transpire upset you. I know that you believe in God, but I want you to believe also in Me. "In My Father's house are many dwelling places; if it were not so, I would have told you; for I go to prepare a place for you."[3] Jesus was saying that in the place where His Father dwells or abides there is plenty of room.. Remember, He had said, Where I am going, you cannot come now, but you will

---

[1] John 13:38
[2] John 13:38 & John 14:1
[3] John 14:2

follow later. The reason that I am going is to prepare a place for you. "And if I go and prepare a place for you, I will come again, and receive you to Myself; that where I am, there you may be also."[1] Moreover, this is the linchpin connecting all that had been said before.

The popular exegesis of this passage has been that the place that Jesus was going to prepare for us was heaven. Therefore, the only way that we could go to that place was by dying. However, Jesus did not die on the cross primarily to go and prepare a place for us in heaven. In fact, the emphasis of the Bible is not about dying and going to heaven. The central theme of the Bible refers to us living and bringing heaven to earth. Jesus had taught the disciples to pray, "Your kingdom come, Your will be done on earth, as it is in heaven."[2] Heaven needed no further preparation. The kingdom of God and the will of God do not need to be restored in heaven: it has never been lost there. Even Peter and the disciples seemed confused about this. Misinterpreting what Jesus was talking about, Peter had said that he was ready to follow Jesus by dying. In addition to this, Jesus had told the disciples where He was going. He did not say, I am going to heaven, He said He was going to the Father. That is the place that was lost by Adam. Adam did not lose heaven. He lost the place of unbroken relationship and fellowship with the Father.

Assuming the disciples had heard Him say that He was going to the Father, we should not be surprised that Jesus said, "And you know the way where I am going."[3] Nevertheless, Thomas, one of the twelve said to Him, "Lord, we do not know where You are going, how do we know the

---

[1] John 14:3
[2] Matthew 6:10
[3] John 14:4

way?"[1] In other words, Lord, if we do not know where you are going, how can we know the way? What good is a map without a destination? The response of Jesus to Thomas's question is one of the most popular verses in the Bible. Jesus said, "I am the way, and the truth, and the life; no one comes to the Father, but through Me."[2] "I am the way!" I am the way to what – heaven? Well, of course, but that is not what He is talking about in this passage. He is not saying that He is the way to heaven, the truth about heaven and the life of heaven. We know this, because He continued by saying that no one can come where? "No one can come to the Father"—not to heaven—"but by me." He had said, "Where I am going you cannot come now, but you will be able to come later." Jesus went on to say, "If you had known Me, you would have known My Father also; from now on you know Him, and have seen Him." Again, He makes no reference to knowing about heaven. Jesus' purpose on earth was to show us the Father. The way to the presence of the Father is through Jesus. There is no other way.

Now another disciple, Philip, enters the conversation. Philip said to Him, "Lord, show us the Father, and it is enough for us."[3] Philip still did not understand, and perhaps some of us missed it, too. Philip's desire was commendable. He wanted to see the Father. Philip did not say, Show us heaven and that will suffice. Appearing a bit puzzled by all this, Jesus said, "Have I been so long with you, and yet you have not come to know Me, Philip? He who has seen Me has seen the Father; how do you say, 'Show us the Father?' "[4] The place that Jesus was going to and returning from has to do with

---

[1] John 14:5
[2] John 14:6
[3] John 14:8
[4] John 14:9

fatherhood, not with heaven. Jesus spoke further to the disciples, "I will not leave you as orphans; I will come to you,"[1] as if to say, You will all have a father. **Note, again in this instance, Jesus did not say that He would not leave us homeless in reference to a place. Rather, Jesus said that He would not leave us Fatherless in reference to a relationship.**

A third disciple, Judas (not Iscariot), then inquired, "Lord, what then has happened that You are going to disclose Yourself to us, and not to the world? Jesus answered and said to him, 'If anyone loves Me, he will keep My word; and My Father will love him, and We will come to him, and make Our abode with him.' "[2] Judas was asking Jesus, How is it that we alone have this revelation, and others do not? Jesus replied, My Father loves you, because you love Me and keep My word. Since My Father loves you, He and I will come to you and abide with you. Clearly, that nails down what has been said previously. The place that Jesus was going to prepare was a place in the presence of His Father. For this reason, Jesus came to be the Son of Man. He reopened the door that had been closed as a consequence of Adam's sin. He said, "You heard that I said to you, 'I go away, and I will come to you.' If you loved Me, you would have rejoiced, because I go to the Father..."[3] Jesus would open the path for us to once again abide in the everyday presence of the Father. That is the context of John 15. It is the call to abiding with the Father continually. It is the dwelling place prepared for us in the Father's heart, referred to at the beginning of chapter 14.

Understanding the Jewish practice of adoption gives us

---

[1] John 14:18
[2] John 14:22-23
[3] John 14:28

insight into the latter part of chapter fourteen, and it continues in chapter sixteen. The Jewish practice of adoption, referenced by Paul in his letter to Corinth,[1] was that a child was given over to a tutor, normally a rabbi, and this rabbi would teach him to be a son. The Holy Spirit is called the Spirit of Adoption, who would be sent to teach us and remind us of all things that Jesus taught us. Clearly, this would fit into our understanding of learning to be sons, and then becoming fathers by modeling sonship for our children. This will be more clearly explained later in this book.

As I wrote earlier, the great intercessory prayer of Jesus, which follows in John 17, further validates this point. This prayer, offered before the crucifixion, reads, "I glorified Thee on the earth, having accomplished the work which You have given Me to do. I manifested Your name to the men whom You have given Me out of the world; Yours they were, and You have given them to Me, and they have kept Your word."[2] Jesus said that he had glorified the Father on earth, having accomplished the work given to Him to do. That work was to manifest, incarnate or flesh out, the name (Father) to the men that God had given to him. Again, I contend that it has always been God's desire that His word become flesh. I interpret this to mean that the greatest way to glorify God is to manifest His fatherhood to the persons that He gives us.

After the resurrection, Mary Magdalene came to the garden tomb. Unexpectedly, she found the tomb empty. She concluded that the body of Jesus had been stolen. Jesus appeared to her and asked her why she was weeping. Thinking that she was speaking to the gardener, she shared with Him the cause of her grief. When Jesus spoke her name,

---

[1] 1 Corinthians 4:15
[2] John 17:4 & 6

Mary shockingly replied, "Master!" Then He said, "Stop clinging to Me, for I have not yet ascended to the Father; but go to My brethren, and say to them, 'I ascend to My Father and your Father, and My God and your God.' "[1] As the spotless Lamb of God, Jesus was about to go to the Father to present Himself as the sacrificial substitute for the sin of mankind. Again, His destination is even clearer. Basically He said, I am about to go to My Father and Your Father, so Mary, do not touch Me because I have not yet done this. Later, as He appeared to the disciples, He said to Thomas, "Reach here your finger, and see My hands; and reach here your hand, and put it into My side; and be not unbelieving, but believing."[2] To Mary, Jesus had said, Don't touch Me; now to Thomas he says, Go ahead and touch Me. What had changed? He had gone to the Father; the Father had been satisfied and accepted the sacrifice made by the Son for us. Jesus said, I will go and I will return. He returned and showed Himself to over five hundred people. Perhaps, therefore, when we speak of the "second coming," we should reconsider our terminology. He came a second time, but be assured He will come again. The next time He comes, it will not be as the Lamb of God, but rather as the Lion of Judah.

Now in the presence of the Father, where Jesus dwells, we have an open door again. The restoration of Father and earthly sons is complete. A place has been prepared for us, not just in heaven after we die, but here on earth where we live. He went to prepare a place for us, and He came again after His resurrection, that where He was, there we can be also. No longer is access to the presence of the Father limited to only one priest, once a year.

---

[1] John 20:17
[2] John 20:27

20

A Father's Desire for a Family

*T*he vast majority of adult males throughout the world have at least one thing in common. They carry a desire to have children. I do not believe that this is coincidental. The DNA of the Godhead is Father, Son and Holy Spirit, a mystery predating time. What fascinates me is that Father God desired a family on the earth. In fact, His very first command to Adam (mankind) was to reproduce, "...be fruitful, multiply, fill the earth..."[1] Reproduction requires men and women. God wanted Adam and Eve to have children, and they did. However, simply reproducing children does not make a family. Through the disobedience of Adam, "sin entered the world and death by sin."[2] The breakup of the family was one of the first consequences of sin. In Genesis 4, Eve gives birth to a boy whom she named Cain. As detailed earlier, the first human death recorded in Scriptures was fratricide. Cain murdered his brother Abel over an issue of acceptable worship. Atonement for sin, which ushers us into worship, requires a blood sacrifice. Cain's sacrifice was not a blood sacrifice, and God rejected it. Sadly, sin destroyed the family of Adam through Adam's first son. Cain's punishment was separation from his family: he was cursed to be a vagrant

---

[1] Genesis 1:28
[2] Romans 5:12

and drifter.

As sin increased on the earth, God grew increasingly saddened by human behavior. Yet, this did not alter God's purpose to have an earthly family. By the sixth chapter of Genesis, we see that the Lord saw that the wickedness of man was great on the earth and that every intention and every thought of his heart was continually evil. The Lord was actually grieved in His own heart, and He was sorry that He had made man on the earth. Because of man's evil behavior, the Lord said, "I will blot out mankind whom I have created from the face of the earth... for I am sorry that I have made them. But Noah found favor [or grace] in the eyes of the Lord."[1] God saved Noah and his family out of the flood. Soon after, sin reared its ugly head and caused a problem in the family. We read in Genesis that Ham was Noah's youngest son. As a son, Ham had an open door into his father's presence, including his tent. One day Noah became drunk with wine and apparently was running around naked inside his tent. Ham, the father of Canaan, saw the nakedness of his father and went out and told the whole world. Of course, the whole world consisted of those who survived the flood, his two brothers Shem and Japheth.[2] Shem and Japheth backed into the tent with a garment and covered the nakedness of their father. Ham failed to realize that it was a position of privilege to be close enough to his father to see his frailties. A commonly stated idiom is "Familiarity breeds contempt." Notice that the word *familiarity* comes from the root word *family*. Ham dishonored his father Noah. The result was that Ham's son Canaan was cursed to be a servant in the clan of Noah. I am struck with God's silence concerning Noah's

---

[1] Genesis 6:5-8
[2] Genesis 9:21-22

behavior. His apparent disregard for Noah's drunkenness, in light of His severe judgment of Ham, should cause the fear of God to rise within many of us.

Even after the family breakdown of Adam and Noah, God remained steadfast in His determination to have a family on the earth. God desired not only a family on the earth but one that would bless all the families of the earth. Therefore, He once again searched the earth for a father. God turned His attention toward a father and son, Terah and Abram whom He called from Ur of the Chaldeans (currently Iraq) by way of Haran. Abram's father Terah died in this journey. In the twelfth chapter of Genesis, Father God comes to speak to the newly orphaned seventy-five year old man called Abram. God said, "Go forth from your country, from your relatives, and from your father's house to the land that I will show you; And I will make you a great nation, I will bless you, and make your name great; And so you shall be a blessing; I will bless those who bless you, and the one who curses you, I will curse. And in you, Abram, all the families of the earth will be blessed."[1] This is an amazing promise for God to make to a man. Then look at what God asks Abram to do.... Leave everything behind, your country, your relatives, and even your brothers and sisters, and go to a land that I will show you. God says, I have some plans for you and you alone, Abram. Nevertheless, Abram took Lot along.

At the end of chapter 14 of Genesis, after rescuing Lot from his kidnappers, Abram met Melchizedek. As mentioned earlier, the writer of Hebrews leads us to infer that Melchizedek is a pre-incarnate appearance of Jesus Christ. Melchizedek offers Abram bread and wine (the elements of the covenant) and blesses him. As chapter 15 begins, Father

---

[1] Genesis 12:1-3

God once more appears to Abram, promising that he would not only give him an heir, but that his descendants would be like the stars in the heaven. Moreover, we are told that Abram "believed the Lord; and He reckoned it to him as righteousness."[1] Strangely enough, Abram's name translates as "Exalted Father." This is ironic because Abram and Sarai had no children. In ancient times, barrenness was considered a divine curse. In fact, the very "first mention" of the word *prayer* is when Abraham prayed to God, and God healed Abimelech, his wife and his maidservants, so that they bore children.[2]

In chapter 16 of Genesis, we can learn a lesson about taking matters into our own hands. In an effort to assist God, Sarah came up with a scheme to solve the problem of her barrenness. She gave her maidservant, Hagar, to Abram, which resulted in the birth of Ishmael. This foolish decision, based upon pragmatism and expediency, tragically resulted in family turmoil, estrangement and division. To this day the descendants of Ishmael, including the Palestinian people, strive with the descendants of Abraham's grandson Israel.

In chapter 17, once again God appears to Abram, now ninety years old, and says, "I am El Shaddai, Almighty God; walk before Me and be blameless. I will make My covenant between Me and you, and will multiply you exceedingly."[3] At this, Abram fell on his face—a good posture for any of us whenever we encounter Almighty God. Then God spoke further to him saying, "As for Me, My covenant is with you."[4] As I mentioned earlier, the words "as for me" are covenant words. Covenant begins as a unilateral commitment stated in

---

[1] Genesis 15:6
[2] Genesis 20:17
[3] Genesis 17:1
[4] Genesis 17:4

these terms, "As for me," not "I will if you will." God said, "I will make you to be a father of many nations."[1] Remember that Abram was now ninety years old, and after thirteen years still had not received the promise of an heir. However, here is El Shaddai, God Himself, coming to Abram and telling him, I have a new name for you. "No longer shall your name be called Abram."[2] I believe that this blessed Abram to hear that God was about to change his name. Imagine all the teasing he must have received, having no children and having the name "Exalted Father." Abram probably said, Thank God! I doubt, however, that it brought Abram much relief when he heard, "Your name shall be Abraham; for I have made you a father of many nations."[3] The literal translation of this new name is "Father of Many Nations." Herein lies an interesting insight into God's hidden treasures.

In the Bible, the Holy Spirit is often referred to as a fire, a wind[4] or breath.[5] In fact, the Hebrew for breath, for wind, and for spirit is the word *ruwach*. When this word is pronounced, it sounds like a guttural 'rah.' Notice, by changing the name Abram to Abraham (Ab 'rah' ham), and Sarai to Sarah (Sa 'rah'), God added that sound to these two names. I am convinced that when God added this syllable [rah] the Spirit was breathed into the name. Look what took place! The barren couple became fertile. This reassures us that the Holy Spirit is well equipped to take that which is barren by nature and breathe life into it, thereby making it fruitful. God continued, "I will make you exceedingly fruitful; I will make nations of you, and kings shall come from you. I will establish

---

[1] Romans 4:17-18
[2] Genesis 17:5
[3] Romans 4:17-18
[4] Acts 2:2-4
[5] John 20:22

My covenant between Me and you and your descendants after you in their generations, for an everlasting covenant, to be God to you and your descendants after you. Also I give to you and your descendants after you the land in which you are a stranger, all the land of Canaan, as an everlasting possession; and I will be their God."[1]

More than a decade after the promise of God, Abraham and Sarah finally had a son and named him Isaac. Although Abraham and Ishmael were circumcised on the same day, and God promised to bless Ishmael, the covenant blessings of Abraham would be upon Isaac. As mentioned, Isaac serves as an Old Covenant shadow of Jesus. Abraham had prepared to sacrifice Isaac, but God provided a ram in his place. The example of Isaac's willingness to put his life in the hands of his father in such a dramatic manner has few comparisons outside the Lord Himself.

The names of Abraham and Sarah are recorded in the New Covenant "Hall of Faith" found in Hebrews 11.[2] Abraham is not remembered as a great warrior like David, a great prophet like Isaiah, a great liberator like Moses or as a prominent political figure like Joseph. Instead, the Biblical saga of Abraham's life focuses primarily around him, his wife, a son, and a grandson. Still today, his name ("Exalted Father" and "Father of Many Nations") remains a household word throughout the world. Conceivably, two things caused God to choose him for such an important role in history. First, he was a man of faith. Note that it does not simply say that Abraham believed in God, but it says, "Abraham believed God!"[3] I feel that there is a great difference in these two ideas.

---

[1] Genesis 17:6-8
[2] Hebrews 11:8-12
[3] Romans 4:3; Galatians 3:6; James 2:23

To believe God goes far beyond simply believing in God. Second, God saw Abraham's potential as a father. When Abraham received his name from God, he had no children. Apparently, it was God's opinion that if this man were given children, he would be a good father. At the time that God was prepared to destroy Sodom and Gomorrah for their perversion of family and society, He decided to first visit Abraham. We find this story recorded in Genesis. "And the Lord said, 'Shall I hide from Abraham that thing which I am about to do; Seeing that Abraham shall surely become a great and mighty nation, and all the nations of the earth shall be blessed in him? For I know him, that he will command his children and his household after him, and they shall keep the way of the Lord, to do justice and judgment; that the Lord may bring upon Abraham that which He has spoken of him.' "[1] God saw Abraham as a man of faith, and God had confidence that Abraham would command his children and his household to keep the way of the Lord. Therefore, the criterion for God's choice of Abraham was that he would be a faithful and responsible father. As it always is, God's assessment was correct. Surely, history has clearly vindicated God's choice of Abraham. Hundreds and even thousands of years have come and gone, and still today, Judaism, Islam, and Christianity all consider and revere Abraham as an important figure. Amazingly, we know Abraham for little else than his faith and his fatherhood. So let us take encouragement from Abraham's example. If the legacy we leave is simply to be men of faith who worked hard at being faithful fathers and sons, perhaps we are walking in the "footsteps of Abraham."[2]

---

[1] Genesis 18:17-19
[2] Romans 4:10-12

21

Sonship: The Path to Fatherhood

*A*t times, I fear that many have made Jesus appear like a "cosmic humanist," a mystical philanthropist out to save humanity. I absolutely and unequivocally believe in the gospel message of salvation, and I hold fast that Jesus Christ is my Savior. In addition, I believe Jesus offered Himself as the Savior of the world. Having said this, I feel a subtle danger of putting ourselves at the center of Jesus' mission and ministry. John Piper, noted author and pastor, has said that many of us are willing to be God-centered so long as we are convinced that God is man-centered. Numerous times, we have heard the message, "He came to save us!" Well, yes, He did, but His ultimate passion and obsession was "...to do the will of Him who sent Me and to finish His work."[1] Jesus said that His food, His very sustenance, was to do His Father's will and to complete His Father's work. Yes, we are blessed that our salvation was within the will and purpose of what the Father sent Him to do. However, the fact remains that the vital task undertaken by Jesus and the primary purpose in his first coming was to glorify His Father and then to reveal His Father to us.

Earlier I mentioned that God the Father had promised that He would again send a prophet with the spiritual mantle

---

[1] John 4:34

of Elijah.[1] He did this by sending John the Baptist. When John came, it was to prepare the way for the Lord Jesus Christ. It is often overlooked, yet it is important to note, that John was not sent to prepare the way for a father to come but rather for a son. Allow me to reiterate: this son Jesus Christ and His Father, who is God, had enjoyed the perfect father and son relationship throughout eternity. Now, into this time-space world the Father would send His Son. It was a son who came to bring the message of God's fatherhood. It was Jesus His Son, who showed us that our God is a Father (or better yet, *the* Father.) This is one of the simplest, most obvious, yet most fascinating revelations that I have ever received. God sent us His Son.[2] Moreover, the primary motivation and passion of Jesus was to reveal to us who are His followers that our God is a Father.[3]

Since the obsession of Jesus was to reveal His Father to men and women, it would seem that His disciples would have caught this vision. As mentioned earlier, it appears that Philip, one of Jesus' twelve disciples, did recognize the importance of seeing and knowing the Father. However, Philip did not realize that the Father was revealed through seeing and knowing the Son. Let us look again at a portion of their conversation. Jesus began by saying, " 'If you had known Me, you would have known My Father also; from now on you know Him, and have seen Him.' Then Philip said to Jesus, 'Lord, show us the Father, and it is enough for us.' Jesus said to him, 'Have I been so long with you, and yet you have not come to know Me, Philip? He who has seen Me has seen the Father; how can you say, "Show us the Father"?' "[4] The

---

[1] Malachi 4:5-6
[2] John 3:16
[3] John 17:4-6
[4] John 14:7-9

response that Jesus gave to Philip reveals a measure of His frustration regarding this issue. The passages above imply that if you were to see Jesus and His Father, you would not be able to tell them apart.

For my sixtieth birthday, Kathy surprised me with a party. She asked the guests to come dressed in the attire that I normally wear, which includes a t-shirt, jeans and a ball cap. My son, Sean, stepped out further. He shaved his chin, took out his decorative metal earrings and even put a spot on his lower lip that mirrored my appearance. As most of you know, Sean and I are somewhat similar in appearance, being a bit short and deprived of hair. Several times during that celebration, even Kathy mistook Sean for me. This example simply illustrated a physical likeness. Jesus was and is the exact image of His Father in all ways. They look alike, talk alike, think alike and are alike. Therefore, when the Father sent Jesus, it was as if the Father had come Himself.[1] As mentioned before, it was the responsibility of Jesus as the Son to reveal the nature of God as a Father. For this reason, we say with confidence that the Biblical path to an understanding of fatherhood is through understanding sonship. Jesus Christ is the archetype and the model for us in all things, including this.

Jesus became a father by being a son. This, too, is how we become fathers and understand fatherhood: that is, by first being sons. When we as men or women come to embrace the "spirit of sonship," we begin to understand fatherhood. Many men spend years attempting to be better fathers, failing to understand that Biblical fatherhood happens as a consequence of modeling sonship. God's purpose in sending a son was to show us how to be sons. The most

---

[1] John 8:19; John 14:7

effective manner in which to teach sonship is to model it. Example will trump advice every time. Through demonstrating right relationships with our fathers, we can show our children, not simply tell them, how to relate to us as fathers. We are obliged to allow our sons to see our example.

Here is an illustration: Let us suppose that a child speaks to his father in an inappropriate manner or voice. There are at least two possible ways to correct the child. I have found the most common correction is for a father to say to the child, "Don't ever speak to me like that again! I am your father." There may be times when this is appropriate to say. However, on some occasions I suggest that there is another way to address this child. Consider, if you will, a father saying to his child, "I would never speak to my father the way you are speaking to me." The first example demands rather than commands honor and respect. This method of correction will have a tendency to cause a child to turn downward and inward. The second approach is more apt to call a child up to a higher example. Understandably, in order to use the second approach requires that the father had already demonstrated his own sonship in some manner. Not long ago I was spending time with Sean, when one of his children began to pout and complain. Sean spoke these words: "Have you ever seen me behave like that around Grandpa?" There was no need for a response, since the answer was obvious.

Demonstration and example were two essential elements of Jesus' teaching method. It is helpful to note that Luke, who authored the book of Acts, speaks of Jesus first doing and then teaching. "The first account I composed, Theophilus, about all that Jesus began to do and teach..."[1] Often in His ministry, Jesus would do something, such as a

---

[1] Acts 1:1-2

miracle, a healing, or some other demonstration of His power. Afterwards, He would use what he had done as an opportunity for teaching. Later, Jesus would send His disciples out both to perform and to proclaim. Notice here, once again, the order given. "He called the twelve together, and gave them power and authority over all the demons, and to heal diseases. And He sent them out to proclaim the kingdom of God, and to perform healing."[1] They were to teach and to do, or to proclaim and perform. Jesus had been discipled by correctly posturing Himself toward His Father. The method that Jesus used to father His disciples was by being a faithful Son to His Father. He lived among them, and used the events of each day to teach them spiritual lessons and principles. The disciples were spiritual apprentices. They learned by observing His example. In short, when we use this model as leaders or fathers we say, "Son, listen to me, watch me and do as I do."[2] With this in mind, if you want to know how to be a father, you must first learn how to be a son. You then demonstrate sonship to those who look to you for fatherhood.

Now let us look at how modeling sonship might affect our leadership style. I once saw a cartoon with a man chasing after a crowd. The caption read, "Wait for me, I'm your leader." It may be of some help for pastors to consider that we drive cattle, but we lead sheep. If someone calls himself a leader, his followers will see more of his back than of his face. Additionally, if nobody is following him, he is not a leader; he is just out for a walk. The word *leader* describes a person who says, "Step where I have stepped." Personally, I would be a bit reluctant to follow the advice of a marriage counselor

---

[1] Luke 9:1-2
[2] John 5:19-20; John 8:28-29

who has been through several divorces.

Another advantage of modeling sonship to those who are looking to us for fathering is that it gives us a sense of empathy. As a high school English teacher one of the most helpful pieces of advice I ever received was "Never forget what it was like to be a student." When I prepared exams or gave out homework, I regularly used this principle to help govern my actions. Most fathers could benefit by using this advice when it comes to dealing with their children.

The best leaders are those who set examples for their followers. That is why modeling sonship is a practical expression for leadership and fatherhood. By embracing this model, we lead by serving. We are able to lead those who look to us, by serving the one who is over us.

For many years Dan Wolfe has emphasized the point that humility is a virtue we should find in every leader. Serving, also, is a visible and practical way for one to express humility. Jesus was the epitome of a servant-leader. However, as I have stated previously, His primary focus of service was not toward His followers. Jesus saw that His priority was to serve His Father. His purpose for coming to earth was to bring glory to His Father. He did this by being perfectly obedient to finish the work His Father had sent Him to do.[1]

---

[1] John 17:4-6

22

A Portrait of Jesus

You would probably agree that few people know us better and trust us more than our best friend. The Bible refers to John as the "beloved disciple," using that phrase in his own gospel at least five times.[1] Since Jesus loved all of the disciples, I have concluded that this was a distinguishing name for John. More than likely, he was Jesus' best friend. From the cross, Jesus committed the care of His mother Mary to John. Having this relationship with the Lord would have given him a deeper understanding, perhaps a more intimate knowledge, and a more penetrating insight into Jesus. Significantly, more than the other gospel writers, John addresses the ambition, attitude, and motivation of Jesus' life and ministry. The magnificent obsession of Jesus Christ may be summed up in this phrase: Jesus' passionate pursuit was to please His Father. Using passages from John's gospel, I want to attempt to paint for us his portrait of Jesus. This is not a physical portrait, but rather one that attempts to shed light on His nature and being. As we read the following texts, we get a glimpse into the heart of a Son who is dedicated to the goal of fulfilling the task for which His Father sent Him.

Jesus obeyed His Father. Jesus said, "My food is to do

---

[1] John 13: 23; John 20:2; John 21:7, 20 & 24

the will of Him who sent Me, and to accomplish His work."[1] Satisfying His spiritual hunger to please His Father was far more important to Jesus than gratifying His human appetite. Jesus desired doing the will of His Father more than He craved his necessary food. He clearly demonstrated this during His temptation in the wilderness. After Jesus fasted for forty days, the devil came and tempted Him to turn the stones into bread. Jesus responded to the temptation by quoting Moses saying, "Man shall not live by bread alone, but by every word that proceeds from the mouth of God."[2]

Jesus was discipled by the Father Himself. Addressing an angry mob, Jesus said, "Truly, truly, I say to you, the Son can do nothing of Himself, unless it is something He sees the Father doing; for whatever the Father does, these things the Son also does in like manner. For the Father loves the Son, and shows Him all things that He Himself is doing; and greater works than these will He show Him, that you may marvel."[3] We learn from these words that discipleship involves relationship (love), demonstration, and imitation. The primary purpose of discipline is sonship. It is through discipline that one becomes a son. "But if you are without discipline, of which all have become partakers, then you are illegitimate children and not sons."[4] The advantage of discipline is learning that a genuine father wishes for his son to do greater works than he himself does.

Jesus did nothing on His own initiative. Jesus said, "I can do nothing on My own initiative. As I hear, I judge; and My judgment is just, because I do not seek My own will, but

---

[1] John 4:34
[2] Deuteronomy 8:3; Matthew 4:3-4
[3] John 5:19-20
[4] Hebrews 12:8

the will of Him who sent Me."[1] This is an amazing statement to me. Let me repeat; Jesus never used His power and authority to initiate His own agenda. The compass that Jesus used to set His own course was His Father's will. Additionally, the will of the Father was the plumb line that Jesus would use to judge everything.

Jesus pointed out that the validation of His ministry came from accomplishing the works that His Father had sent Him to do. He said, "...the witness which I have is greater than that of John the Baptist; for the works which the Father has given Me to accomplish, the very works that I do, bear witness of Me, that the Father has sent Me."[2] He did not attempt to validate his ministry with the endorsement of John the Baptist, who was the most famous preacher to arrive in over four hundred years. Accomplishing the work that His Father sent Him to do authorized and confirmed Him as the One who was sent.

Jesus clearly understood and declared His purpose for coming to earth. He originated from heaven, and earth was His destination. "For I have come down from heaven, not to do My own will, but the will of Him who sent Me."[3] Jesus was sent on an assignment, which he completed without flaw or corruption in any manner. He demonstrated that His duty was not related to His comfort or convenience, but only to His Father's will. He never sidetracked from His commitment to establish His Father's kingdom, the governmental order of God, and with it to display His Father's glory.

Jesus only taught what His Father had taught Him. Jesus said, "My teaching is not Mine, but His who sent Me."[4]

---

[1] John 5:30
[2] John 5:36
[3] John 6:38
[4] John 7:16

Jesus had studied under the greatest of all teachers, the Father and the Holy Spirit themselves. He embodied knowledge and wisdom. That which He had learned from His Father, He taught to us. He had not only been a Son, but also a disciple and a student of His Father. Of course, this relationship defies human understanding and explanation.

Jesus was not seeking His own glory. "He who speaks from himself seeks his own glory; but He who is seeking the glory of the One who sent Him, He is true, and there is no unrighteousness in Him."[1] Jesus focused on bringing glory to His Father, the one who had sent Him. Whatever He said or undertook to do was never motivated by selfish ambition or self-realization. His entire focus was always and entirely upon His Father's reputation.

Jesus implied that a spiritual revelation is needed for us to know Him. For us simply to concur with the fact that Jesus was a historical figure is not true knowledge of Him. We need the Holy Spirit to reveal to us that Jesus came in the exact image of the Father in heaven. When Jesus asked His disciples, who do men say that I am, Peter said, "You are the Christ, the Son of the living God." Jesus responded, "Flesh and blood has not revealed this to you, but My Father in heaven has revealed this."[2] The religious leaders of the day knew Him in the natural, but as He was teaching, "Jesus cried out in the temple, 'You both know Me and know where I am from; and I have not come of Myself [of my own initiative], but He [the Father] who sent Me is true, whom you do not know.' "[3] The Scribes and Pharisees of Jesus' day proved that one could know the book and not know the author.

[1] John 7:18
[2] Matthew 16:13-17
[3] John 7:28

Jesus' assessments of situations were not subject to the biases and prejudices of His day. "But even if I do judge, My judgment is true; for I am not alone in it, but I and He who sent Me."[1] Again, the manner in which He judged things was identical to the position His Father took. Jesus never held an opinion that was opposed to that of His Father. This is especially evident in His conversation with the woman at the well. "The Samaritan woman therefore said to Him, 'How is it that You, being a Jew, ask me for a drink since I am a Samaritan woman?' (For Jews have no dealings with Samaritans.)"[2] Even though Jesus was a Jew, neither He nor His Father are bound to or limited by the cultural prejudices of Judaism.

According to Jesus, confidence in ministry comes from knowing who you are and knowing who it is that is sending you. Jesus said, "I am He who bears witness of Myself, and the Father who sent Me bears witness of Me."[3] The clear implication of what Jesus said is that legitimacy in the ministry is linked to being sent. Jesus did not come to earth primarily because there was a need; He came because He was sent. At least thirty times in the Gospel of John alone, Jesus refers to Himself as being sent. *Apostle* is a Greek word meaning, "one sent forth."

Jesus said, When you've met me, you've met my dad. If we were to look at the Father and the Son together, we would feel like we had double vision. They are not like identical twins; they are identical individuals. "And so they were saying to Him, 'Where is Your Father?' Jesus answered, 'You know neither Me, nor My Father; if you knew Me, you

---

[1] John 8:16
[2] John 4:9
[3] John 8:18

would have known My Father also.' "[1] Philip requested that Jesus show him the Father. I wonder if we do the same. We must understand the full significance of what it means when He said that the Father is revealed in seeing and knowing the Son. Apparently, when Jesus and the Father walk together, they only cast but one shadow.[2] It does not get any clearer than that!

Jesus was and always is a "Father pleaser." As I will expound upon later, the driving force in Jesus' life was to be a "Father pleaser." "Jesus said, 'When you lift up the Son of Man, then you will know that I am He, and I do nothing on My own initiative, but I speak those things as the Father taught Me. And He who sent Me is with Me; He has not left Me alone, for I always do the things that are pleasing to Him.' "[3] These verses, two of the most powerful in all of Scripture, sum up virtually everything that John has said. The last sentence of this passage, "I always do the things that please my Father," is one of the most significant in the entire Bible.

Jesus was not driven in ministry simply to meet needs. As mentioned, Jesus did nothing out of His own initiative. He was touched by need and at times was moved with compassion, but He limited Himself to serving the purpose and desire of His Father. He did not come under the compulsion of meeting existing needs. "Judas Iscariot asked, 'Why was this perfume not sold for three hundred denarii, and given to poor people?' Now he said this, not because he was concerned about the poor, but because he was a thief, and as he had the moneybox, he used to pilfer what was put into it. Jesus therefore said, 'Let her alone, in order that she

---

[1] John 8:19
[2] John 14:8-9
[3] John 8:28-29

may keep it for the day of My burial. For the poor you always have with you, but you do not always have Me.' "[1] Much of ministry has its origin and focus in meeting a need; I believe that filling a need is admirable. However, a wealthy pagan philanthropist can do this.

Jesus did not minister out of a "need to be needed." "But I do not seek My glory; there is One who seeks and judges."[2] Some ministry flows out of ministers who have a need to be needed. Without doubt, there is a certain measure of self-satisfaction that comes with meeting a need. However, Jesus was neither influenced nor affected by the praise of men. His entire focus was to bring glory to His Father. He made no effort to gain attention or recognition for Himself.

Jesus had a clear sense of identity. Undaunted by His detractors, He knew who He was, and what He was called to do. "Do you say of Him, whom the Father sanctified and sent into the world, 'You are blaspheming,' because I said, 'I am the Son of God'?"[3] Jesus was not "name dropping" His Father for some personal agenda. Unlike many of us today, Jesus had no identity issues.

Jesus was the exact echo of His Father's voice. He quoted the Father verbatim. Jesus said "... I did not speak on My own initiative, but the Father Himself who sent Me has given Me commandment, what to say, and what to speak. And I know that His commandment is eternal life; therefore the things that I speak, I speak just as the Father has told Me."[4] Along with many of you, I have been in meetings where someone has said, "Thus says the Lord..." It is my opinion that the Lord often receives the blame for saying things He did not

---

[1] John 12:5-8
[2] John 8:50
[3] John 10:36
[4] John 12:49-50

say. However, in the case of Jesus, everything He spoke was a "Thus says the Lord!" I have sometimes wondered why the whole of the Bible is not in red letters, since Jesus is the Word of God and vice versa.

Jesus, who was sent, became the sender. "Truly, truly, I say to you, he who receives whomever I send receives Me; and he who receives Me receives Him who sent Me."[1] This passage puts the man of God, whom Jesus sends, in a powerful position of authority. Many people say, "God sent me!" Not only does God receive blame for saying things He has not said, but also God is charged for sending people He did not send. The ultimate issue and often the dilemma for us is to clearly recognize and receive only those whom Jesus sends.

---

[1] John 13:20

23

Raising Father Pleasers

As a high school athletic coach, I became interested in the dynamics of motivation. Motivation, in my opinion, is a subject that has been greatly misunderstood. Therefore, during my postgraduate studies I decided to do a thesis on this theme. Subsequent to extensive research, I came to this conclusion: That which many people call motivation is not motivation at all; rather it is actually positive or negative stimulation. Let me explain: If a dog is lying in a doorway that you wish to go through, there are two ways to cause him to move. First, you might offer him a treat; this is an example of positive stimulation. If this does not work, you can kick him; this I would call negative stimulation. I like to call what I have described here the Coaxing or Kicking Model. In each of the two examples, the dog is stimulated, not motivated. In other words: who wants the dog to move, you or the dog? The dog moves, but it is you that desires the dog to move. Hence, you are the one who is motivated. The dog is simply responding to your stimulus. If and only when the dog moves of its own desire, can we say the dog is motivated.

Prompted by my research on the subject of motivation, I began to investigate the life of Jesus more closely. I asked myself, "What motivated Jesus?" "What was the internal passion and drive that moved him?" A careful study of the gospel of John answered this question for me. Jesus Christ needed neither coaxing nor kicking. John taught us that Jesus was, He is and He always will be a Father pleaser. Jesus said, "He who sent Me is with Me; He has not left Me alone, for I always do the things that are pleasing to Him."[1] In basic terms, Jesus simply wanted to please His Dad.

I have often asked people this question: "If you raise your children to be father pleasers, how many rules will you need to make?" Typically, the response is, "Not many." Children raised to be father pleasers will need very few rules. Moreover, the purpose of the rules would simply be to define the heart of their father. The attitudes and conduct of such children would be restrained and modified by the love and respect that they have for their fathers. Subsequently I have asked, "If your children are not father pleasers, how many rules will you need to make?" Well, any answer to this question is probably immaterial. If children do not wish to please their fathers, it matters little how many rules are made, because it is quite unlikely they will be honored and obeyed.

A major problem that we face today is that many in the church are not taught to recognize and to please God the Father, let alone those whom God sends as "spiritual fathers." Consequently, many churches have been inclined to establish strict rules. All too often, these rules define certain forms of acceptable behavior, rarely touching motives and attitudes. Generally, this will force leaders to attempt to enforce these codes of conduct. The result is seldom any more than legalistic compliance with little if any joyful obedience. I venture to say that all too many Sunday sermons qualify under the Coaxing and Kicking Model that I referred to earlier.

---

[1] John 8:29

The love that Jesus had for His Father compelled and constrained Him. Certainly, He was not a crowd pleaser! Jesus refused to be swayed by public opinion or pressure from his natural family, his friends or His disciples. He did not take his cues from those who looked to Him for leadership. He looked to His Father, the One who was over Him, and always pleased Him. Inasmuch as Jesus is our example for every aspect of our life and being, what motivated Jesus should motivate us. He is the perfect model of a son and, as such, a father pleaser. Therefore, we must consider adopting His attitude and pattern for ourselves. We ourselves should be father pleasers, giving our children a pattern to observe and a model to follow. We must consider setting an example ourselves instead of using the current model of coaxing and kicking to raise children. So, how is this accomplished?

Using the example of farming, let us consider the steps necessary to bring forth a bountiful harvest. Let us consider the heart of humanity as the field. A good farmer will select good soil. Regrettably, I construe that in the parable of the sower, three of the four soils were not productive.[1] Also, it is implied that the most important part of sowing is soil preparation. God often begins with a shallow plow, which overturns the weeds and sun-baked surface. Then He sets the plow point deeper, overturning some of the stones and rocks—attitudes and motives—more deeply hidden within us. Finally, He plows deep enough to tear through and turn up roots. Many of us pass through seasons of plowing with great anguish and distress. Sometimes we forget that God never plows deeper than He intends to plant. Once our hearts have been prepared, God can plant the seed. The fields of our hearts—and the hearts of those we help to plow—still need

---

[1] Matthew 13:18-23

cultivation, water and light.

Let us return to the Law of First Mention as it relates to sonship and fatherhood. In the book of Genesis, we have the creation story. On the third day, God created fruit trees, which had the distinct characteristic that the seed for reproduction was in the fruit itself.[1] In each seed is the potential to reproduce the fruit that brings forth more seed. My son Matt expresses it this way: "There is a potential for a large orchard in every five pound bag of oranges." Jesus taught us that the word of God is a seed, and in the seed is the potential to bring forth fruit. The promise that God gave to Abraham was that he would have a son. This son would be a figure of the Son that was to come. Isaac was that son, and he carried the seed of the promise given to Abraham.[2]

Now let us apply this to our model for fatherhood, which is fathers producing sons by first being sons. Three times it is mentioned that the seed brings forth or yields fruit "after their kind." We would say, "Like produces like." You have probably heard the phrase, "Like father, like son." After Jesus told the parable of the sower, He offered the parable of the wheat and the tares. The soil in this instance is the world. The seeds are the sons of the Kingdom. The enemy sowed tares in the wheat field. Tares are harmful weeds that resemble wheat. Rather than separating the two immediately, Jesus said He would allow both to grow up together, so that the wheat would not be uprooted.[3] It is not always easy to distinguish between genuine sons of the Kingdom and imposters. It is interesting to note that as wheat grows and matures the weight of the grain causes the head to bow; but

---

[1] Genesis 1:11-13
[2] Galatians 3:16
[3] Matthew 13:24-30

not so for tares.

Now consider this: we know seed does not grow, sprout and reproduce until it is sown in the proper environment. You can go to any garden store and pick up a packet of seed. Isn't it interesting, that the seeds never sprout in the packet? However, open the packet and put them into fertile soil and the seed will grow. Jesus explained in detail the parable of the four soils. In this parable, the seeds are not different, but the soils are. The soils represent the environment, which in this case is the hearts of men. As mentioned, three-fourths of the soils spoken of would become unproductive. So, let us address the issue of soils. Let me define soil as the environment or atmosphere needed for the reproduction of sons. I remind you that soil, as well as seed, is needed for reproduction. The seed of sonship has the best chance of bearing fruit in an environment that includes the following:

The seed of sonship is most likely to sprout in an atmosphere of unconditional love. God stated His unconditional love in terms of covenant. I mentioned earlier that He said to Abraham, "As for me..." Unconditional love does not demand reciprocity. It is unilateral. Moreover, the basis of it is not performance. It involves loving someone for who they are, not for what they do.

The seed of sonship thrives in an atmosphere of openness. Sometimes children are not open, partly due to their fathers having failed to really listen to them. From time to time, when my sons were young, I would ask Sean and/or Matt, "Are you doing anything that you would not want Dad to know about? I want you to tell me. I will not use what you tell me as an opportunity to punish you." Usually, just looking into their eyes gave me the answer I was looking for. Accusation, shame and guilt can cause children to become isolated in paranoia and the fear of being discovered. Much demonic activity thrives on blackmail. Intimacy can be defined as "in to me see." When I worked in this way with my sons, we were able to develop a more intimate relationship with each other.

The seed of sonship needs an atmosphere of protection and safety. Numerous passages of Scripture speak of the protection that the Lord provides for us His children. Fathers can make children feel that they are safe and protected. One day when Matt arrived home from school, it was evident that he had been crying. He went directly to his room, avoiding any questions from Kathy. Later, when I came home, Sean filled us in on what had happened. While walking home from school, a young boy had threatened Matt by putting a knife to his neck. Well, I became one enraged pastor who was about to blow his testimony. Veins popping in my neck, I headed for the home of the boy who had assaulted my son. When he saw me coming, he ran and hid. His father came to the door, and I explained to him what had happened. Then I said, "I give you this option, are you going to whip him, or am I?" His father said, "I'll take care of it." I said, "I'll wait!" While I waited and observed He called the boy and then he spanked him. Partially satisfied, I turned to leave with these words, "If it ever happens again, I will not give you the option." It never happened again.

The seed of sonship needs an atmosphere of truth, lavishly seasoned with grace and mercy. Truth, grace and mercy have the ability to create an atmosphere of freedom. John wrote, "For the Law was given through Moses; grace and truth were realized through Jesus Christ."[1] This verse is illustrated in John 8 in the story of the woman caught in adultery. Heartlessly using her as bait, the woman's accusers

---

[1] John 1:17

intended to trap Jesus. However, when He asked that the one without sin throw the first stone, the accusers disbanded. And straightening up, Jesus said to her, " 'Woman, where are they? Did no one condemn you?' And she said, 'No one, Lord.' And Jesus said, 'Neither do I condemn you; go your way. From now on sin no more.' "[1] He dismissed the woman with these words. Notice Jesus first said, "Neither do I condemn you." Then He said, "Go and sin no more." Grace came before truth and lays a foundation for it. Surely overemphasizing grace while neglecting the truth is not the way to genuine freedom. However, in light of this example when we err with our children, it might behoove us to err on the side of grace.

The seed of sonship flourishes in an atmosphere free of suspicion, accusation and condemnation. The Scriptures refer to Satan as "the accuser."[2] I like to think about my situation like this: Satan stands against me before God as a prosecuting attorney. Jesus Christ stands with me as my defense attorney. Marvelously, Jesus is not only my defense attorney, but also He is the judge. What is more, thanks be to God, through the work of the cross I am pardoned not paroled. Oftentimes when Sean and Matt were little, I took the opportunity to hear their prayers as I tucked them into their beds. It was a precious time. As they were usually a bit sleepy, it made them more vulnerable. Occasionally, I would ask them individually, "Have I accused you of or punished you for something you did not do?" If I had, I wanted to clear up the incident by quickly apologizing to them. Untended childhood wounds can fester and become gangrenous in the life of an adult.

The seed of sonship will grow in an atmosphere of

---

[1] John 8:10-11
[2] Revelation 12:10

trust and confidence. When Sean was eighteen years old, Kathy had the following conversation with him. "Sean," she said, "you have never caused us any real problems. You have never rebelled. What was your secret?" Sean responded, "I knew that you and Dad trusted me, and as long as you trusted me, I had all the freedom in the world. I also knew that if I lost your trust, I would lose my freedom." Jesus said, "...the truth will make you free."[1] The freedom that Sean enjoyed rose out of our ability to trust him.

I do not believe that we can think of life as a recipe such that if we simply add all the proper ingredients, we will have one continuous feast. If we adhere to this idea, we will most certainly conclude that the great apostle Paul missed the path that God had for him. Paul's journey included beatings, imprisonment, shipwrecks, stonings, and near-drownings. He was subjected to hunger, thirst and nakedness. Moreover, he was nearly always under the scrutinizing and critical eye of the religious leaders of his day.[2] In the life of each believer, there are factors and circumstances that are far beyond our control. I do not believe that the law of sowing and reaping is an overriding and sacrosanct or inviolable law, at least as it pertains to our life here on earth. I continually thank God for the spiritual "crop failures" He has permitted. However, as my wife Kathy has countered, "If you want to reap tomatoes, you better plan to plant tomato seeds." Drought, disease and other things out of our control may affect what we reap, but they do not change the nature of the seed.

---

[1] John 8:32
[2] 2 Corinthians 11:23-27

24

Dads and Daughters

Prior to writing this book, I wrote a seminar manual entitled *Sonship: The Path to Fatherhood*. In the opening of this manual I wrote, "This book is written primarily to men, and for men. It comes after raising two sons, who are now fathers themselves." It was my attempt to describe and relate to others a journey I had been traveling for over three decades. The purpose of this journey was the maturation of boys into men, and sons into fathers. Since then, I began to ask myself, *Where do my daughters-in-law, Wendy and Tina, and my granddaughters fit into this paradigm?* A couple of years ago, the women of Harvest Church planned a women's retreat. Wendy and Tina came to me with a spark of mischief in their eyes. They asked, "Dad, was it not Paul who wrote to Titus telling him to, "...urge the older women to teach the younger women..."[1] Here we see four generations; Paul told Titus to teach the older women to teach the younger women. Based upon that passage, they chose me as the keynote speaker for the Harvest Ladies Retreat. The subject was to be the women's role in the Fatherhood and Sonship message. At the time, I was ill-prepared to do this. I remember nervously walking into a roomful of giggling women. I proceeded to stumble through a

---

[1] Titus 2:3-5

message that I knew so well for men, but had no clue how to give to a group of daughters. I am not certain why this was so awkward for me. Almost every man that I oversee has at least one daughter. Surely, these daughters needed to understand God's Fatherhood, too.

A few years later, Kathy and I were traveling together in Australia. I had shared from the manual *Sonship: The Path to Fatherhood*. A Chinese businesswoman who was hosting Kathy and me asked me this question. "Would you be a father to me?" When I hesitated to answer, she asked, "Does not God have daughters?" A bit of her background may give you a better understanding of the source of this question. She was born into an affluent Chinese family in Malaysia. As a little girl, her Chinese father rejected her simply because of her gender. She was given over to a foster family, and only because her grandfather intervened was she reluctantly restored to her biological family. As she grew up, she constantly was reminded that her father had wanted a boy. After graduating from secondary school, she attended an Assembly of God Bible school. Later, she and her husband served as co-pastors in the Assemblies of God. Finally, they settled in Australia, left the pastorate, and she became involved in business mentoring, which she continues to this day.

For me, this question was complicated by two factors. First, soon after I was converted, the course of my life altered dramatically when a serious failure was discovered in the church leadership. It was through Dan Wolfe's counsel and guidance that I was not totally scandalized. Secondly, Kathy and I had two boys. I have never considered myself an expert on the subject of raising boys, let alone girls. Until January of 2008, we were blessed to have our immediate family living within seven miles of us, three doors from one another. Sean and Matt are grown and married. Wendy and Tina, the respective wives of my sons, are as precious to Kathy and me as if they were our own daughters. What's more, these two couples have provided us with eight grandchildren, three boys and five girls. Still, I pondered the question, "What is the role of girls and women in the message of fatherhood and sonship?"

Obviously, God has daughters and loves them as much as He loves sons. Therefore, I had to conclude that all children of God should have the experience of having a father, including spiritual fathers. Finally, after much prayer and conversation with Dan and with Kathy, I agreed to be a spiritual father to the businesswoman mentioned above. The practical outworking of this, however, has forced me to research this more extensively. My own sons, as well as many of you reading this book, probably have greater insight into this than I do. Nevertheless, here is my feeble attempt to address the gender issue as it pertains to "spiritual sonship."

Earlier I shared that "first means first" and that "all means all." There exists no more than all! For example, when the Bible says, "All authority has been given to Me in heaven and on earth..."[1] that is exactly what it means. There is no authority except that which comes from Jesus Christ. Now let me share a passage of Scripture that opened to me while I was meditating upon the sonship message as it applies to women. "For you are all sons of God through faith in Christ Jesus. For all of you who were baptized into Christ have clothed yourselves with Christ. There is neither Jew nor Greek, there is neither slave nor free man, there is neither male nor female; for you are all one in Christ Jesus. And if you belong to Christ, then you are Abraham's offspring, heirs

---

[1] Matthew 28:18

according to promise."[1] The word *sons* in this passage is the Greek word **huios**, which is masculine. It is not the neutral word **teknon**, which could be translated children. I thought to myself, *So all are "sons (huios) of God through faith in Christ?"* If this is true, then in some instances sonship, especially spiritual sonship, is not gender-specific.

Let us consider another passage: "For all who are being led by the Spirit of God, these are sons (*huios*) of God. For you have not received a spirit of slavery leading to fear again, but you have received a spirit of adoption as sons by which we cry out, 'Abba! Father!' The Spirit Himself bears witness with our spirit that we are children of God, and if children, heirs also, heirs of God and fellow heirs with Christ, if indeed we suffer with Him in order that we may also be glorified with Him."[2] If we agree that the Spirit of God can lead a woman, then we must conclude from this passage as well that in some significant instances the term "sons of God" is not gender-specific. In light of these and other passages, the "spirit of sonship" is what I am attempting to address.

Well, then, does this mean that women can become fathers? Absolutely not! I want my readers to rest assured that I have not jumped into the militant feminist agenda. Still, it would make sense that having an understanding of fatherhood and sonship would be a great asset to a woman, particularly when she is choosing a husband and potential father for her children. A noted feminist once wrote, "Many of us have become the husbands that we wanted to marry." Males and females need to understand what a father is, how to relate to a father and to be able to experience the love and grace of a father. Both need to be fully reassured of their

---

[1] Galatians 3:26-29
[2] Romans 8:14-17

personal worth, their value, as well as their power, passion and purpose in fulfilling God's call and use of them in extending His kingdom. Both need to be able to accurately reflect, represent and reproduce His nature and character to a dysfunctional and lost world.

Therefore, this is my attempt to speak to the godly women, the precious daughters and granddaughters of the family of God. The message of fatherhood and sonship applies to them as well. On the sixth day, God created male and female.[1] Then He said, "It is very good."[2] As the archetype for all fathers, God did not love, respect or prefer mankind on the basis of gender. The relationship with a dad and his sons and daughters should be a powerful reflection of the Father's love for each of us. A genuine father will appreciate, love and care for his daughters every bit as much as he cares for his sons. I have observed Matt and Sean relating to their daughters. I find that there is no preferential treatment given to their sons over their daughters. They offer time, attention, energy, discipline and encouragement without reference to gender. I am certain that any material inheritance will be given in the same manner. Yes, in the Old Covenant only male sons received an inheritance from the father. However, in the New Covenant Paul says that as many as are led by the Spirit of God are "...joint heirs with Christ."[3] What is more, the Old Covenant continued through the circumcision of the males, which made it gender-specific. However, the New Covenant perpetuates through the circumcision of the heart. In actuality, circumcision was always meant to be an issue of the heart.

---

[1] Genesis 1:27
[2] Genesis 1:31
[3] Romans 8:17

Silence is a tool used by Satan to hurt and to divide. Great wounds and hurt have come to both natural and spiritual daughters due to our lack of understanding, error or silence in dealing with this theme. Personally, I believe that much of the militant feminism rises out of the vacuum created by renegade fathers. Therefore, it behooves us to ask, "What is the Father's heart toward this beautiful and precious creation that we call woman?" Surely, we must conclude that God does not call any of us (male or female) to bondage but to freedom. He does not separate or reject, but includes and accepts us. His purpose is not primarily restriction, but release. His call for submission is not to a second-class subservience, but to protection and safety. Since the woman is to be the glory, or reflection of the man, her countenance should reflect the joy and peace of that protection and safety. Any true father reading this book must agree that nearly all of the attitudes, posture of heart and character traits that we desire to impart to our sons would be just as desirable in our daughters. Certainly, we are not raising our daughters to be husbands and fathers, but rather to be wives and mothers. In over thirty-five years of ministry I have never heard a single mother say, "I am so glad that I can now fill the role of being not only a mother but also a father to my children."

Another question that I have been asked is, "Can both married and single women have fathers?" Again, this was a difficult question for me to answer. Although the role of a father differs once a woman is married, I believe that fatherhood is still beneficial, and at times needed. My experience with Kathy has helped lead me to this conclusion. Kathy's father was a cool, aloof and intellectual man. He was not warm and affirming toward her. Through the years, Kathy watched me father people and was somewhat frustrated by the fact that I could be a father to so many others, but not to her. I was her husband, not her father. I have discovered that many women want from their husbands only that which a father can provide. This brings us to the issue of what it is that a father should provide for a daughter. Obviously, this is not meant to be a checklist, nor is it exhaustive; but let me suggest some things that a father can provide whether a woman is single or married.

- ❖ The assurance of her personal worth.
- ❖ The safety of genuine male affection, free of any sexual agenda.
- ❖ The consistency of covenant commitment.
- ❖ The reflection of the Heavenly Father's delight.
- ❖ The patience of guiding her into womanhood.
- ❖ The boundaries that should exist in relationships.
- ❖ The absolute security of provision.
- ❖ The example of a husband to her mother.

We must never confuse worth and function! A woman's function in the home and in the church is addressed in the Scriptures, especially in the writings of Paul. It is beyond the intention and scope of this book to resolve the gender issue; therefore, let me conclude with this. It may sound redundant to state that all men are males. However, I do not believe all males are men. In the Apostle Paul's first letter to the Corinthians, he gives us a clear and simple distinguishing characteristic of a man. He begins with this emphasis, "I want you to understand." We might say, "Pay attention!" Paul wrote, "Christ is the head of every man and the man is the head of a woman, and God is the head of Christ."[1] This statement implies that you only become a man by acknowledging the just, due and rightful headship of Jesus Christ. If Christ is not your head, you are not a man. It is really not clear what you are. You may qualify anatomically to be a male, but by Biblical definition, you are not a man. Also, as implied by the passage above, not all females are women. What qualifies a female as a woman is male headship, especially as it concerns the order of God in the home and in the church. So when we address the issue of male sons becoming fathers, we conclude that only men, not just males, qualify. Nevertheless, clearly the "spirit of sonship" is the spirit of Christ dwelling in the believer, whether male or female. The outward expression of the spirit of Jesus Christ is not gender-specific.

---

[1] 1 Corinthians 11:3

25

A Child Is Born but a Son Is Given

*I*n the preceding chapter I proposed by Biblical definition that not all males are men and not all females are women. Now, I want to suggest that not all male children are sons, nor female children daughters. My intent and purpose for the following is to provide a greater understanding and appreciation for what it means to be a legitimate and genuine son. Children provide an essential element upon which we build the household, or the family. The Hebrew verb **yalad** means "to bear, bring forth, or beget." From a Biblical point of view, there is a difference between a female child (**yaldah**) and a daughter (**bath**) as well as a male child (**yeled**) and a son (**ben**). Notice that the root word for male and female child comes from the Hebrew *yalad*. Of particular interest to us is the fact that both *bath* and *ben* derive from the verb **baanah**, meaning to build. My conclusion is that you conceive and bear children, but you build sons and daughters. Therefore, not only do we build sons and daughters, but also we build upon sons and daughters.

The same is true for the Greek language. The Greek word for children is *teknon*, formed from the verb **tikto** meaning to beget or to bear. The Greek language uses *huios* as the word for son and **thugater** for daughter. *Teknon*, children, is used in both the natural and figurative senses. Generally speaking, *teknon* refers to the fact of birth, whereas the word *huios* stresses the nature of the relationship. As I stated earlier, in the literal sense, that is referring to a legal position, simply being born as a male child does not make one a son. Nor does being born a female child make one a daughter, at least in a Hebraic understanding of the word.

In his letter to the Galatians Paul wrote, "...as long as the heir is a child , he does not differ at all from a slave even though he is owner of everything, but the child is under guardians (tutors or mentors)."[1] In verse four Paul goes on to say, "But at the right time, God sent forth His Son, born of a woman, born under the Law, so that He might redeem those who were under the Law, that we might receive the adoption as sons. So, since you are sons, God has sent forth the Spirit of His Son into our hearts, crying, "Abba! Father!" Therefore you are no longer a slave, but a son; and if a son, then an heir through God."[2] According to Paul a child who is not yet considered a son or daughter, is like a slave. It is the Spirit of His Son sent forth into our hearts that allows us to be sons and therefore heirs. Sonship is not something we can achieve or produce by our own efforts. Rather it is only His Spirit within us that can produce it.

The Bible also teaches that Jesus was forever the Son of God, but He became the Son of Man, who took on flesh and blood in a time-space world.[3] Isaiah wrote, "For unto us a child (*yeled*) is born, and unto us a son (*ben*) is given..."[4] The New Covenant refers forty-three times to Jesus as the Son of God and over eighty times as the Son of Man. In my research, however, I cannot find the term "Son of God" in the Old

---

[1] Galatians 4:1
[2] Galatians 4:4-7
[3] John 1:14
[4] Isaiah 9:6

Covenant, and the only reference to the "Son of Man" (in capital letters) comes in the prophetic word of Daniel. "And behold, with the clouds of heaven One like a Son of Man was coming, and He came up to the Ancient of Days and was presented before Him. Moreover, to Him was given dominion, glory and a kingdom, that all the peoples, nations, and men of every language might serve Him. His dominion is an everlasting dominion which will not pass away; And His kingdom is one which will not be destroyed."[1] This, of course, is a reference to Jesus, the Messiah and King. As I wrote earlier, Jesus was, is and always will be the preexisting one, the alpha and omega, the eternal creator, co-equal and co-substantial with the Father and the Holy Spirit. Nevertheless, He emptied Himself and became as one of us, born as a child, and maturing into His role as the only begotten Son. "And Jesus kept increasing in wisdom and stature, and in favor with God and men."[2]

To help us further understand the difference between children and sons, we must study the Greek word *huiothesia*, which we translate as *adoption*. *Huiothesia* comes from *huios*, "a son," and *thesis*, "a placing." To the church in Corinth Paul wrote, "For if you were to have countless tutors [*paidagogos*] in Christ, yet you would not have many fathers; for in Christ Jesus I became your father through the gospel."[3] The English word translated here as "tutor" is the Greek word *paidagogo*. Its literal meaning is "boy-leader." As mentioned earlier, a *paidagogo* was a servant whose task it was to take the children to school; that is to say, he became responsible for the child's instruction and

---

[1] Daniel 7:13-14
[2] Luke 2:52
[3] 1 Corinthians 4:15

education. In ancient days, a Jewish child was given over to a rabbi whose responsibility was to teach him the character of a son. A corruption of this practice occurred when the rabbi refused to return the son to his father. In modern day terms, it could be a Sunday school teacher or a youth leader, who rather than turn the hearts of the children back to the fathers, would draw them as disciples after himself, unless they have been called to be their spiritual fathers.

Paul is the only writer in the Scriptures to use the word "adoption." According to Paul, believers have received "the Spirit of adoption," that is, the Holy Spirit, who is given as the firstfruits of all that is to be theirs. This Spirit of adoption produces in them the realization of sonship.[1] They receive "the adoption of sons"; in other words, sonship bestowed in distinction from a regeneration. The Bible clearly states that one "must be born again."[2] In the sense of Western world understanding of adoption, God does not adopt believers as children; they are begotten as such by His Holy Spirit through faith.

Adoption is a term involving the dignity of the relationship of believers as sons; it is not a putting into the family by spiritual birth, but a putting into the position as a son. Even today, when a Jewish boy or girl reaches the age of twelve or thirteen, he or she goes through a ceremony known as a **bar mitzvah** (for girls a **bat mitzvah**.) The word *mitzvah* is translated *law*; it is a command or a charge. This rite of passage, the bar (son of) mitzvah (the law), makes him the son of the Law. It means that the child has graduated to where he is now responsible before God under the Law, and should therefore know a large part of it. From that time forth,

---

[1] Romans 8:15
[2] John 3:3; John 3:7; 1 Peter 1:3

he would advance to a fuller instruction in matters of the Law.

Again taken from Isaiah: "...and the government shall be upon his shoulder: and his name shall be called Wonderful, Counselor, The mighty God, The everlasting Father [ab], and The Prince of Peace."[1] One can see a succession here; Messiah went from boy child or *yeled*, to son (*ben*), to father (*ab*). As I have mentioned earlier, Jesus was always the Son of God, but through the incarnation He is revealed as the Son of Man, and through His sonship, He is identified as the everlasting Father. Jesus is known as an everlasting Father by successfully qualifying as a son, and then raising up His disciples as sons. This journey resembles the one that we must also take. We are born as children, we become sons through the discipline of fathers, and then we become fathers through repeating reproducing children as sons.

As mentioned earlier, Kathy and I had two boys but no girls. Kathy was a registered nurse; but when Sean was born, we decided that she should give herself fully to being a wife and mother. Kathy was the primary caregiver, and therefore the most influential person for both Sean and Matt in their early years. She took what was in my heart and carefully placed it into them. The Proverb that guided Kathy's child-rearing philosophy was, "Train up a child in the way he should go, and when he is old he will not depart from it."[2] Kathy's interpretation of this was that we should train up and prepare Sean and Matthew as sons "to go." Leading the list to becoming a son is the issue of obedience. It is difficult to understand, but even Jesus learned obedience. The purpose of training should be to bring to maturity for the purpose of

---

[1] Isaiah 9:6b
[2] Proverbs 22:6

release. The difference between a boy child and a son must include reliability, credibility and responsibility.

26

Maturing As Sons

C ertainly you are aware that many of the principles I share in this book could be modified and applied to help understand and to improve the relationship between any category of leaders and followers, including employers and employees, teachers and students and pastors and congregations. Although none of these relationships can duplicate the relationship between a father and children, you might want to consider substituting these positions in this listing. A male child differs from a son, just as a man differs from an adult male. I have come to realize that growing old is inevitable, but growing up is a choice. God wants us to grow up and not just to grow old. Paul wrote, "When I was a child, I used to speak like a child, think like a child, reason like a child; but when I became a man, I did away with childish things."[1] As adult males, whether we consider ourselves as fathers or sons, we need to learn to behave as grown men. Women must learn to behave as daughters of the King, as wives and mothers.[2] Although our faith is to be childlike, our conduct, attitudes, and behavior are not.

The writer of Hebrews speaks of two types of spiritual food: Milk and solid food (meat). Milk is for children and

---

[1] 1 Corinthians 13:11
[2] Ephesians 4:14-15

solid food is for adults. He writes, "...by this time when you ought to be teachers, you have need again for someone to teach you the elementary principles of the oracles of God; you have come to need milk and not solid food. For everyone who partakes only of milk is not accustomed to the word of righteousness, for he is a babe. But solid food is for the mature, who because of practice have their senses trained to discern good and evil."[1] Kathy made an interesting and insightful observation. She shared that women are the source of milk for babies and infants, but normally men were the hunters who brought meat home for the family. As we grow older, our diet must change in order for us to develop and mature physically. For strong and healthy children to grow into strong and healthy adults, or for strong boys to become strong men, I believe certain character traits must be nourished. I am quite certain that the desired characteristics below are not to be gender-specific. Of course, this list is by no means exhaustive, but it might help us as we select our spiritual menu.

Be committed to Jesus Christ. In order to become a mature man or woman, the primary prerequisite is to become a devoted follower of Jesus Christ. The real question is not whether we can count on God; instead it is whether God can count on us. In these days, apathy and indifference have become an obstacle to commitment in all types of relationships. Elijah forced the issue with Israel when he cried out, "How long will you hesitate between two opinions? If the LORD is God, follow Him; but if Baal, follow him..."[2]

Be honest and tell the truth. Someone has said, "A liar needs a good memory." When Sean and Matt were children,

---

[1] Hebrews 5:12-14
[2] 1 Kings 18:21

Kathy and I emphasized and encouraged that they tell the truth. If I found them in a lie, discipline would be much more severe. The reason for this is that the Bible clearly identifies truth and lies in the respective persons of Jesus and Satan. We should note that Jesus said, "I am the truth."[1] As mentioned earlier, He does not simply say, "I speak the truth." Conversely, Jesus refers to Satan as a liar and as the father of lies.[2] A dishonest father who expects his children to be truthful could be compared to the man who says, "I've told you a million times not to exaggerate."

Live in reality. I have heard it said that disillusionment is a positive thing; it liberates us from living in an illusion. During my years as an athletic coach, I became increasingly aware that there were many alumni who refused to realize and accept the fact that they were not great athletes, nor would they ever be. Much of their spare time was spent hanging out at the gym; thus, the nickname for such men was "Gym Rats." Some of them had been relatively big fish in a small pond. Often, if these men were fathers, they would put an unrealistic pressure upon their sons to perform. Every father should desire for their sons to reach heights beyond themselves, but not with the purpose of living vicariously through them. As fathers, we must learn to accept our weaknesses, as well as our strengths. Then we can teach our sons to do the same.

Learn to moderate opinions and judgment with grace and mercy. The Bible says that "...judgment will be merciless to one who has shown no mercy; mercy triumphs over judgment."[3] In our effort to be right, it is essential for us

---

[1] John 14:6
[2] John 8:44
[3] James 2:13

to understand that truth without grace and mercy is likely to be harsh and rigid. Grace is God giving us the good things we do not deserve, while mercy is God withholding from us the justice, judgment and punishment we do deserve. At the risk of creating a stereotype, a father's tendency would be to emphasize truth, while a mother is more apt to emphasize grace. Truth, mercy and grace are essential qualities for maturation, as embodied in Jesus Christ. Referring to Jesus, John wrote, "...the Word became flesh, and dwelt among us, and we beheld His glory, glory as of the only begotten from the Father, full of grace and truth."[1]

Accept responsibility for choices made. If we could kick the fellow most responsible for our problems, we would not be able to sit down for a long time. As stated earlier, Sigmund Freud did not invent shifting the blame or "passing the buck." Adam did it thousands of years earlier. In regards to this, I have often heard the excuse, "I came from a dysfunctional family." Although I may not verbalize it, my thought is that we all came from dysfunctional parents— Adam and Eve. That's everyone's problem, so let us deal with it rather than perpetuate it. In refusing to accept personal responsibility, many around the world have embraced a victim mentality. Countless people excuse their attitudes and behavior by putting blame upon others. Ownership of responsibility is one of the keys to maturity.

Everyone must give an account to someone. Thousands of people populate correctional institutions, prisons and jails who adamantly believed, "No one can tell me what to do." Each week numerous church pews fill with adults who say, "I don't answer to any man, I answer to God." Of course, if a child said that to his father when he was told to take out the

---

[1] John 1:14

garbage, he would probably be in line for a good spanking. Accountability is a reality not only in this life, but also in the life to come. The author of Hebrews wrote, "Obey your leaders, and submit to them; for they keep watch over your souls, as those who will give an account. Let them do this with joy and not with grief, for this would be unprofitable for you."[1] Paul wrote, "...each one of us shall give account of himself to God."[2]

Quitting is not an option. A slogan that I often shared during my years as a football and basketball coach was this, "Quitters never win; winners never quit." Jesus, of course, has set the example for us. Jesus saw the task and the goal set before Him and set His face like a flint to accomplish His Father's purpose. He simply refused to quit.[3] As Sean and Matt attended school, I did not require that they join an athletic team. However, if they chose to do so, and if they started the season, they were obliged to finish the season. One year Sean joined the high school baseball team. Unlike many who were on the team, Sean faithfully attended every practice. Several of the players, who were more talented than Sean, regularly missed practices, yet the coach chose to play them anyway. Sean sat on the bench and kept the scorebook the entire season. I was proud of him for not quitting. Years later, I would see how this would benefit Sean. Ironically, while serving me in the ministry and trying to provide for his wife and five children, Sean had to walk through two business ventures that failed. Repeatedly, he refused to quit. His perseverance is more than admirable. True sons of God will stick to the task until either the task is finished, or they

---

[1] Hebrews 13:17
[2] Romans 14:12
[3] John 17:4; John 19:30

are. That is endurance. Paul left a legacy in these words to his spiritual son, Timothy: "I've fought the good fight, I've finished the course, and I've kept the faith. Henceforth there is laid up for me a crown of righteousness, which the Lord, the righteous judge, shall give me at that day:"[1] Baseball players and sons need to learn that to stop at third base adds no more to the score than striking out. Blessed are the finishers.

Be tenacious and resolute. Charles Spurgeon said, "Through perseverance even the snails reached the ark." Commitment, especially covenant commitment, requires tenacity, diligence and endurance. I would describe my son Matt as tenacious. I remember an incident when Matt was a teenager. He was working to perfect a one-and-a-half somersault off the diving board of a nearby pool. In his attempts, he bloodied his nose, but he persevered until he could do it. Later, as an adult he became a self-taught rock climber. Once again, his tenacity quickly paid off, and he won the first indoor competition that he entered. Matt learned the skill of paintless dent removal for automobiles. A few years ago, he founded his own business called *ProVision*. Soon after this, at a national convention for dent removal technicians, Matt placed first in their competition. Proverbs says, "The plans of the diligent lead to advantage, or steady plodding brings prosperity."[2] Paul writes that in order to complete his destiny he had struggled to remain faithful. It has been said, "If Christopher Columbus had turned back, no one would have blamed him; however, no one would have remembered him, either." He who would wish to move mountains starts by carrying small rocks.

Learn to handle rejection. As I have proposed,

[1] 2 Timothy 4:7-8
[2] Proverbs 21:5

rejection is probably one of the most destructive and even lethal forces on earth. Jesus was well acquainted with rejection. He was the rock, the chief cornerstone, rejected in His own generation and by His own people.[1] In the Bible, the fear of rejection is associated with the fear of man. Fear has the ability to cripple and enslave children and adults. It will tempt one to choose being trendy, accepted or popular, rather than to be ostracized for integrity and righteousness. Rejection and the fear of rejection are the underlying forces that empower peer pressure. I really like the slogan: "You wouldn't worry so much about what people thought of you, if you realized how seldom they do." In everyday life, a father's acceptance can be an effective and forceful alternative to the power of peer pressure and rejection.

Do not indulge in self-pity. Self-pity is emotional quick-sand, sucking its victims into a suffocating quagmire of pouting, grumbling and complaining. It has its origin in questioning the goodness of God. Self-pity is an ungodly response to difficulties, because its tendency is to judge circumstances and events by their effect upon one's self. A person who succumbs to the habit of regularly wallowing in the muck of self-pity will see all suffering as evil. This is contrary to a Biblical attitude toward suffering.[2] Fathers who allow their children to indulge in self-pity promote a victim mentality. The threat, attempt or act of suicide is the supreme expression of self-pity. Like a venomous serpent, it should be crushed, not pampered. I have heard Dan Wolfe tell those of us related to him, "You have less than twenty-four hours to get out of self-pity."

Be decisive. Choice, not chance, determines destiny. A

---

[1] Luke 20:17; 1 Peter 2:7
[2] James 5:10-11; 1 Peter 2:19-20

pollster asked, "What is your opinion on ignorance and apathy?" The answer given was, "I don't know and I don't care." Ignorance and apathy are two great causes for indecision. We've heard, "Not to decide is to decide!" It is like saying, "My answer is 'maybe,' and that's final." Elijah said, "How long will you hesitate between two opinions? If the Lord is God, follow Him; but if Baal, follow him. But the people did not answer him a word.' "[1] Indecision concerning accepting Jesus Christ as Lord and Savior will cause many to enter into a Christless eternity. The Bible speaks of indecision as a form of mental paralysis causing instability in men and all that they touch.[2]

Be passionate. The word *enthuse* comes from the root "in theos" or "in God." Therefore, to be enthusiastic means to be in God. If we are in God, that should be enough to make us passionate. If you have no fire or spark, you will never be able to ignite others. The warning in the book of Revelation is, "I know your deeds, that you are neither cold nor hot; I would that you were cold or hot. So because you are lukewarm, and neither hot nor cold, I will spit you out of My mouth."[3]

When you fall down, get up. When I was coaching football, I gave our offensive backs this instruction: When you are tackled, always get to your feet before your tackler does, and help him up. It was a psychological statement that no matter how hard he hit you, you would be back for more. The Bible says, "The righteous or just man falls seven times, and rises up again."[4] Seven is the number of perfection. Therefore, even when we fall perfectly seven times, we must get up seven times, not six.

---

[2] 1 Kings 18:21
[2] James 1:8
[3] Revelation 3:15-16
[4] Proverbs 24:16

Remain humble. Humility is the antonym of pride. It includes the qualities of modesty, being unassuming, unpretentious and meek. James wrote, "God resists and opposes the proud, but He gives grace to the humble."[1] Arrogant behavior is a sure way to pick a fight with God. The Bible says to humble ourselves before God and He will exalt us. Derek Prince said, "If we do God's job, and exalt ourselves, He will do our job, and He will humble us."

Overcome the fear of failure. Linked very closely to the subject of being indecisive is the fear of failure. Someone has said, "Don't be afraid of going out on a limb, because that is where the fruit is." Paul wrote to his spiritual son Timothy, "God has not given us a spirit of fear, but of power and love and of a sound mind."[2] The fear of failure can hinder us from the pursuit of the adventure of following God. The presence of a strong father in the home will do much to alleviate such fears that plague children. However, as fathers, if our love and approval has its foundation in performance, we will cause our children to avoid risks.

Learn the importance of being crossed. Let me attempt to explain what it means "... to take up our cross daily."[3] The daily cross that Jesus spoke of is giving someone the permission to cross our will. In simpler terms, taking up our cross means that we give someone the right to correct us and to say no to us. One of the most important questions that any leader or father must consider is, "Who can say no to me?" Jesus told us that no one could be a disciple unless he could learn how to be crossed.[4] This becomes obvious to us if we reflect upon the basic meaning of being a disciple. Being

---

[1] James 4:6; 1 Peter 5:5, Proverbs 3:34
[2] 2 Timothy 1:7
[3] Luke 9:23
[4] Luke 14:27; Matthew 10:38

crossed involves learning to subject our personal desires and interests to someone else. Obviously, if nobody can cross your will, you cannot be discipled. In the Garden of Gethsemane, Jesus spoke of two wills, His Father's and His own. "Jesus went a little beyond them, and fell on His face and prayed, saying, 'My Father, if it is possible, let this cup pass from Me; yet not as I will, but as You will.' "[1] Earlier Jesus had taught his disciples to pray this way. "Your kingdom come, Your will be done, on earth as it is in heaven."[2] Satan, rather than doing the Father's will, spoke of doing his own will.[3] Satan's pride was his downfall. The basic problem with pride in each of us is it makes us unable to receive correction. We must teach others by our example how to embrace the cross. Embracing the cross involves breaking a person's will. Breaking someone's will without breaking someone's spirit is one of the most important and delicate responsibilities that a father or leader carries.

Learn where to lay down our lives and then do it. Laying down one's life is the ultimate act of love.[4] Anyone who has not learned to lay down his life will place a premium on survival in any conflict or struggle (verbal or physical). I have often shared with men that if we have not found something worth dying for, we have not found anything worth living for, and vice versa. I have yet to find a program worth dying for. Bear in mind, we cannot lay down our physical life daily. The life that we lay down daily is our soul life. The soul is the seat of our volition (I want or I choose), intellect (I think) and emotion (I feel). Jesus said that a disciple must learn the daily task of laying down his "soul

---

[1] Matthew 26:39
[2] Matthew 6:10
[3] Isaiah 14:12-15
[4] John 15:13

life." Genuine men, fathers and leaders, will demonstrate a willingness to lay down (or die to) the demands of their soul. (What I want..! What I think...! What I feel...!) Keep in mind also: Jesus emphasized the importance of this being a deliberate and voluntary act. He said, "No one takes my life, I lay it down."[1]

Everyone should have a place of appeal. One of the most important benefits for men submitting their lives to someone is that it gives those under them a place of appeal. If one wishes to lead without modeling submission, his followers can be easily abused or misused; they have little if any recourse. Because we are imperfect, we—knowingly or ignorantly—can be unjust. A man, a father or a leader who refuses to submit to anyone allows no recourse to those who look to him when he is unjust. However, a man who is under authority will understand what it feels like to be corrected. I believe that every person, man, woman or child, member of a church or employee should have a place of appeal. By now I am sure you have grasped my conviction is that a real man is a man submitted to authority.

Emphasize and appreciate character over gifts. The Bible clearly distinguishes between fruit and gifts. Fruit rather than gifts are to distinguish us. Talent and ability most often are gifts. A gift speaks nothing about the person that receives it. Gifts only demonstrate the generosity of the giver. Character is what the Bible refers to as fruit. One does not grow a gift, but he does grow character. The primary emphasis of the Scriptures is on our *fruit*, not our *gifts*. God is more concerned with our character than He is with our comfort or charisma. Real men will learn to demonstrate, to recognize, to encourage and to reward attitude and obedience above

---

[1] John 10:17-18

talent and ability.[1] The current trend in the church to profile gifts over character has caused great confusion and harm. "Many will say to me in that day, Lord, Lord, have we not prophesied in Your name? And in Your name have cast out devils? And in Your name done many wonderful works? And then will I profess unto them, I never knew you: depart from me, ye that work iniquity."[2] Since it is obvious that Jesus is omniscient and knows everyone, a better translation of "I never knew you," would be "I never approved of you." Notice also, in the above passage that Jesus referred to prophecy, deliverance, and wonderful works (miracles), all of which would be considered distinctively charismatic in nature. I believe that which we profile is what we will reproduce. Unfortunately, much of the church is profiling gifts rather than fruit. Let me illustrate this by the following question: "Should my pastor be a man of integrity, a good husband and father, or should he simply be a gifted and scholarly speaker?"

Learn the importance of true wisdom. A primary theme in the book of Proverbs is to encourage young men to search out wisdom. In fact, the word *wisdom* is used over fifty times in Proverbs. Genuine wisdom is not primarily academic, but relates to the correct use of knowledge. Much wisdom is gained through learning from the experiences that God allows us to go through. In addition, we can gain wisdom from those whom God sends, especially good parents.[3] Learning from another's experience is often less painful and less costly than learning at our own expense. The Prodigal Son learned that when two people meet, one with experience

---

[1] Matthew 7:20
[2] Matthew 7:22-23
[3] Proverbs 1:7-9

and one with money, the one with the experience ends up with the money. The one with the money ends up with the experience. Wisdom rather than age is the best criteria for judging maturity. Solomon wrote to his son, "Wisdom is the principal thing; therefore get wisdom: and with all Your getting get understanding."[1]

Learn to differentiate between obedience and submission. Once again let us remember, obedience has to do with behavior and activity, while submission has more to do with a posture of spirit, heart, and attitude. Samuel said, "Has the Lord as much delight in burnt offerings and sacrifices as in obeying the voice of the Lord? Behold, to obey is better than sacrifice; and to heed than the fat of rams. For rebellion is as the sin of divination, and insubordination is as iniquity and idolatry. Because you have rejected the word of the Lord, He has also rejected you from being king."[2] Principles of submission and obedience were never meant to give fathers a license for domination and control. Obedience may be demanded, but submission cannot. As I've stated before, however, one can disobey and still have a submitted heart, especially when it involves being asked to do something illegal, immoral, or unscriptural. Always remember that Jesus was one child who knew more than His parents did, yet He still submitted to them and obeyed them.[3] Real men know the difference.

Learn how to be dominant without being domineering. Closely related to the matter of submission and obedience is the issue of authority. There is a humongous difference between spiritual authority and an authoritarian

---

[1] Proverbs 4:7
[2] 1 Samuel 15:22-23
[3] Luke 2:51

spirit. Exercising authority is a poor substitute for leadership. Authority is like a bank account; the more you draw upon it, the less you have of it. We have authority by being under authority. As a case in point, a father who is under authority can rule his household by letting them see and follow his example. In order for spiritual authority to be effective, two things are necessary. It must be recognized and not required. It is always voluntarily submitted to and very rarely compelled or forced. Jesus said, "The kings of the Gentiles lord it over them; and those who have authority over them are called benefactors. But it should not be so with you; rather let him who is the greatest among you become as the youngest, and the leader as the servant.' "[1] Being macho is a smokescreen attempting to cover up a lack of genuine manhood.

Learn the value of keeping your word. I once read of a father who told his son, "Be so dependable that if you say you will be somewhere and you don't show up, they will send flowers to the funeral home." One of the greatest compliments that I ever received came from my brother-in-law, Bill Peddie. He once said to me, "Many promise more than they deliver, but you deliver more than you promise." I have heard that Henry Ford would seal contracts with a handshake. When the Psalmist speaks about dwelling in the presence of the Lord, one of the requirements was that we must keep our word. "Lord, who shall abide in Your tabernacle? Who shall dwell in Your holy hill? ...He that swears to his own hurt, and changes not."[2] In today's social climate of broken contracts, broken covenants and broken promises, we have spawned an epidemic of mistrust. Unscrupulous lawyers prosper at finding loopholes to release

---

[1] Luke 22:25-26
[2] Psalm 15:1 & 4b

men from their vows. Solomon, reputably the wisest man who ever lived, wrote, "When you make a vow to God, do not be late in paying it, for He takes no delight in fools. Pay what you vow! It is better that you should not vow than that you should vow and not pay."[1] Jesus warned, "I say to you, that every careless word that men shall speak, they shall render account for it in the Day of Judgment. For by your words you shall be justified, and by your words you shall be condemned."[2] If you wish to be a man, be a man of your word. At the least, deliver what you promise.

Avoid making comparisons. Making comparisons is like racing to a railroad crossing to beat a train; even if you tie, you lose. In the following passage, Peter drew a comparison between himself and the apostle John. The response of Jesus can be seen as a reprimand. "Peter therefore seeing him said to Jesus, 'Lord, and what about this man?' Jesus said to him, 'If I want him to remain until I come, what is that to you? You follow Me!' "[3] Nearly always, comparisons will only lead to pride or envy. If we feel we compare favorably against another, it can lead to pride. If we fall short when we are compared to another, it can lead to jealousy and envy. Paul wrote, "For we are not bold to class or compare ourselves with some of those who commend themselves; but when they measure themselves by themselves, and compare themselves with themselves, they are without understanding."[4] Imagine the temptation to compare that James, the brother of Jesus, faced. Yet James taught that jealousy produces a downward spiral of bitterness, envy and strife. It begins as "earthly" (carnal); then it

---

[1] Ecclesiastes 5:4-5
[2] Matthew 12:36-37
[3] John 21:21-22
[4] 1 Corinthians 10:12

becomes "sensual" (soulish); but if it continues it can become "demonic" (spiritual).[1] Jealousy is a terrible evil. It is born out of ingratitude and breeds envy, and is closely related to selfish ambition. The fruit of jealousy will never be good. It is important to nip jealousy as it buds in childhood, before it blossoms during the teenage years and comes to fruition during adulthood. In today's world, competition has deteriorated from doing your absolute best to doing whatever it takes to beat the other guy.

Forgive quickly. Derek Prince taught us that forgiveness is not an emotion, it is a decision. When someone says, "I can't forgive," what he means is "I won't forgive." Unwillingness to forgive is very dangerous. Jesus said, "If you don't forgive others, I won't forgive you."[2] In other words, unforgiveness is like drinking poison and expecting the other person to die. On the other hand, genuine forgiveness may be described as the fragrance that a flower leaves on the heel of the boot that crushes it. Unforgiveness and bitterness have the ability to defile one's self as well as others.[3] Offenses are unavoidable, but real men—and especially fathers and leaders—will not be easily offended. They will allow God to avenge or to vindicate them, as He sees fit.

Learn to be content. There is a difference between being content and being satisfied. Contentment is a direction, not a destination. Paul said, "...for I have learned to be content in whatever circumstances I am. I know how to get along with humble means, and I also know how to live in prosperity; in any and every circumstance I have learned the secret of being filled and going hungry, both of having abundance

---

[1] James 3:14-16; James 4:1-2
[2] Matthew 6:15
[3] Hebrews 12:15

and suffering need."[1] Notice that Paul learned to be content. I believe that murmuring, grumbling and complaining are a sure recipe for provoking the anger of our Father.

Have a good work ethic. The root word for *worship* and *work* are the same. Before the curse, man was set in the garden to cultivate it. After sin entered the world, work became more wearisome, painful and tiring, because the ground was cursed. However, work was not the curse. The first day following the creation of man was a day of rest. Man's first full day on earth was a day of rest. The world works and then rests, but believers should work from a place of rest. When we work, we work as unto the Lord, and remember, "Nobody has ever drowned in sweat." Real men know how to work, and they do it all to the glory of God.

Finally, let us always keep in mind that this life is a journey, but it is not our destination. Let us remember that when men are most concerned with product, God appears to be more concerned with process. The Bible emphasizes faithfulness far more than success.

---

[1] Philippians 4:11-12

27

Learning to Serve

*T*wo of the foundational principles of the kingdom of God are love and service. Greatness is found in the kingdom of God on the handle of a shovel or a broom. Luke wrote, "And there arose also a dispute among them as to which one of them was regarded to be greatest. And He said to them, 'The kings of the Gentiles lord it over them; and those who have authority over them are called Benefactors. But not so with you, but let him who is the greatest among you become as the youngest, and the leader as the servant. For who is greater, the one who reclines at the table, or the one who serves? Is it not the one who reclines at the table? But I am among you as the one who serves.' "[1] A servant is one who puts the welfare of his master first. Jesus, although He is master of all, demonstrated His willingness to serve anyone. We can gain from this that it is essential for fathers to teach their children to serve by setting the example for them. Serving will help deal with pride and selfish ambition. It will touch the very heart of "jockeying for position," a problem that plagued even the disciples of Jesus.

It has been said you can give without love, but you cannot love without giving. In the same manner that one can obey without having a submitted heart, one can serve

---

[1] Luke 22:24-27

without being a servant. Paul taught, "It was for freedom that Christ set us free; therefore keep standing firm and do not be subject again to a yoke of slavery. For you were called to freedom, brethren; only do not turn your freedom into an opportunity for the flesh, but through love serve one another."[1]

The vast majority of what I have believed and taught about serving over the years came from Canadian-born friend Paul Petrie, who now serves as a leadership strategist and consultant in Brussels, Belgium.[2] In January 1979, *New Wine Magazine* published an article by Paul entitled "The Privilege of Serving."[3] With Paul's permission, I have gleaned a great deal of what I write from the contents of that article. Here are some characteristic attitudes that are important when we serve.

We should attempt to serve anonymously. With the exception of Jesus, probably no person served more quietly and faithfully than Joseph. He did not bemoan his fate, but rather demonstrated his character from the house of Potiphar, to the prison cells of Egypt, and finally to Pharaoh himself.

We should attempt to serve lavishly. Mary took the nard, an extremely expensive fragrant ointment, and to the dismay of the disciples, seemingly wasted it on Jesus' feet.[4]

We should attempt to serve faithfully. In the parable of the talents Jesus says, "Well done, good and faithful slave."[5] He uses the word *doulos*, which means *slave* in Greek, as

---

[1] Galatians 5:1&13

[2] www.paulpetrie.com

[3] Archives of New Wine articles are now available from Charles Simpson Ministries at www.csmpublishing.org.

[4] John 12:3-8; Mark 14:3-8

[5] Matthew 25:14-30

opposed to *diakonos*, translated *servant*. The faithful "slave-like" service brought increase and reward. The man who hid the single talent had a maintenance mentality and was considered slothful and wicked.

We should attempt to serve selflessly. Few examples of serving are more graphic than the following: "Now three of the thirty chief men went down to the rock to David, into the cave of Adullam, while the army of the Philistines was camping in the valley of Rephaim. And David was then in the stronghold, while the garrison of the Philistines was then in Bethlehem. And David had a craving and said, 'Oh that someone would give me water to drink from the well of Bethlehem, which is by the gate!' So the three broke through the camp of the Philistines, and drew water from the well of Bethlehem which was by the gate, and took it and brought it to David; nevertheless David would not drink it, but poured it out to the Lord; and he said, 'Be it far from me before my God that I should do this. Shall I drink the blood of these men who went at the risk of their lives? For at the risk of their lives they brought it.' Therefore, he would not drink it. These things the three mighty men did.' "[1] Notice that they risked their lives simply to satisfy a desire of their master. David was so touched by what they did that he poured out the water onto the ground.

We should attempt to serve sensitively. We must discern whether our service needs to be urgent or leisurely and relaxed. We should concentrate on doing the right things with the right heart. We must prepare by anticipating the needs of those we are serving.

We need to attempt to serve courteously, always giving esteem and respect to others. You may have heard

---

[1] 1 Chronicles 11:15-19

that people must earn our respect. If we believe that people need to earn our respect, then disrespect becomes the norm. People need not earn our respect, but they can earn our disrespect.

We must learn to serve when it is not convenient. This helps differentiate the person who simply serves from the person who is a servant. Jesus explained it this way, "But which of you, having a slave plowing or tending sheep, will say to him when he has come in from the field, 'Come immediately and sit down to eat?' But will he not say to him, 'Prepare something for me to eat, and properly clothe yourself and serve me until I have eaten and drunk; and afterward you will eat and drink?' He does not thank the slave because he did the things which were commanded, does he? So you too, when you do all the things which are commanded you, say, 'We are unworthy slaves; we have done only that which we ought to have done.' "[1]

Fathers have the responsibility to help set children free from the pattern of self-orientation. By now, you know that I believe that Jesus did not come primarily to serve us; He came to serve His Father. He then taught His disciples to serve; "You go and get a donkey. You get the upper room ready. You go and preach the gospel of the Kingdom." By the way, these were not suggestions.

Paul explained the focus of service when he wrote, "And let the one who is taught the word share all good things with him who teaches, So then, while we have opportunity, let us do good to all men, and especially to those who are of the household of the faith."[2] In this passage, we see that Paul addresses the priority of service: First, we should serve those

---

[1] Luke 17:7-10
[2] Galatians 6:6, 10

responsible for us in God. A major focus of service is to liberate the one who oversees us by doing things for him that he could do for himself, if he were not watching over us. We rejoice in doing this when we realize that a leader can do for us what we cannot do for ourselves. Think about what is included in all good things. Undoubtedly, this would include giving of our time, energy, attention, finances and support.

Second, Paul instructs us, as we have opportunity, to do good things for the household of faith. As with most all spiritual principles, service should begin at home. There is a tremendous need in our society to teach the children to release the parents, instead of vice versa. For example, children can be taught to release their mother, so that their mother is free to strengthen and release their father. The result of this order is that it allows the father freedom to serve the Kingdom in society. Having learned and practiced doing good to those close to us, we can then go out and do good things to those in the world, our neighbors.

Maturity in service is also progressive. Initially, we serve by saying, If there is anything I can do for you, just let me know. Then we move to the point where we say, I know this needs to be done, so can I do it for you...? This is exactly what the three did for David in the passage above. Finally, we perceived that the need and desire is there, and we just do it. Notice the example set by Joseph in the house of Potiphar. "So he (Potiphar) left everything he owned in Joseph's charge; and with him there he did not concern himself with anything except the food which he ate."[1]

When it comes to serving, we will see the principle of exchange take place. For nearly four decades, I have attempted to practice what I have just preached by making an

---

[1] Genesis 39:6

effort to serve my pastor and spiritual father, Dan Wolfe, in some practical areas. Here is one illustration I trust will be beneficial. Early in my relationship with Dan, I had gathered about thirty men who looked to me for leadership. Together with these men, I was able to help paint and then to replace a roof on Dan's house. I was well aware that Dan was willing and able to paint and to roof his own house. However, I felt that in doing this practical thing for him, I was able to release him to do things that were more important. I am convinced that Dan can do spiritual things for me that I am not capable of doing for myself. One of these things was to provide spiritual oversight of me, giving me guidance and advice. He can help me with problems that may arise in my personal life, marriage, family, or the church. He can provide my wife, my family, and the church a place of appeal. These, I cannot do for myself. When I serve Dan in practical areas of his life, I am able to release him to help me in spiritual areas of my life. Both of us benefit from this exchange. I am convinced that, as I made it a priority to be faithful to serve Dan in practical areas, God increased my understanding and my sphere in spiritual areas. The spiritual heritage that I currently enjoy has been primarily a consequence of this process. The Scriptures reinforce the principle of serving as described above. The principle is demonstrated in the relationship between Joshua with Moses, Joseph with Pharaoh, Elisha with Elijah, Timothy with Paul, and most importantly Jesus with His Father. In each of these examples, promotion came after faithful service.

28

Training to Honor

*V*ery closely related to the previous chapter on learning to serve is the Biblical mandate concerning honor. Lack of honor and respect has reached epidemic levels in the family, the school, society and the church. Many people today find it difficult to understand why some choose to defer to others. This is due to the prevalence of self-centeredness, self-interest and self-determination that exists even in Christian circles. I believe that mutinous and insubordinate attitudes need to be addressed through training. Training involves consistency and repetition, as well as teaching. Many parents want the schools or military to do what they themselves have neglected. Beginning in the family, we must reinforce the command of God, which is, "Render to all what is due them… honor to whom honor."[1] "Honor" means, "To regard someone with love, respect, and esteem." It includes manifest tokens of respect paid to others. It implies that we voluntarily and happily defer to someone in an attitude of genuine humility.

To whom should we give honor? **Obviously, we must first honor God.**[2] In the Bible, genuine honor is nearly always expressed with substance. The prophet Malachi

---

[1] Romans 13:7
[2] 1 Chronicles 16:23-29

addressed the issue of honor. Malachi wrote, "A son honors his father, and a servant his master. Then if I am a father, where is My honor? And if I am a master, where is My respect?' says the Lord of hosts to you, 'O priests who despise My name.' But you say, 'How have we despised Your name?' 'You are presenting defiled food upon My altar.' But you say, 'How have we defiled Thee?' In that you say, 'The table of the Lord is to be despised.' 'But when you present the blind for sacrifice, is it not evil? And when you present the lame and sick, is it not evil? Why not offer it to your governor? Would he be pleased with you? Or would he receive you kindly?' says the Lord of hosts."[1] God said the value, condition, and quality of the animals brought by the people for sacrifice were expressions of honor. Because Israel was offering lame, blind, and sick animals for sacrifice, they were accused of despising His name (Father). The Lord said, "If your governor would refuse it, don't give it to me."

When the nation of Israel was smitten with a plague, David demonstrated how careful he was to honor God. "Araunah said, 'Wherefore is my lord the king come to his servant?' And David said, 'To buy the threshing floor of thee, to build an altar unto the Lord, that the plague may be stayed from the people.' And Araunah said unto David, 'Let my lord the king take and offer up what seems good unto him: behold, here are oxen for burnt sacrifice, and threshing instruments and other instruments of the oxen for wood.' All these things did Araunah, as a king, give unto the king. And Araunah said unto the king, 'The Lord Your God accept thee.' And the king said unto Araunah, 'Nay; but I will surely buy it of thee at a price: neither will I offer burnt offerings unto the Lord my God of that which doth cost me nothing.' So David bought the

---

[1] Malachi 1:6-8

threshing floor and the oxen for fifty shekels of silver. And David built there an altar unto the Lord, and offered burnt offerings and peace offerings. So the Lord was entreated for the land, and the plague was stayed from Israel."[1] David said, "I will not offer to God that which costs me nothing." Genuine honor has a cost. Sacrifice is a part of this cost.

Secondly, we are to honor parents. Expressing honor toward our parents is an integral and vital part of being a son. The fifth commandment is, "Honor your father and your mother, that your days may be prolonged in the land which the Lord your God gives you."[2] Paul told children to obey their parents, and links obedience with honor. "Children, obey your parents in the Lord, for this is right. Honor your mother and your father (which is the first commandment with a promise), that it may be well with you, and that you may live long on the earth."[3] This passage mentions two specific blessings: (1) "...that it may go well with you," and (2) "...that you may live a long life on the earth." If we refuse to honor our parents, we can expect some unusual hardships and difficulties, and we may die prematurely. Jesus gave us these sobering words to show us the importance of parental honor. "For God said, 'Honor your father and your mother, and, he who speaks evil of father or mother, let him be put to death.'"[4] Observe from these passages how blatantly God speaks regarding this subject. Virtually, He says children who dishonor their parents are as traitors or murderers, deserving of capital punishment.

Thirdly, we should honor all spiritual authority. We should serve those who honor God and honor those who

---

[1] 2 Samuel 24:21-25
[2] Exodus 20:12
[3] Ephesians 6:1-3
[4] Matthew 15:4

serve God. The manner in which we receive and honor the "man of God" can greatly affect God's ability to touch our lives. When God sends a man of God, or a spiritual father, we should be careful to recognize, welcome, and accept him. As I have written, it is important to recognize the messenger, as well as the message. In the following passages, Jesus clearly states that receiving the one whom God sends is directly related to receiving the Son and the Father. "He who receives you receives Me, and he who receives Me receives Him who sent Me. He who receives a prophet in the name of a prophet shall receive a prophet's reward; and he who receives a righteous man in the name of a righteous man shall receive a righteous man's reward. And whoever in the name of a disciple gives to one of these little ones even a cup of cold water to drink, truly I say to you he shall not lose his reward."[1]

Fourthly, Paul teaches us that we are to honor all civil and governmental authority. "Let every person be in subjection to the governing authorities. For there is no authority except from God, and those which exist are established by God. Therefore he who resists authority has opposed the ordinance of God; and they who have opposed will receive condemnation upon themselves."[2]

Finally, let me address the issue of establishing the principle of honor in the home and family. To do this, wives must honor their husbands.[3] Husbands must love, and therefore show honor to their wives.[4] This lifestyle then becomes a model for the children. In an atmosphere of honor, love and respect, the children learn by seeing it. I mentioned manifest tokens of respect in defining honor. Let us look at

---

[1] Matthew 10:40-42
[2] Romans 13:1-2
[3] Ephesians 5:33b
[4] Ephesians 5:23-33a

some very practical ways in which children who wish to be sons in the house can be trained to recognize and apply these tokens.

We will call the first token "the seat of honor," taken from the example in Luke.[1] A child should learn to give his parents the preferred seat at the table, and the most comfortable chair in the family room. He should learn to say, "Here, Mom," or "Here, Dad, you take this chair."

By example, the child should learn that firstfruits belong to those who oversee us.[2] Children can be trained to honor and respect parents and others by using the "you first" principle in something as simple as a buffet line. The child, in offering his or her parents the choicest piece of meat or the first slice of pie, learns simple ways to render due honor. Of course, parents can always give these back to the child, and as the child practices this, most parents would do so.

Children can learn the importance of honoring with words. In some languages, such as Spanish and German, the vocabulary changes between formal and familiar. In the home, children, if they wish to be sons in the house, should learn tone of voice and protocol.

Honor is demonstrated by attending to proper etiquette. Children can learn to be courteous in such simple things as opening and holding the door for their parents, for the elderly and for women, even in the home.

Children can be trained to demonstrate deference to their elders. Children need to be trained to allow parents to take initiative in their lives. This can happen by having our calendars and schedules open to adjustment by those over us. Many parents need to be trained to listen in order to

---

[1] Luke 14:7-11
[2] Proverbs 3:9

demonstrate the skill of deference.

Finally, children can learn the importance of honor with substance by "picking up the check from time to time." As Paul wrote, "And let the one who is taught the word share all good things with him who teaches."[1] Remember, "all good things" includes time, money, talent and energy. Again, fathers and leaders should demonstrate this before they attempt to teach it.

---

[1] Galatians 6:6

29

The Example of the Rechabites

*I*n His effort to speak to Judah, God used the Rechabite's obedience to their father as an example. Jeremiah 35 records the account of the Rechabites. I trust that this account will help to illustrate much of what I have written. The prophet Jeremiah is sent by God to attempt to entice the grandsons of Rechab to break a vow they had made to their father, Jonadab. A portion of the vow was that they agreed not to drink wine. "The word which came to Jeremiah from the Lord in the days of Jehoiakim the son of Josiah, king of Judah, saying, 'Go to the house of the Rechabites, and speak to them, and bring them into the house of the Lord, into one of the chambers, and give them wine to drink.' "[1]

Even though Jeremiah was sent by God to do this, the sons of Jonadab refused to break their word to their father. "Then I set before the men of the house of the Rechabites pitchers full of wine, and cups; and I said to them, 'Drink wine!' But they said, 'We will not drink wine, for Jonadab the son of Rechab, our father, commanded us, saying, You shall not drink wine, you or your sons, forever.' "[2] Not only had the sons obeyed their father, but their entire families did so as well. "And we have obeyed the voice of Jonadab the son of

---

[1] Jeremiah 35:1-2
[2] Jeremiah 35:5-6

Rechab, our father, in all that he commanded us, not to drink wine all our days, we, our wives, our sons, or our daughters."[1]

Next, we see God drawing the analogy between the simple obedience of Rechabites to their father, to the disobedience of Judah to the Lord. The Rechabites obeyed their natural father. The tribe of Judah refused to obey their Heavenly Father. "Then the word of the Lord came to Jeremiah, saying, Thus says the Lord of hosts, the God of Israel, 'Go and say to the men of Judah and the inhabitants of Jerusalem, Will you not receive instruction by listening to My words?' declares the Lord. 'The words of Jonadab the son of Rechab, which he commanded his sons not to drink wine, are observed. So they do not drink wine to this day, for they have obeyed their father's command. But I have spoken to you again and again; yet you have not listened to Me. Indeed, the sons of Jonadab the son of Rechab have observed the command of their father which he commanded them, but this people has not listened to Me.' "[2]

God now pronounces judgment on Judah and Jerusalem, because they would not heed His voice. "Therefore thus says the Lord, the God of hosts, the God of Israel, 'Behold, I am bringing on Judah and on all the inhabitants of Jerusalem all the disaster that I have pronounced against them; because I spoke to them but they did not listen, and I have called them but they did not answer.' "[3]

Because they set an example by choosing to honor and obey their natural father, God promised the Rechabites an eternal standing. The Scriptures say, "Then Jeremiah said to the house of the Rechabites, 'Thus says the Lord of hosts, the

[1] Jeremiah 35:8
[2] Jeremiah 35:12-14&16
[3] Jeremiah 35:17

God of Israel, Because you have obeyed the command of Jonadab your father, kept all his commands, and done according to all that he commanded you; therefore thus says the Lord of hosts, the God of Israel, Jonadab the son of Rechab shall not lack a man to stand before Me always.' "[1] The point God makes to Judah is this: "Why couldn't you honor Me like this?"

Later, we see that Jonadab (also spelled Jehonadab) the son of Rechab was taken up into the chariot of Jehu. "Now when he had departed from there, he met Jehonadab the son of Rechab coming to meet him; and he greeted him and said to him, 'Is your heart right, as my heart is with your heart?' And Jehonadab answered, 'It is.' Jehu said,' If it is, give me your hand.' And he gave him his hand, and he took him up to him into the chariot. And he said, 'Come with me and see my zeal for the Lord.' So he made him ride in his chariot. And when he came to Samaria, he killed all who remained to Ahab in Samaria, until he had destroyed him, according to the word of the Lord, which He spoke to Elijah."[2] Jehu was the man that Elijah had anointed to destroy Jezebel. Jezebel was the greatest enemy of Elijah. Elijah's spirit was "to turn the hearts of the fathers back to the children." Jezebel opposed this spirit. So, Jonadab was used by God to help Jehu fulfill Elijah's prophecy against Ahab and Jezebel. Jehu, as mentioned, was the one responsible for Jezebel's death.

Finally, we see Jonadab help Jehu to clean idolatry out of Israel. "And Jehu went into the house of Baal with Jehonadab the son of Rechab; and he said to the worshipers of Baal, 'Search and see that there may be here with you none of the servants of the Lord, but only the worshipers of Baal.' Then

---

[1] Jeremiah 35:18-19
[2] 2 Kings 10:15-17

they went in to offer sacrifices and burnt offerings. Now Jehu had stationed for himself eighty men outside, and he had said, 'The one who permits any of the men whom I bring into your hands to escape, shall give up his life in exchange.' Then it came about, as soon as he had finished offering the burnt offering, that Jehu said to the guard and to the royal officers, 'Go in, kill them; let none come out.' And they killed them with the edge of the sword; and the guard and the royal officers threw them out, and went to the inner room of the house of Baal."[1]

The historical success and the blessing of the Rechabites are linked to one simple choice. The sons and daughters, and their children, had decided to honor and obey a vow that their father made with their grandfather. Part of the vow regarded the use of alcohol. Because they honored their natural father, God used them as an example for Israel. This decision established their legacy and directed them into their destiny.

---

[1] 2 Kings 10:23-25

30

The Principle of Exchange

Perhaps no subject that I could address carries more controversy than the issue of finances. It is not my intention within the scope of this book to resolve this controversy. I will leave that to the experts. I confess that I have been hesitant to address this issue. Then I was reminded of the apostle Paul who wrote, "I did not shrink from declaring to you the whole purpose [or counsel] of God."[1] Recently, I heard that Jesus spoke six times more often about financial areas than about any other area. Possibly, it is because of His statement, "No one can serve two masters; for either he will hate the one and love the other, or he will hold to one and despise the other. You cannot serve God and mammon [riches]."[2] Interestingly enough, in this passage Jesus speaks of God as one master, but He speaks of riches, not the devil, as the other master. Paul wrote, "For the love of money is a root of all sorts of evil, and some by longing for it have wandered away from the faith, and pierced themselves with many a pang."[3] In each of these passages, the issue is our attitude toward riches, not riches. Money and riches themselves are not evil, but the love of money is evil. One can

---

[1] Acts 20:20 & 27
[2] Matthew 6:24
[3] 1 Timothy 6:10

be poor and love money.

In a previous chapter, I spoke of showing honor. Financial support is one of many ways in which New Covenant saints use substance to show honor. In his letters to the church in Corinth, Paul explained and then defended his position regarding the issue of financial support.

First, Paul laid out his relationship to the church of Corinth. "For if you were to have countless tutors in Christ, yet you would not have many fathers; for in Christ Jesus I became your father through the gospel."[1] Paul was a spiritual father to the church in Corinth. His status likely emerged as a result of his proclaiming the gospel of the kingdom of God.

Being a spiritual father to the Corinthians gave Paul authority with them. "Am I not free? Am I not an apostle? Have I not seen Jesus our Lord? Are you not my work in the Lord? If to others I am not an apostle, at least I am to you; for you are the seal of my apostleship in the Lord."[2] Notice that the seal of Paul's apostleship was not in certificates, degrees or titles but was evidenced by the people that he fathered. His credentials were not papers but people. Of course, apostleship is not limited to spiritual fatherhood, but in the case of the church in Corinth Paul uses his spiritual fatherhood to make his point.

In Paul's second letter to the Corinthians, he restated this relationship. "Are we beginning to commend ourselves again? Or do we need, as some, letters of commendation to you or from you? You are our letter, written in our hearts, known and read by all men; being manifested that you are a letter of Christ, cared for by us, written not with ink, but with the Spirit of the living God, not on tablets of stone, but on

---

[1] 1 Corinthians 4:15
[2] 1 Corinthians 9:1-2

tablets of human hearts."[1] Again, Paul said that his credentials were the fruit in the lives of the people that he had fathered.

Then Paul addressed the criticisms concerning the financial support that he was receiving. "My defense to those who examine me is this: Do we not have a right to eat and drink? Do we not have a right to take along a believing wife, even as the rest of the apostles, and the brothers of the Lord, and Cephas [Peter]? Or do only Barnabas and I not have a right to refrain from working?"[2] Paul spoke of the offerings, which he received as a right; and he defended his position by pointing to the example of the rest of the apostles, including the brothers of Jesus and Peter. Paul said that they were even receiving sufficient support to bring their wives on their missionary journeys.

To further justify his position, Paul drew analogies using a soldier, an owner of a vineyard, and a shepherd. "Who at any time serves as a soldier at his own expense? Who plants a vineyard, and does not eat the fruit of it? Or who tends a flock and does not use the milk of the flock?"[3] Obviously, his questions are metaphorical and rhetorical; they need no response. A soldier receives wages from the government he serves. A person who plants a vineyard is free to eat the fruit (grapes) from it. A shepherd is permitted to drink the milk taken from his goats. No one would question the right of each of them to live from and enjoy the produce of their labors.

To drive home his point, Paul turned to the writings of Moses. "I am not speaking these things according to human judgment, am I? Or does not the Law also say these things?

---

[1] 2 Corinthians 3:1-3
[2] 1 Corinthians 9:3-6
[3] 1 Corinthians 9:7

For it is written in the Law of Moses, 'You shall not muzzle the ox while he is threshing.' God is not concerned about oxen, is He? Or is He speaking altogether for our sake? Yes, for our sake it was written, because the plowman ought to plow in hope, and the thresher to thresh in hope of sharing the crops."[1] Using Deuteronomy for his text, Paul explains the analogy of the ox that eats freely while it treads out the grain. The Old Covenant commanded, "You shall not muzzle the ox while he is threshing."[2] Paul said this passage was not written for the benefit of an ox. Once again, in his letter to Timothy, Paul used the analogy of the ox. He wrote, "Let the elders who rule well be considered worthy of double honor, especially those who work hard at preaching and teaching. For the Scripture says, 'You shall not muzzle the ox while he is threshing,' and 'The laborer is worthy of his wages.' "[3] He defined "elders who rule well" as those who work hard at preaching and teaching. Concerning them, he said they are worthy of "double honor." Pointing to the Law of Moses, he concluded with the statement that the laborer is worthy of his wages. This phrase connects each of the analogies of the ox eating while threshing with financial support.

Paul revealed to them the principle of exchange. "If we sowed spiritual things in you, is it too much if we should reap material things from you? So also the Lord directed those who proclaim the gospel to get their living from the gospel."[4] Clearly, Paul was saying that the Lord directed those who sow into our lives spiritual seed (or feed us spiritually) should expect material things in return. This principle of exchange is clearly demonstrated when Abram met Melchizedek. "And

---

[1] 1 Corinthians 9:8-10
[2] Deuteronomy 25:4
[3] 1 Timothy 5:17-18
[4] 1 Corinthians 9:11&14

Melchizedek king of Salem brought out bread and wine; now he was a priest of God Most High. And he [Melchizedek] blessed him and said, 'Blessed be Abram of God Most High, Possessor of heaven and earth; and blessed be God Most High, Who has delivered your enemies into your hand.' And he [Abram] gave him a tenth [or tithe] of all."[1] The book of Hebrews leads one to the conclusion that Melchizedek was a pre-incarnate appearance of Christ. Melchizedek offers Abram bread and wine and then gives him a blessing. Bread and wine represent the elements of Covenant (the Lord's Supper). Covenant and blessing are spiritual things. Abram responded by giving Melchizedek a tenth of all, a portion of which were the spoils of battle. These would be material things.

We see in these passages the first mention of the covenant elements (bread and wine), along with the first use of the word "tithe." In the example of Abram and Melchizedek, we see the exchange of spiritual things (a blessing and the elements of covenant) and material things (tithes of all). This principle of exchange is repeated in Paul's letter to the Galatians. "And let the one who is taught the word share all good things with him who teaches."[2] The Galatian disciples were being taught the word of God (spiritual things). Therefore, Paul encouraged them to share good things (material or natural things) with the one who was teaching them. Since they were being taught spiritual things, their response should be to share "all good things," like time, energy, finances, and other expressions of help and encouragement. This was not to be a wage, but a way of honoring.

---

[1] Genesis 14:18-20
[2] Galatians 6:6

In regards to honor, Solomon wrote, "Honor the Lord from your wealth, and from the first of all your produce; So your barns will be filled with plenty, and your vats will overflow with new wine."[1] Plainly, we are admonished to honor from our wealth. Notice that barns (where we store grain) and vats (where we store wine) are linked to the elements of covenant, grain and grapes or bread and wine. The so-called firstfruits, or in Hebrew, *t'rumah*, *offering*, was set aside for the Levitical priesthood. The firstfruits are what sanctified the other tithes and offerings. I cannot go into further teaching on firstfruits, but if you are interested in this subject, I recommend a series by Tony Fitzgerald called *God's Interest in Your Financial Interests*.[2] Tony is the founding father of Church the Nations, and has done extensive research and teaching on the subject of tithes and offerings.

---

[1] Proverbs 3:9-10
[2] www.cotn.org

31

Storehouses

This leads us to the very controversial and divisive issue of tithing. As I have shown earlier, the first mention of tithes was linked to the spiritual blessing of covenant. The Scripture that is most often quoted in reference to tithing is found in Malachi. " 'From the days of your fathers you have turned aside from My statutes, and have not kept them. Return to Me, and I will return to you,' says the Lord of hosts. But you say, 'How shall we return?' 'Will a man rob God? Yet you are robbing Me!' But you say, 'How have we robbed Thee?' 'In tithes and offerings. You are cursed with a curse, for you are robbing Me, the whole nation of you. Bring the whole tithe into the storehouse, so that there may be food in My house, and test Me now in this,' says the Lord of hosts, 'if I will not open for you the windows of heaven, and pour out for you a blessing until it overflows. Then I will rebuke the devourer for you, so that it may not destroy the fruits of the ground; nor will your vine in the field cast its grapes,' says the Lord of hosts. 'And all the nations will call you blessed, for you shall be a delightful land...' "[1]

Over the years, I have heard the argument that tithing is an Old Covenant principle and that "we are under grace and not under the law." I absolutely agree that we are under grace

---

[1] Malachi 3:7-12

and not under the law. However, let me mention two things. First, the practice of tithing was introduced by Abram and Melchizedek long before the law. Of even greater importance is the fact that Jesus did not teach that tithing ended with the Old Covenant. In fact, when the Pharisees were being exacting and legalistic about tithes of the smallest seeds and herbs, Jesus said, "Woe to you, scribes and Pharisees, hypocrites! For you tithe mint and dill and cumin, and have neglected the weightier provisions of the law: justice and mercy and faithfulness; but these are the things you should have done without neglecting the others."[1] His rebuke was aimed at their neglect of the weightier issues of justice, mercy, faithfulness, and love. He was not rebuking them for paying their tithes in an exacting and careful manner; instead, He said, "...these things you should have done." But He went on to say that they should demonstrate the same exacting care when it comes to justice, mercy and faithfulness. Second, under the New Covenant, everything belongs to the Lord, not just the tithe. James Kraft, founder of the Kraft foods conglomerate, regarding giving purportedly said, "I don't believe in tithing, but it's a good place to start."

When Malachi wrote about tithes, he used the word *storehouse* in his analogy. "'Bring the whole tithe into the storehouse , so that there may be food in My house, and test Me now in this,' says the LORD of hosts, 'if I will not open for you the windows of heaven, and pour out for you a blessing until it overflows.' "[2] One must define the word "storehouse." A natural storehouse, or depository, would be the place you would go to get food and to get seeds for sowing. A spiritual storehouse would be where you would go to be fed spiritually

---

[1] Matthew 23:23; Luke 11:42
[2] Malachi 3:10

and to be provided spiritual seed for sowing. For the vast majority, the storehouse is the pastor who cares for you in the local church that you attend. However, some feel that their local church pastors do not meet these criteria. For more than three decades Dan Wolfe, my pastor, mentor and spiritual father has been the recipient of my tithes. Now Tony Fitzgerald receives a portion of my tithe, as well. I have looked to the two of them for oversight, for spiritual food and for spiritual seed for sowing. Charles Simpson, Dan's pastor, receives a tithe of my tithe. Finally, those whom God sends to bless and encourage, especially of the five-fold ministries, receive my firstfruits. This allows for each of them to use a portion of it to help defray expenses incurred by trans-local responsibilities, which includes caring for me. You see, we all benefit from this.

I believe in the principle of exchange. However, this must not be an obligation. Each person must determine this for himself. We must not feel beholden to anyone. "If others share the right over you, do we not more? Nevertheless, we did not use this right, but we endure all things, that we may cause no hindrance to the gospel of Christ. But I have used none of these things. And I am not writing these things that it may be done so in my case; for it would be better for me to die than have any man make my boast an empty one. What then is my reward? That, when I preach the gospel, I may offer the gospel without charge, so as not to make full use of my right in the gospel."[1] Paul wrote that he would rather die than to have his motivation for preaching misconstrued and the ministry of the gospel compromised. Here are some final principles that I have used to guide me in the area of tithes and offerings.

---

[1] 1 Corinthians 9:12, 15 & 18

As a spiritual son, it should be seen as a privilege, not an obligation, to honor a father. "For I testify that according to their ability, and beyond their ability they gave of their own accord, begging us with much entreaty for the favor of participation in the support of the saints, and this, not as we had expected, but they first gave themselves to the Lord and to us by the will of God."[1] Notice that language used here: they *begged* for the favor of participation. What's more, before they offered anything, they gave themselves to the Lord. Finally, they gave themselves to the apostles by the will of God.

"Let each one do just as he has purposed in his heart; not grudgingly or under compulsion; for God loves a cheerful giver."[2] Bob Mumford once said, "Don't give until it hurts; give until it stops hurting." I believe that God loves a cheerful giver, and that a cheerful giver is one who loves God.

"...for where your treasure is, there will your heart be also."[3] I desire for the affections of my heart to be in the right place. I want to invest in those who are making a difference, not only in my own life, but also in the nations.

As mentioned previously, I have written this with a measure of reluctance, for fear that my motives would be misconstrued. Ezekiel gives a severe warning to those leaders who oversee the people of God and misuse or abuse their support. "Son of man, prophesy against the shepherds of Israel. Prophesy and say to those shepherds, thus says the Lord God, 'Woe, shepherds of Israel who have been feeding themselves! Should not the shepherds feed the flock? You eat the fat and clothe yourselves with the wool; you slaughter the

---

[1] 2 Corinthians 8:3-5
[2] 2 Corinthians 9:7
[3] Matthew 6:21

fat sheep without feeding the flock. Those who are sickly you have not strengthened, the diseased you have not healed, the broken you have not bound up, the scattered you have not brought back, nor have you sought for the lost; but with force and with severity you have dominated them.' "[1] Paul's testimony was, "I have coveted no one's silver or gold or clothes. You yourselves know that these hands ministered to my own needs and to the men who were with me. In everything I showed you that by working hard in this manner you must help the weak and remember the words of the Lord Jesus, that He Himself said, 'It is more blessed to give than to receive.' "[2]

In conclusion, in regards to firstfruits (*t'rumah*), tithes and offerings, I appreciate the advice of Tony Fitzgerald. Each person must decide for himself what things ended with the cross, what things are altered by the cross, and what things pass through the cross unchanged. I leave this decision to you, the reader.

---

[1] Ezekiel 34:2-4
[2] Acts 20:33-35

32

What Every Child Needs

*I*t is my personal opinion that we live in an anxiety-ridden world. Paul wrote to the Philippians, "Do not be anxious about anything, but in everything by prayer and supplication with thanksgiving let your requests be made known to God."[1] Prayer is the manner in which we communicate with our heavenly Father. It is fascinating to me that, speaking about prayer, the Bible says, "...your Father knows what you need before you ask Him."[2] Often I feel that we might be guilty of telling God what we need, as if He does not already know. Perchance this is a result of our feeling that our natural fathers were clueless to what we felt we needed.

In Matthew 6, Jesus implies that the primary root for anxiety arises out of the mistrust that a father does not know what we need. Five times in chapter six alone, Jesus entreats us not to be anxious.[3] He includes as the source of our anxiety such common necessities of life as clothes, food and drink. Obviously, every father should know instinctively that his children need these things and that he should provide them. Yet, due to the breakup of the family, many renegade fathers have failed to provide these very things. In the seventh

---

[1] Philippians 4:6
[2] Matthew 6:8
[3] Matthew 6:25-34

chapter of Matthew it is written, "If you then, being evil, know how to give good gifts to your children, how much more shall your Father who is in heaven give what is good to those who ask Him!"[1] Even an evil father should understand this: What a child needs is a father who knows what a child needs.

Nurture and care of children are not only the responsibility of a mother, but are also the responsibility of a father.[2] According to this reference, nurturing includes *exhorting*, *encouraging* and *imploring*. In plain English, this means that fathers should be cheering their children on. Children need to hear from their fathers such phrases as, "Go for it!" – "You can do it!" – "You're going to make it!" – "Keep it up!" – "Great job!" – "I'm so proud of you!" However, these cannot be limited to efforts of achievement; rather they must be phrases that express confidence in the child regardless of performance.

One of the greatest examples of such fatherly encouragement occurred during the 1992 Summer Olympics in Barcelona. Derek Redmond, a sprinter from Great Britain, had won his preliminary races and was expected to win a medal in the 400-meter race. The start of the race was uneventful. Just before the halfway point, Derek Redmond "heard a pop," the result of a torn hamstring in his right leg. He pulled up in tremendous pain, and the other racers passed him. When he saw the stretcher-bearers rushing towards him, Redmond jumped up and began hobbling forward despite the intense pain. Suddenly His father, Jim, came out of the stands and onto the track to help his son. Redmond initially tried to push him away, not realizing who he was, but

---

[1] Matthew 7:11
[2] 1 Thessalonians 2:11-12

then heard a familiar voice. "Derek, it's me," his father said. Redmond told his father, "I've got to finish this race." His father said, "If you're going to finish the race, we'll finish it together." With arms over each other's shoulders, they continued down the track with Derek sobbing, agonizing in pain. Just before the finish line, Jim let go of his son and Derek completed the race on his own. The crowd of 65,000 gave him a standing ovation, and the photo of his finish went around the world.

Many fathers—even renegades—have provided food, clothing and shelter and in so doing feel that they have fulfilled their responsibility. Yet every father should know that material things alone are not all that his children need. A genuine father knows that his children need love. It is a father's foremost duty to represent God to his children. He does this is by showing love, since "God is love."[1] As I have said, the first mention of the word *love* in Scripture does not refer to a husband and wife. Rather it occurs in the context of the relationship between Abraham and Isaac, a father and a son.[2] Love is the oxygen that a family needs to breathe. When I speak of love, I am speaking of the Biblical description of it. In the writings of Paul we read, "Love is patient, love is kind, and is not jealous; love does not brag and is not arrogant, does not act unbecomingly; it does not seek its own, is not provoked, does not take into account a wrong suffered, does not rejoice in unrighteousness, but rejoices with the truth; bears all things, believes all things, hopes all things, endures all things."[3] Here is a simple exercise for you to do. In the above passage, instead of using the word *love*, say *my Father*,

---

[1] 1 John 4:8
[2] Genesis 22:2-3
[3] 1 Corinthians 13:4-7

since the Bible says that God is love. Therefore, we can read it in this manner, "My Father is patient, my Father is kind, my Father...," etc. After doing this, in place of the word *love*, use the name *Jesus*. Finally, use the pronoun *I* in place of the word *love*. Do we fit this description? If we wish to be like Christ, we should!

According to the writer of Hebrews, the evidence of a father's love for his children is his willingness to *train*, to *correct*, and to *discipline* them.[1] In these references, only a child who has received and accepted discipline is considered legitimate. Solomon was even more emphatic about a father's responsibility to discipline his child, as he wrote, "He who spares the rod hates his son, but he who loves him disciplines him diligently."[2]

---

[1] Hebrews 12:7-11
[2] Proverbs 13:24

33

What Sons Need to Hear

I have spoken of things a father should know. Now I want to address the subject of things a father should say. A popular saying when I was a child was, "Sticks and stones may break my bones, but words will never hurt me." Few axioms are as erroneous as this one is! The Bible says, "Life and death are in the power of the tongue."[1] A father's words have the power to transform a son's life. **The spoken word has power to bless and to curse, to build up or to tear down and to confine or release.** As John baptized Jesus, the Father spoke from heaven saying, "This is my beloved Son, in whom I am well pleased."[2] His Father did not say, "This is my beloved prophet, evangelist, pastor or apostle." These words of blessing and affirmation would forever link the public ministry of Jesus to His position as a son. Pure and simple, the credential for Jesus' ministry related to His success as a son. Later, these words are repeated by the Father to Jesus on the Mount of Transfiguration. In Matthew 17, we find Jesus on a mountain with three of His closest disciples, Peter, James, and John. As Jesus was transfigured before their very eyes, Moses and Elijah appeared. The Scriptures reveal to us that Jesus was the fulfillment of the law and the prophets.

---

[1] Proverbs 18:21
[2] Matthew 3:17

Moses represents the law, and Elijah the prophets. Peter, insensitive to the moment, suggested that shrines be built on the spot for Jesus, Moses and Elijah. At that moment, the Father spoke from heaven, interrupting Peter in his good intention. In an audible voice, the Father said, "This is my beloved Son, with whom I am well-pleased; listen to Him."[1] The Father's blessing, embodied in these three statements, addresses some of the most critical needs that people face today. Jesus lived and died to hear these words. Therefore, let us examine these three phrases more closely.

"This is my beloved Son..."

Speaks of Relationship and Worth

Recognition – "This is my Son" has to do with recognition. Notice that the Father did not say this simply for the benefit of Jesus. He did not say, "You are my Son..." but rather He said, "This is my Son..." This was an announcement to all who would hear. A father has the ability to give recognition to his children, and he should do so, not only privately, but also publicly. He was publicly recognizing Jesus as His beloved Son. Every child needs recognition, since this relates to our self worth. We gain a sense of worth when we are singled out and honored by those whom we love and respect.

Affection – "This is my beloved Son" refers to affection. Of course, affection is closely linked to love, but I like to differentiate it this way. God loves everyone, but He appears to like some people more than He likes others. Isaac's relationship with Jacob and Esau are a prime example of this idea. Look at the natural relationship that Jacob had with

---

[1] Matthew 17:5

Joseph. The desire for affection is a normal appetite. Legitimate male affection should come from a father to his sons and daughters. Countless men have told me that their fathers never hugged them and/or told them that they loved them. Many children have never felt the safe, clean touch or embrace of a father. Fathers who withhold affection can cause their children to search for it in illegitimate ways. One major cause of sexual exploration and experimentation among youth is an illegitimate search for affection.

Identity – Identity is and always should be linked to sonship. Having identity is one of the most significant effects of fatherhood. These five words, "This is my beloved Son," have the potential to give us identity. Jesus had a clear sense of identity. He knew who He was, and He knew who His Father was, too.[1] Jesus found His identity in the clarity of His relationship with His Father. Today, due to a lack of fatherhood, millions of youth are in an identity crisis. Many have joined athletic teams, clubs, fraternal organizations, cults, or even street gangs searching for an identity. In most instances, the result has been frustration, disillusionment, anger and rebellion. Our identity relies heavily upon our being validated. Validation comes from being recognized and accepted as a member of a family. Unfortunately, in the church today too many people are attempting to find their identity through their ministry, gifts or calling. This can be a serious problem. True identity should come out of our relationships. We must be willing to recognize that identity comes from our natural and/or spiritual family.

The story of David and Goliath is one of the most familiar in the Old Covenant. After David defeated Goliath, King Saul wanted to know the identity of this young warrior. Three

---

[1] John 8:18

times Saul inquired about David's lineage. Saul wanted to know whose son David was.[1] Furthermore, as the Pharisees were attempting to identify Jesus, our Lord asked them the following question: "Whose son do you think I am?"[2]

Security – The result of receiving recognition, proper male affection, and a sense of identity is security. Security is the foundation for peace and a sense of well-being. Often I have observed that the most secure people are the risk takers. Pastor Mark Batterson wrote, "Quit living as if the purpose of life is to arrive safely at death. Go after the dream that is destined to fail without divine intervention. Your greatest regret at the end of your life will be the lions you didn't chase."[3] Personally, I regret the things that I have not done and should have, as much as I regret some of the things I have done and should not have. Indiana poet Kenneth C. Kaufman expresses this better than I:

TAME DUCK

There are two tame ducks in our back yard,
Dabbling in mud and trying hard
To get their share, and maybe more,
Of the overflowing barnyard store.
Of eating and sleeping and getting fat.
But whenever the free wild ducks go by
In a long line streaming down the sky,
They cock a quizzical, puzzled eye
And flap their wings and try to fly.

---

[1] 1 Samuel 17:54-58
[2] Matthew 22:42-46
[3] Mark Batterson, *In the Pit with a Lion on a Snowy Day.* (Colorado Springs, CO: Multnomah Books, 2006)

I think my soul is a tame old duck,
Dabbling around in barnyard muck;
Fat and lazy, with useless wings,
But at times, when the North wind sings
And the wild ones hurtle overhead,
It remembers something lost and dead,
Then cocks a wary, bewildered eye,
And makes a feeble attempt to fly.
It's fairly content with the state it's in,
But it's not the duck it might have been.

　　– Kenneth Kaufman[1]

Finally, let me add that we must not confuse identity with self-realization. We must use our identity as sons to glorify our Father. Like the prodigal son who "came to himself," self-realization awaits each of us in the pigpen.

"With whom I am well pleased"

Speaks of Being Tested and Approved

Approbation – Many people in the world are seeking approval from those who admire them. Ironically, when movie stars gain the popularity they seem to crave, they start wearing dark glasses to avoid recognition. Desiring approval from those who admire us is upside down. Look at some of those who have become professional athletes, rock stars or famous in business. Many who have climbed the ladder of success have found it was leaning against the wrong wall. The very nature of leadership requires that the leader must turn his back to those who are following. Jesus did not look for approval from those who followed Him but rather sought and

---

[1] <u>Milwaukee Milk Producer</u>, Vol. 2, No. 6, September, 1929, p. 4

received approval from His father. We too will be able to find genuine affirmation from those whom God sends to us as leaders and fathers.

Appreciation – In today's society, performance has become the rule of law for appreciation. The remedy is to be appreciated for who we are instead of what we do. We live in a world that is addicted to performance. When we are only appreciated for what we do, it will cause us to become "human doings" instead of "human beings." It is well to note here that in the King James Version of the Bible the word success is mentioned only once, whereas the word faithful is mentioned over eighty times. Based upon this observation, fathers might also do well to show their appreciation for things such as endurance, effort and consistency, as opposed to final scores, medals and trophies. Remember the words that we hope await us are, "Well done, good and faithful [not successful] slave."[1]

Acceptance – If rejection is one of the most destructive forces in the earth, then acceptance could have the opposite effect. At the baptism of Jesus, before He had given a sermon, done any public ministry, or performed any miracles the Father spoke these words: "This is my beloved Son, in whom I am well-pleased." His Father was expressing a relationship between Him and His Son. The Bible makes it clear that God chose us, not based on merit, but according to grace, which is His unmerited favor. We must always remember: "Our acceptance as children of God is based not on what we have done, but is based upon what He has done!"

Liberation – One of the great benefits of approbation, appreciation, and acceptance is liberation. Since genuine fatherhood does not promote a performance orientation, we

---

[1] Matthew 25:21,23

are free to be ourselves in Christ, recognized for who we are and not for what we do. Someone wrote, "Freedom is not the right to do as a person pleases, but the liberty to do as he ought."

"Listen to Him"

Speaks of Being Authorized and Sent

Elevation – Conscientious fathers will look to provide a platform of expression for their children. Having the opportunity to be heard gives us status among others. Elevation also is experienced through promotion. All legitimate promotion comes from Him and from those over us.

Affirmation – We are affirmed when people feel we have something worthy of hearing. Fathers are in a unique position to give their children the chance to be heard. Being heard affirms our position in the family, the church, and society. Militant street marches and demonstrations are most often born out of the desire to be heard.

Authorization – The words, "Listen to Him..."[1] authorized Jesus as a spokesman. Let us look at some verses from the gospel of Matthew that address the subject of authorization: "So then, you will know them by their fruits. Not everyone who says to Me, 'Lord, Lord,' will enter the kingdom of heaven; but he who does the will of My Father who is in heaven. Many will say to Me on that day, 'Lord, Lord, did we not prophesy in Your name, and in Your name cast out demons, and in Your name perform many miracles?' And then I will declare to them, 'I never knew [approved of] you:

---

[1] Matthew 17:5

depart from me, you who practice lawlessness.' "[1] Prophesying, casting out demons and performing miracles are considered to be elements of charismatic ministry. In the passage, please note that these ministries are all done in His name. However, it implies that they are done without authorization. Jesus says that many (not just a few) will ask, "Did not our gift and ministry authorize us?" His answer is clearly, "No!" Not gifts but fruit must be our credentials for ministry. In addition, Jesus warned us, "Not everyone who says, 'Lord, Lord,' will enter the kingdom."[2] What's more, we read, "And why do you call Me, 'Lord, Lord,' and do not do what I say?"[3] Doing His will corroborates and confirms His Lordship in our lives. The result of this warning is frightening. Many, not just a few, will hear, " 'I never knew [approved of] you; depart from me, you who practice lawlessness.' "[4] Once more, we know that God knows everyone; therefore, we must assume that He was not saying, "I didn't _know_ you," but rather, "I never _approved_ of you," or "I never authorized you." Going out, without being sent out, is a critical problem in ministry today. In John's Gospel, Jesus repeats at least twenty-seven times that "He was sent."[5]

Spheres – Elevation, affirmation, and authorization are important parts of the process that help us to define our spheres of influence, authority and responsibility. We have learned that promotion should come from above. Therefore, those men to whom we look to for oversight should help us define our spheres. When we have help with defining our spheres, it leaves minimal room for making comparisons,

---

[1] Matthew 7:20-23
[2] Matthew 7:21
[3] Luke 6:46
[4] Matthew 7:23
[5] (Examples) John 4:34; John 5:24

jockeying for position, power struggles, jealousy, and competition. In an effort to avoid such conflict of spheres, Paul wrote, "And thus I aspired to preach the gospel, not where Christ was already named, that I might not build upon another man's foundation..."[1] We must understand that our field of influence and authority, or measure of rule, has limits. Since the issue of spheres is so important in defining purpose, I want to look more closely at it.

---

[1] Romans 15:20

34

Recognizing Our Sphere

*H*aving spoken on the subject of spheres in the previous chapter, let me now address the issue of *metron*. My understanding of *metron* has come largely through the teaching of my friend and fellow laborer, Michael Puffett. The word *metron* means our "measure of rule"; *i.e.*, the sphere, the field, and the boundaries that determine the limits and extensions of one's authority and influence. God sets our *metron*. For some this sphere is larger than for others. Paul wrote, "For we are not bold to class or compare ourselves with some of those who commend themselves; but when they measure themselves by themselves, and compare themselves with themselves, they are without understanding. But we will not boast beyond our measure, but within the measure of the sphere which God apportioned to us as a measure, to reach even as far as you."[1] It is vital that sons understand their sphere of authority and remain within it.

For each *metron* of ministry, there is a special measure of grace. When we function inside our sphere of authority, we see the favor and grace of God. Paul wrote, "... to each one of us grace was given according to the measure of the gift of

---

[1] 2 Corinthians 10:12-13

Christ."[1] Paul understood that his *metron* included preaching the gospel of the Kingdom to the Gentiles.[2] Faithfulness within our *metron* can increase our sphere and bring favor and promotion. In fact, our *metron* is where our faithfulness is required, expected and tested. Therefore, let us look at what the Bible describes as characteristics of faithful or trustworthy people. "He who is faithful in a very little thing is faithful also in much; and he who is unrighteous in a very little thing is unrighteous also in much. Therefore, if you have not been faithful in the use of unrighteous wealth, who will entrust the true riches to you? And if you have not been faithful in the use of that which is another's, who will give you that which is your own?"[3] In these three verses lie three important principles that we should teach our successors.

It is important to be faithful in very little things. The minuscule must be as important as the magnificent. Detail is critical. The inference is that if we are careless with small things, we will also be careless with great things.

It is important how we acquire and manage material wealth. Before we are entrusted with spiritual understanding and wisdom, we should show ourselves to be trustworthy with money and material possessions. In Proverbs, wisdom and knowledge are described as having much more value than gold and silver. If we do not know how to handle gold and silver, we probably will not know how to handle wisdom and knowledge.

Finally, we should learn to be faithful with another's things before we have our own things. A child must be taught to be faithful with his parents's things, so he can be

---

[1] Ephesians 4:7
[2] Romans 1:5
[3] Luke 16:10-13

entrusted with his own things. This is clearly a principle used in apprenticeship and in discipleship. As mentioned, the Bible speaks volumes more about faithfulness than it does about success.

As we look at raising our children to be faithful, these three principles should be a check and balance for each of us. Fathers and leaders should always be faithful in little, faithful with money and material possessions and faithful with another's things. Their example clears the way and creates a path for their followers to walk in their ways.

Conversely, when we are outside of our measure of rule, we function outside the grace of God. Grace is the enabling power of God to do what He called us to do without striving in our human efforts. The boundaries that God sets are not to limit us, but rather to protect us. If we move beyond the grace of God, we will function in areas where we are out of order. We will not have the legitimacy or the capacity to maintain that sphere. Whenever we move beyond our sphere, we will have a tendency to become arrogant and presumptuous. This causes us to move into a performance mode, which may satisfy our self-image, but rarely will it be effective with helping others. When we are functioning outside of our sphere, those who follow us will often become offended, unfulfilled and disillusioned.

Moreover, we should not interfere within the sphere of another without expressed invitation and permission. The family situation is a classic example. The father and mother are responsible for their children. Other people who have no authority in that home have no right to challenge or adjust that household unless such authorization is given. Of course, all authority is delegated to us by God, including within the home. Where we have authority, we also have the right to delegate that authority, as parents may do so with a baby sitter.

There are two types of *metrons*; one has to do with geographical area, and the other has to do with people. Some people serve in local towns, while others are called to go around the world. Some are called to be responsible for ten, some to one hundred and some to thousands. As God is the one who determines our *metron*, He knows our capacity and our limitations. When we prove to be faithful in our assigned spheres, God can promote us and extend our boundaries.[1] The point is to be faithful in whatever sphere that God places us. At the close of the age, we hope to hear our Master say, "Well done [not well said], good and faithful servant; you were faithful with a few things, I will put you in charge of many things; enter into the joy of your master."[2]

A father who wishes to expand the *metron* of his son should look at the youth's faithfulness, stewardship, integrity and the dimension of the gifting and calling. Helping our sons determine their *metron* is critical. Before passing the mantle of authority to our sons and broadening their spheres, we must teach, train and equip them. Sons (and daughters) of God who are raised and equipped well will then have the capacity to do greater works than their fathers have done.

---

[1] Luke 19:11-27
[2] Matthew 25:23

35

The Example of Paul and Timothy

We can learn a lot about a father by observing his son. Most of us are familiar with the old saying, "The apple does not fall far from the tree." Another way to phrase this is to say, "Like father, like son." It means that sons will often become a reflection of their fathers. Unfortunately, it may not be a compliment for a son to hear these words: "He looks and acts just like his dad." Repeatedly, in the Old Covenant history of the kings of Israel and Judah, we see that the kings followed the example of their fathers. "So while these nations feared the Lord, they also served their idols; their children likewise and their grandchildren, as their fathers did, so they do to this day."[1] When these fathers drifted away from following God, their sons, and often even their grandsons, followed their example.

Let us concentrate on a successful Biblical example of a spiritual father and his spiritual son by taking a closer look at the relationship between Paul and Timothy. Paul profiled Timothy's model as an example for us. In his second letter to Timothy, Paul wrote "...to Timothy, my beloved son: ...I thank God, whom I serve with a clear conscience the way my forefathers did, as I constantly remember you in my prayers night and day, longing to see you, even as I recall your tears,

---

[1] 2 Kings 17:41

so that I may be filled with joy. For I am mindful of the sincere faith within you, which first dwelt in your grandmother Lois, and your mother Eunice, and I am sure that it is in you as well."[1] Prior to becoming a spiritual son to Paul, Timothy was raised by a godly mother and grandmother. We do not know what happened to his biological father, since the Scriptures are silent with regard to him. It is my hope that this example will encourage many single mothers today. In the absence of natural fathers, God is able and willing to provide spiritual fathers. In fact, James wrote that caring for the fatherless and widows, who often end up as single mothers, is "...pure and undefiled religion."[2]

From Paul's letter to the Philippians, we can glean some characteristics of a spiritual son. "But I hope in the Lord Jesus to send Timothy to you shortly, so that I also may be encouraged when I learn of your condition. For I have no one else of kindred spirit who will genuinely be concerned for your welfare. For they all seek after their own interests, not those of Christ Jesus. But you know of his proven worth that he served with me in the furtherance of the gospel like a child serving his father."[3] What follows are some thoughts that we can glean from this passage.

"I hope in the Lord Jesus to send Timothy to you shortly..."[4] Remember, when God wished to demonstrate to us that He was a Father, He did not send a father; He sent His Son. Here we see that Paul followed the exact pattern. When Paul could not visit, he sent his spiritual son. What's more, Paul commended Timothy to the church at Corinth. He calls him his "beloved and faithful child (son) in the Lord."

---

[1] 2 Timothy 1:2-5
[2] James 1:27
[3] Philippians 2:19-20
[4] Philippians 2:19a

"...so that I also may be encouraged when I learn of your condition."[1] From this statement, we see that Timothy was to visit the church, learn how it was faring and then return and bring a report back to Paul. Timothy was sent as a young man under Paul's authority, with a clear mission.

"For I have no one else of kindred spirit..."[2] This is what qualified Timothy for his mission. He was a genuine son. However, we see from this statement that there are few who aspire to be genuine spiritual sons. A couple of years ago Kathy said to me, "It seems nearly all men want to be fathers, or to be fathered, but few desire to be sons." This is to say, they desire what a father provides but do not wish to position themselves in the place where they can receive it. I believe this is a revelation from God, and that it gives us profound insight into our subject. The great apostle Paul said that he had no one else who had the kindred spirit of Timothy. The word *kindred* is translated from the Greek word **isosuchops** which means of equal soul. In English the root word of *kindred* is *kin*, meaning *family*. Perhaps this is why Paul wrote to the Corinthians, "... you have not many fathers..."[3] because so very few desire to be genuine sons.

"... who will be genuinely concerned with your welfare."[4] A genuine son must embrace and care for the concerns of his father. The concerns of Jesus always were in alignment with His Father's interests. Paul said that Timothy would demonstrate a genuine reflection of Paul's heart toward the Philippian church. In Paul's letter to Timothy he repeated his exhortation regarding priority and focus of service as he wrote, "No soldier in active service entangles himself in the

---

[1] Philippians 2:19b
[2] Philippians 2:20a
[3] 1 Corinthians 4:15
[4] Philippians 2:20b

affairs of everyday life, so that he may please the one who enlisted him [chose him] as a soldier."[1] It is implied by this passage that one should attempt to please the one who recruited him for the ministry of the gospel. In Timothy's case, that was Paul.

"For all seek after their own interests...."[2] Isaiah wrote, "All of us like sheep have gone astray, Each of us has turned to his own way; But the Lord has caused the iniquity of us all to fall on Him."[3] Isaiah defines the word "iniquity" for us as "turning to your own way or doing your own thing." The word translated *iniquity* is derived from the Hebrew verb *awoh* meaning to bend or deviate from the way. It is my contention that many have deviated from the path of sonship and fatherhood, doing their own thing. Being a spiritual son will deal with a man's tendency toward iniquity. Timothy was not on a mission doing his own thing. He was doing what Paul sent him to do.

"... not those of Christ Jesus."[4] This is a key point. Paul equates Timothy's service of himself with serving Christ. That is to say, as Timothy served Paul, he was serving Christ. Here we have a spiritual son serving his spiritual father, and that service is compared with serving Christ. Once more, Jesus is the archetype of this example.

"You know the proof of him, that as a son with the father, he has served with me in the gospel."[5] One significant evidence of sonship is the priority of service to a father. We may infer that Timothy had been tested and found faithful. Therefore, all of the qualities mentioned authorized Timothy

---

[1] 2 Timothy 2:4
[2] Philippians 2:21a
[3] Isaiah 53:6
[4] Philippians 2:21b
[5] Philippians 2:22

as a spiritual son, sent to represent his spiritual father.

Referring again to Paul's relationship with Timothy, we read, "I exhort you therefore, be imitators of me. For this reason I have sent to you Timothy, who is my beloved and faithful child in the Lord, and he will remind you of my ways which are in Christ, just as I teach everywhere in every church."[1] This is a direct contradiction to those who say, "Don't look at men, look only at Jesus." In fact, Paul said, "...be imitators of me." He continued by saying that the reason he could send Timothy was that he would remind them of Paul and his ways. This shows us that Timothy was imitating Paul. Timothy said and did what he saw Paul say and do. Furthermore, Paul instructed Timothy to use their relationship as a model for generations to come. "And the things which you have heard from me in the presence of many witnesses, these entrust to faithful men, who will be able to teach others also."[2] In this passage, four generations are mentioned: 1) The things you (Timothy); 2) have heard from me (Paul); 3) commit to faithful men; 4) who will be able to teach others. Whatever Paul taught Timothy became the curriculum for others. Derek Prince taught a number of principles that have helped me, especially as I have sought to invest into the next generation.

True faith not only manifests in what you can produce, but also what you can help to reproduce in another. In this manner, Timothy was encouraged to reproduce what he and Paul had experienced together.

To extend your ministry and advance the kingdom of God, you should not begin by looking for a need, but rather by looking for a man. Invest in people, not programs.

---

[1] 1 Corinthians 4:16-17
[2] 2 Timothy 2:2

When you come across a man, your function and duty is to help him discover his destiny and attempt to equip him for it. Paul taught us that the primary purpose of the five-fold ministry is to equip others. "He gave some as apostles, and some as prophets, and some as evangelists, and some as pastors and teachers, for the equipping of the saints for the work of service, to the building up of the body of Christ; until we all attain to the unity of the faith, and of the knowledge of the Son of God, to a mature man, to the measure of the stature which belongs to the fullness of Christ."[1] Paul was one of these gifts of men sent by God. Paul boldly challenged men to imitate his faith and to follow him as he followed Christ. Therefore, whether in the family or in the church, one of the primary roles of any leader should be to equip those who are following. Genuine fathers, whether natural or spiritual, should desire to equip their children to be more productive than themselves.

---

[1] Ephesians 4:11-13

36

Jacob's Advantage

The genealogies in the Bible are in effect a family tree. These genealogies provide the linkage that connects the generations of the people of God. Numerous passages in both the Old and New Covenants refer to God as the God of Abraham, Isaac, and Jacob. "God said to Moses, 'Thus you shall say to the sons of Israel, The Lord, the God of your fathers, the God of Abraham, the God of Isaac, and the God of Jacob, has sent me to you. This is My name forever, and this is My memorial name to all generations.' "[1] God said that His children would remember Him forever as "the God of Abraham, Isaac and Jacob."

In the New Covenant Matthew wrote, "I am the God of Abraham and the God of Isaac, and the God of Jacob."[2] This name identifies God as the God of a distinct family or genealogical order. I cannot imagine what it would mean to have God use my family name like this. Think of the ramifications: "I will call Myself the God of Jim, Sean, and Matt, and their children." Abraham was the patriarch of this family. God identified Himself not only with Abraham, but also with his son and grandson. That is three generations. God's covenant blessing did not end with Abraham. It was

---

[1] Exodus 3:15
[2] Matthew 22:32

ordained to be passed down through his family line. Moses instructed Israel to teach the commandments and statutes of the Lord specifically to their sons and grandsons. Once again, we see an emphasis on three generations.[1] This pattern was set for us. As I mentioned earlier, Abraham (the first generation) was chosen because God trusted him to lead or manage his family. Isaac (the second generation) was the son that God promised to Abraham. Jacob (the third generation) was Abraham's grandson.

Isaac exhibited an incredible example of sonship on Mount Moriah. While Abraham was over one hundred years old, Isaac was probably in his thirties. I suggest that Isaac voluntarily allowed himself to be bound and laid upon the altar by his father. Isaac entrusted his very life to his father. He lay down on the altar and watched as his father prepared to kill him.[2] This remarkable scene is often presented as an illustration of Jesus laying down His life at His Father's request. Just imagine, as the three of them sat around a campfire, how often Jacob might have heard the story of his father's obedience on Mount Moriah.

Moreover, think of Abraham's faith. He was prepared to kill and burn his son—and in burning him to destroy all the evidence that Isaac had ever existed!—that carried the seed from which Messiah would come. But God intervened. "And He [God] said, 'Do not stretch out your hand against the lad, and do nothing to him; for now I know that you fear God, since you have not withheld your son, your only son, from Me.' Then the angel of the Lord called to Abraham a second time from heaven, and said, 'By Myself I have sworn, declares the Lord, because you have done this thing, and have not

---

[1] Deuteronomy 6:1-2
[2] Genesis 22:1ff

withheld your son, your only son, indeed I will greatly bless you, and I will greatly multiply your seed as the stars of the heavens, and as the sand which is on the seashore; and your seed shall possess the gate of their enemies. And in your seed all the nations of the earth shall be blessed, because you have obeyed My voice.' "[1]

Later, we see that God came to Jacob in a dream and spoke to him about completing the promise He had made to his father and to his grandfather. "And behold, the Lord stood above it and said, 'I am the Lord, the God of your father Abraham and the God of Isaac; the land on which you lie, I will give it to you [Jacob] and to your descendants. Your descendants shall also be like the dust of the earth, and you shall spread out to the west and to the east and to the north and to the south; and in you and in your descendants shall all the families of the earth be blessed. And behold, I am with you, and will keep you wherever you go, and will bring you back to this land; for I will not leave you until I have done what I have promised you.'[2] As the grandson of Abraham, Jacob became the heir of God's promise to his grandfather.

Here we see the unique advantage that comes to the third generation. The third generation is the first generation that can watch their father relate to their grandfather. Jacob had the advantage of observing the relationship his father Isaac had with his grandfather Abraham. The patriarchs born of Jacob were the fourth generation. I do not believe it is coincidental that it was through Abraham's great grandsons, fourth generation, a family and a tribe became a nation, that being Israel.[3],[4] We have looked at the Old Covenant, but now

---

[1] Genesis 22:12 & 15-18
[2] Genesis 28:13-15
[3] Genesis 35:10-12
[4] Hebrews 11:9

let me repeat an earlier theme. When Paul instructs Timothy to find faithful men who will instruct others, we are looking at four spiritual generations. If we are to be a spiritual family, we must have a generational view as we build for the future. Franchises and programs are often instituted for their immediate rewards. God is not building a franchise. God is building us as a family. God's view, as demonstrated above, was and remains a generational view. Three generations can be loosely calculated as one hundred twenty years. That which we sow today may not be harvested completely for over a century. Few innovative programs will still be relevant a century from now.

Less than a century ago in America, it was normal for three generations to live and work on the family farm together. In this setting, it was easy for the son to watch his father relate to his grandfather. Under these conditions, modeling fatherhood and sonship was not a program but a daily lifestyle. Two modern day examples of "Jacob's Advantage" have been very inspirational to me; one is an expression in the business world, and the other is an expression in ministry. In his book, *Loving Monday*,[1] Christian industrialist John Beckett speaks of his decision to follow his father into business. Upon his father's death, John inherited the R. W. Beckett Corporation, which he has since given over to his son Kevin (third generation) to oversee. Charles Simpson, internationally known Bible teacher and founder of Charles Simpson Ministries, often uses illustrations that revolve around his relationship with his late father, Vernon. Today, Charles's sons, Stephen and Jonathan, are deeply involved in their dad's ministry, while his daughter Charlyn and her husband have opened their home to orphan children

---

[1] www.lovingmonday.com

in Costa Rica.

With my sons, Sean and Matt, I have attempted to build a relationship that they would desire to reproduce with their children. I have tried to do the same with my spiritual sons. To do this, it has been my goal to posture myself toward my leaders in a manner that I would desire for my sons to replicate. I have tried to walk as a spiritual son to those spiritual fathers that God has sent my way. Therefore, the evidence of the success of my journey will be confirmed or invalidated by the third and fourth generation, not only through my natural sons, but through my spiritual sons as well.

As I have illustrated, Jacob's ability to observe his father's relationship with his grandfather was "Jacob's (Israel's) Advantage." At least in the life of Jacob, the legacy of Abraham and Isaac was the seed of Jacob's destiny. Jacob became the heir to the blessings God promised to Abraham and Isaac. Perhaps this is the reason such care is given to genealogies in both the Old and the New Covenants. What's more, we know that the promises were not simply given to a natural genealogical lineage. The gene of Abraham's faith in God's covenant faithfulness, which was to be passed down through faith into his spiritual family, qualifies us to become a part of the genealogical order of Abraham, and today we carry that gene.

Therefore, according to Paul, "Christ redeemed us from the curse of the Law, having become a curse for us for it is written, 'Cursed is everyone who hangs on a tree' in order that in Christ Jesus the blessing of Abraham might come to the Gentiles, so that we might receive the promise of the Spirit through faith."[1] Paul continues, "If you belong to Christ,

---

[1] Galatians 3:13

then you are Abraham's offspring, heirs according to promise."[1] So what is so spectacular about the blessing of Abraham and being an heir of Abraham? Moses wrote, "Now Abraham was old, advanced in age; and the LORD had blessed Abraham in every way (some translations say everything)."[2] Can we even imagine being blessed in "every way and everything?" Besides this, "And Abraham breathed his last and died in a ripe old age, an old man and satisfied with life, and he was gathered to his people."[3] I doubt that there is much more we could hope for than to die at a ripe old age, being satisfied with life, and then for us to be welcomed home by those who have gone before us. Now, that's what I call a successful life!

[1] Galatians 3:29
[2] Genesis 24:1
[3] Genesis 25:8

37
Legacy and Inheritance

*H*istorically, the vast majority of fortunes are dissipated before reaching the third or fourth generation. The children and grandchildren of numerous wealthy families often squander the wealth left by their parents or grandparents. Since many who have received an inheritance were never properly trained or equipped to manage it, let alone increase it, inheritances are lost through poor stewardship practices. However, through proper training and equipping in stewardship, inheritances and important legacies can be preserved and perpetuated.

Some time ago, I found myself sitting in a hospital waiting room with Theresa Stone and Marian Gross. Both Marian and Theresa are extremely gifted and intelligent businesswomen. Theresa has been a successful accountant, and Marian is a personal assistant to a senior executive of Boeing Corporation. Nervously waiting for Marian's husband Michael to come out of a lengthy surgery, the three of us began to talk about the manual I wrote, *Sonship: The Path to Fatherhood*. I was interested in their insight on how I might take the principles of sonship into the workplace arena. As we talked, these two women came up with a brilliant idea. Their idea was to develop and offer a seminar to the corporate community, emphasizing the importance of equipping heirs. They shared that many in the corporate world dedicate a great amount of time and money into estate planning in an effort to protect and pass on their fortunes. In her role as a personal assistant, Marian had even attended some seminars covering this subject.

It is sad but true that people spend time, effort and money preparing to protect and give an inheritance, but they fail to make the same effort in preparing the inheritor. Tragically, they leave an inheritance and legacy to one who is not prepared to steward it. In fact, the Bible has numerous examples of those men who failed to pass along their inheritance to the third generation. Moses raised up Joshua, but it appears that Joshua failed to raise up a successor, and responsibility fell upon a group known as the Judges. The Bible has this to say about the period in which the Judges ruled. "In those days there was no king in Israel; everyone did what was right in his own eyes."[1] Isaiah defined iniquity as people doing their own thing. "All of us like sheep have gone astray, each of us has turned to his own way; But the LORD has caused the iniquity of us all to fall on Him."[2] The book of Ruth sums up the results of Joshua's failure to raise up a successor. "Now it came about in the days when the judges governed, that there was a famine in the land."[3]

Jacob, later known as Israel, had a tremendous model in the relationship between Abraham and Isaac, but he failed to raise his oldest son Reuben in that manner. As Jacob's oldest son, Reuben failed to protect Joseph from his jealous brothers. Later, during the time of Jacob's mourning for Rachel, Reuben further forfeited his rights as the firstborn

---

[1] Judges 21:25
[2] Isaiah 53:6
[3] Ruth 1:1

when he disgraced his father: "And it came about while Israel was dwelling in that land, that Reuben went and lay with Bilhah his father's concubine; and Israel heard of it."[1]

One further example of what I am attempting to explain comes from King David's son and successor, Solomon. Throughout the book of Ecclesiastes Solomon speaks of the vanity of living this lifetime as an end in itself. As we all know, there is a vast difference between gifts and fruit. Remember, Solomon had a "gift of wisdom," but when he was old, this gift failed to reflect in his character. Solomon's son Rehoboam, third generation, rejected the wisdom and advice of his elders and instead took the counsel of his peers. The advice of his peers resulted in the splitting of the kingdom. What David and Solomon built was left to and lost by this third generation, a foolish son. Soon, I began to realize the relevance of Solomon's words when he wrote, "...I hated all the fruit of my labor for which I had labored under the sun, for I must leave it to the man who will come after me. And who knows whether he will be a wise man or a fool? Yet he will have control over all the fruit of my labor for which I have labored by acting wisely under the sun. This too is vanity. Therefore, I completely despaired of all the fruit of my labor for which I had labored under the sun. When there is a man who has labored with wisdom, knowledge and skill, then he gives his legacy to one who has not labored with them."[2]

In the New Covenant, Paul raised up Timothy and Titus, but we are not privileged to know if they in turn raised up spiritual sons. The list of beneficiaries who squandered their inheritance is endless. Still, God's plan does not vary. The

[1] Genesis 35:22
[2] Ecclesiastes 2:18-21

Father sent Jesus as a son to raise up sons who are to raise up sons. God the Father desires to have innumerable sons that can be beneficiaries as well as stewards of His abundant supply. Jesus came, "...that He might be the firstborn among many brethren."[1] We have received that which we must pass along, that is our spiritual heritage.

In many instances, including the above, the haphazard manner in which inheritances have been passed on has reaped tragic consequences. So let us look at what makes one eligible to receive an inheritance. The Bible teaches that inheritances and legacies are meant for sons, not for children or slaves. "Now I say, as long as the heir is a child (*teknon*), he does not differ at all from a slave although he is owner of everything, but he is under guardians and managers until the date set by the father. So also we, while we were children (*teknon*), were held in bondage under the elemental things of the world. But when the fullness of the time came, God sent forth His Son, born of a woman, born under the Law, in order that He might redeem those who were under the Law, that we might receive the adoption as sons. And because you are sons, God has sent forth the Spirit of His Son into our hearts, crying, 'Abba! Father!' Therefore you are no longer a slave, but a son; and if a son (*huios*), then an heir through God."[2] According to Paul, children (*teknon*) do not have the legal right to an inheritance; inheritance is reserved for sons (*huios*.) A point I wish to make here is that, according to Paul, a child who is not yet considered a son is likened to a slave. To be sure, God loves us as children, but He does not want us to remain infants.[3] As I explained in a previous chapter, you

---

[1] Romans 8:29
[2] Galatians 4:1-7
[3] 1 John 3:1-2

may bear children, but you must build sons. Sonship, and sonship alone, is the requirement for inheritance.

Implied in the above passage is the thought that many who are born again may remain as children. However, if we desire our inheritance, we should take the steps of adoption, the *huiothesia*, that qualify us to be sons. It is impossible to imagine the inheritance available to the sons of God. Being an heir of His is unworthy of comparison to being an heir of the wealthiest man on earth. Even the wealth of Warren Buffett or Bill Gates pales in relation to what is available to the children of God. Our inheritance is boundless in Him. The Bible teaches us that we have an inheritance available to us that has been passed down by previous generations. Believing that each of us who are in Christ owes a debt to previous generations, we must not serve only our generation. We have a responsibility to the generations that will follow. It has been said, "There is no success without a successor."

Paul wrote, "If you belong to Christ, then you are Abraham's offspring, heirs according to promise."[1] Since we belong to Christ, we have the potential to become the heirs of the promise to Abraham. As we think about legacy and inheritance, let us consider how we might equip our successors, which preferably and hopefully are our children. Let us look to the Scriptures in this regard. To the Corinthians Paul wrote, "It is required of stewards, that a man be found faithful."[2] That is to say, it is required of one given a trust that he be trustworthy.

An inheritance is a trust, and it would be wise to give it to one who is trustworthy. In effect, legacies ought to be built on trustworthy men. Trustworthy, faithful stewards, are

---

[1] Galatians 3:29
[2] 1 Corinthians 4:2

described by this passage: "He who is faithful in a very little thing is faithful also in much; and he who is unrighteous in a very little thing is unrighteous also in much. If therefore you have not been faithful in the use of unrighteous mammon, who will entrust the true riches to you? And if you have not been faithful in the use of that which is another's, who will give you that which is your own?"[1] Legacies and inheritances are safest in the hands of those who are faithful in little, those who are faithful with material wealth and those who have proven faithful with someone else's possessions. Finally, a company president or CEO can bless anyone, but only a father can give a son an inheritance and leave a legacy.

---

[1] Luke 16:10-12

38

The Unfatherable Spirit

*T*he initial catalyst that set my feet on a journey to discover the path of sonship to fatherhood will probably seem a bit strange to you. I will attempt to explain what birthed this obsession for this path. Over three decades ago, I heard a teaching on the spirit of Jezebel. I had been attempting to address some serious problems with a woman in my congregation. At first, I felt that this teaching was a solution to the problems that I was facing with her. However, as this teaching went forth, I observed that the countenance of all the women fell. Of course, no woman wanted to be labeled a Jezebel. I began to research the subject, and came to this conclusion. She was not the source of the problem; her husband was. The primary problem was not an overbearing and strong woman; it was with a passive and irresponsible man. Well over a quarter of a century later, as I am writing this book, I am more convinced than ever that this is the issue. Jezebel is the symptom, but Ahab is the disease. Perhaps the following will help us understand that the spirit of Ahab is one of the most destructive forces against the revelation of sonship as the path to fatherhood.

It was during the ungodly reign of Ahab, that Elijah came. Elijah's name means, "The Lord, He is God." Elijah called Israel back to the God of Abraham by restoring fatherhood to Israel. The manner in which we prepare the way for the Lord to return is through recovering the concept of fatherhood and sonship. John the Baptist, who came in the spirit of Elijah, prepared the way by addressing the need for this restoration. Although Elijah was a prophet, Elisha saw him as a father. Herein lies the problem. Ahab would not allow himself to be fathered by Elijah. Years ago I came across an article that said Ahab's name can be loosely translated *unfatherable*. Ahab refused to allow Elijah to speak into his life. Imagine what might have happened if Ahab had received and acknowledged Elijah as his "spiritual father" rather than turning to the idolatrous worship introduced by his wife and father-in-law.

The name *Jezebel* has Phoenician roots and may be loosely translated in two ways. The first is "isle of the dung-hill." I doubt that anyone reading this material would choose this name for his daughter. *Jezebel* may also be translated *unhusbanded*. Allow me to suggest that there is a great difference between being unmarried and unhusbanded.

The spirit of Ahab desires to be mothered instead of fathered. This has caused serious problems in numerous marriages. If men allow their wives to mother them, the wives will become confused about their role in the home. They will begin to speak to and to treat their husbands as children. We can see how this happened with the incident regarding Naboth's vineyard. Ahab was pouting, and Jezebel scolded him. Then, as "Big Mama," she took over.

There is no Biblical record that Elijah ever spoke to Jezebel. Every verbal confrontation Elijah had was with Ahab. We see this as a pattern that began with God in the Garden of Eden, where Eve initiated the sin, yet God addressed Adam first. This leads me to believe that we are primarily respons-ible to confront men by placing an emphasis in our teaching on the spirit of Ahab and not on the spirit of Jezebel.

Men with the spirit of Ahab will always have a conflict with spiritual authority. Although God had sent Elijah to be His prophet to Ahab, Ahab was convinced that Elijah was his enemy. Often, like Ahab, men with this spirit will turn their wives loose to attack the man of God.

After the confrontation between Elijah and the prophets of Baal on Mount Carmel, Ahab went home and told Jezebel all that Elijah had done, not all that God had done. In other words, he went home and tattled to his wife as a child would tattle to his mother.

On Mount Carmel, Elijah mocked five hundred false prophets, and then called down fire from heaven. Then he slew all of these men. Nevertheless, when one woman (Jezebel) confronted him, he ran eighty miles, hid in a cave and asked God to kill him. A renegade husband unleashes tremendous spiritual evil. Jezebel did not simply take Naboth's vineyard; she took Naboth's life, too. The "spirit of Jezebel" did what the prophets of Baal could not do to Elijah. It did what the Philistines were unable to do to Sampson. Delilah's witchcraft caused Sampson to lose his vision.

Men under the influence of the spirit of Ahab are prone to indulge in pouting and self-pity. Ahab is described as being sullen and vexed. Again using the incident of Naboth's vineyard, the Bible says, "He lay down upon his bed, turned his face to the wall, and wouldn't eat."[1] I have told wives, "If your husband does this, let him starve! Do not give way to the temptation to take over."

Jezebel dies under the assignment and the anointing Elijah gave to Jehu. At the end, she is pictured painting her eyes, probably in an effort at further seduction. Notice that

---

[1] 1 Kings 21

Jezebel had surrounded herself with eunuchs. Eunuchs are emasculated men. One of the major roles of fathers is to reproduce sons. Obviously, these men would not be able to do that.

Ahab dies of an arrow, shot at random, entering a "chink in his armor." We find Ahab in the condition of many men today. Ahab died looking like a warrior. The truth is that he was disguised as someone else; dead, he was propped up in a chariot. In the end, this couple literally went to the dogs.

The unfatherable spirit of Ahab is one that spawns and then tolerates the spirit of Jezebel. It comes into the Kingdom and the church like a temple prostitute, seducing the hearts of men. In conjunction with the spirit of anti-Christ, it wars against legitimate spiritual authority. In the final book of the Bible, the Lord gives messages to the seven churches. One of them is the church in Thyatira.[1] The picture of the Lord here is one of judgment. He is portrayed with eyes like a flame of fire and feet of bronze. In the Scriptures, bronze refers to judgment. First, the Lord commends the Church of Thyatira for its deeds, love, service, perseverance, and progress. I would view this as quite a commendation from God. In my view, many churches would be content only to hear these words of approbation. However, the Spirit then addresses the spirit of Jezebel in Thyatira. The indictment is that they "tolerate Jezebel." "But I have this against you, that you tolerate the woman Jezebel...who calls herself a prophetess, and she teaches and leads My bond-servants astray, so that they commit acts of immorality and eat things sacrificed to idols. And I gave her time to repent; and she does not want to repent of her immorality."[2] I cannot say it more clearly than

---

[1] Revelation 2:18-19
[2] Revelation 2:20-21

this. Ahab is the one who tolerated Jezebel. This is why I believe that Ahab is the disease; Jezebel is the symptom.

Jezebel called herself a prophetess. I have rarely heard anyone in modern day call herself a prophetess except in charismatic circles of ministry. Being a charismatic congregation does not make us immune to the spirit of Jezebel. The passage says that she teaches and leads God's bondservants astray. The bondservants here are spoken of as belonging to Him. They include—but are not limited to—charismatic believers. Like the wheat and the tares in the parable, God says that it can be difficult to differentiate between the people of God and the heathen. Finally, God said, I have given her plenty of opportunities to repent, but she refused to do so. Samuel said that stubbornness is as idolatry and rebellion is as witchcraft.[1] The spirit of Jezebel is the spirit of witchcraft. The result of tolerating Jezebel is severe judgment coming from the Lord. "Behold, I will cast her upon a bed of sickness, and those who commit adultery with her into great tribulation, unless they repent of her deeds. And I will kill her children with pestilence; and all the churches will know that I am He who searches the minds and hearts; and I will give to each one of you according to your deeds."[2] I find it interesting that they must repent of _her_ deeds. The judgment and punishment of God includes sickness, tribulation, death, and destruction. Then the Lord equates the tolerance of Jezebel with holding to the "deep things of Satan." We know that Adam, like Ahab, did not take his proper position as spiritual head of his household, and the deep things of Satan entered.

The right to rule comes with the ability to conquer. Those who conquer are those who are overcomers. Notice,

---

[2] 1 Samuel 15:23
[3] Revelation 2:22-23

therefore, that the ultimate issue regarded authority. "Nevertheless what you have, hold fast until I come. And he who overcomes, and he who keeps My deeds until the end, to him I will give authority over the nations; and he shall rule them with a rod of iron, as the vessels of the potter are broken to pieces, as I also have received authority from My Father; and I will give him the morning star. He who has an ear, let him hear what the Spirit says to the churches."[1] The inheritance of those who overcome is the authority to rule over nations. We see from this passage that the model is intact. Jesus received authority from His Father. Fatherhood is and remains the source of all authority, not only in heaven but also on the earth. There exists no authority outside of fatherhood. I would venture to suggest that the "unfatherable person" who operates in leadership lacks authorization and is likely to be illegitimate.

---

[1] Revelation 2:28-29

39

Restoring Our DNA

*A*uthority is to society as gravity is to the universe. I believe that this applies to the family. The authority of the father in the home must be the nucleus around which all else finds its orbital sphere. All fatherhood on earth derives its genetic code from the heart and mind of God. The Father in heaven is the source or origin of all authority and structure including family. Fatherhood reflects and reveals an image of God to us on earth. This image of God as Father has been clouded by current trends in church and society. As we have mentioned, the Hebrew word *ab* can be translated as both *father* and *source*. Prior to creation God had already structured heaven as a family, in the sense that there existed a Father and a Son in fellowship and community with the Holy Spirit. God our Father is the source of family. For reasons only known to God, He structured heaven as a family, and He desires to see family revealed through His children on earth.

When I wrote about the derivatives of names, I quoted Paul's words to the church in Ephesus. "For this reason, I bow my knees before the Father, from whom every family in heaven and on earth derives its name..."[1] If every family derives its name from the father, the implication is, "No

---

[1] Ephesians 3:14-15

father, no family!" I submit that this is the reason that care of widows and orphans was an emphasis in both the Old and New Covenants. We must see that sonship is the path to fatherhood and that fatherhood must be the nucleus for the family cell and the Kingdom. Later, we will see that the family cell is the nucleus of the church. How we view family structure affects how we grow and structure the church.

The family and the church should provide two of the fundamental building blocks for society. Therefore, the pattern we choose for the family and the church will have implications for the society in which we live. Now let us look at two models that can be used to structure the church. There may be other models for configuring the church, but I will limit my remarks to these: 1) the ancient Hebraic model and 2) the ancient Hellenistic model. Before we do, let us remember the warning given us by Paul: "According to the grace of God which was given to me, as a wise master builder I laid a foundation, and another is building upon it. But let each man be careful how he builds upon it."[1]

We shall look first at what we will call the "Hebraic model." This model has its roots in Judaism and is the pattern seen throughout the Bible. A patriarchal model, it emphasizes fatherhood and family; authority is seen as resting in fathers and/or elders. The twelve sons of Jacob we call the Patriarchs. Each of these sons became the head of a family, and later the descendants of these sons of Jacob fathered the twelve tribes of Israel. Using this model, we structure the church as members of a "spiritual family," not a denomination. Members are bound together through "covenant commitment." They are brothers and sisters because they look to a common father. As with any family, one becomes a

---

[1] 1 Corinthians 3:10

member by birth, not by adhering to a philosophy, a doctrine or a set of rules. One does not hire and fire a father. A spiritual father must not be viewed as a salaried employee. Jesus used the Hebraic model with His disciples. Daily life was the classroom. His example served as their model. They learned from Him as they walked and talked together. His Father was His pastor, His pulpit a boat, His credentials His life: He changed the course of history.

Now let us look at the Hellenistic (or ancient Greek) model. A distinctive difference between the Hebraic and the Hellenistic cultures may be found in their languages. Greek is noun-based; Hebrew, verb-based. This makes Greek culture more centered on the abstract, conceptual and theoretical. Compare this to Hebrew culture, more pragmatic and action-based. Jews are quite pragmatic, and Jesus is a Jew. A further significant and distinctive difference between the Hebraic and the Hellenistic model is the structure of authority and government. The advocates of the Hellenistic model use democracy for their structural basis. In a democracy, final authority rests with the desires of people. *Democracy* is a Greek word meaning: "people rule" (*demo* = people + *cracia* = rule). Using this model would mean to structure the church under congregational government. Furthermore, the Hellenistic model allegiance to the family was replaced by allegiance to the state (or organization). Some of the distinctive characteristics of this Hellenistic model include the following:

Egalitarianism: This concept suggests that all people are created equal. When people ask me, "Doesn't the Bible say that all men are created equal?" I say, "No, it does not." Rather, this is a popular quote from America's Declaration of Independence, later used by Abraham Lincoln in his Gettysburg Address. The Bible says God has created vessels of honor and dishonor. It would do great violence to the Scriptures to attempt to use them to promote an egalitarian, classless and genderless society. Certainly, all are equal in the eyes of God in their value as His creation and in their need for redemption.

Relativism: This is a belief that claims there are no absolutes. Ironically, if we say that there are no absolutes, we are in fact stating an absolute. The result of this relativism is an unholy tolerance of wicked and unclean practices.

Intellectualism: It puts a great emphasis on academics and intellectual study. Even though Paul studied under the highly esteemed master rabbi Gamaliel, he viewed his fruit in his followers as his credentials.

Majority Rule: Leaders are chosen by election. The principle of majority rule can be reduced to might makes right. As I stated earlier, if Israel had been a democracy, the vote would have been six million to three to return to Egypt.

Humanism: This idea states that man has his own solutions and needs not a Savior. This hardly warrants a comment. History is replete with stories of man's inhumanity toward man.

Dualism: This practice separates the spiritual from the secular. Therefore, if we view Christianity as simply a religion instead of a monarchy (the kingdom of God), we marginalize its importance and relevance.

Ramifications of a cultural focus on the concepts listed above have led to our emphasis on membership in an institution, as opposed to citizenship in a kingdom. We can join an institution, but we must be born into a family. Comparing the Hebraic and Hellenistic models, we find two ways of viewing the structure of the church. I call these the organic (family) model and the organizational (business) model. Paul warned the Corinthians to be careful how they built.

Organic (Family) Model	Organizational (Business) Model
A life to be lived	A system to be implemented
Fatherhood and family	Owners and investors
Growing through birthing and nurturing	Growing through recruiting
Training up the children	Hiring and firing workers
Relationally centered	Program centered
Held together by covenant	Held together by contract
Character oriented	Gift and talent oriented
Emphasis is on faithfulness	Emphasis is on success
Generational emphasis	Immediate results and

Now, let us suppose we use a cafeteria as our organizational (business) model, and compare it to the organic (family) model. The model, which we choose to structure the church, will have certain characteristics of these two.

Family Model	Cafeteria Model
Fathers are honored	Bosses or managers are paid
Place set for you	Pick your own place
Eat what is prepared and set before you	Select from a menu
Balanced diet	Choose what you want to eat
Concerned with health	Concerned with taste or flavor
Come when you are called	Come when you like
Eat or go hungry	Switch restaurants
Pitch in and help	Pay as you go—others do the work

Family Model	Cafeteria Model
Depends on sons and daughters	Depends on clients and customers
Growth by relationship	Growth by advertising
Family tree	Restaurant chain or franchise
Takes time to grow	Overnight success
Given to heirs	Sell to highest bidders
Food specially prepared	Food continuously laid out
Struggle through in lean times	Leave and find a new place to eat
Responsible and accountable	Only responsible for your own bill
Intimate relationships	No relationship with owners
Process oriented	Product oriented

Paul structured the church according to the Hebraic Model. In the Hebraic model, the church was simply an extension of the family. As a Jew sent to the Greeks, his task would be similar to ours. He had to teach Kingdom principles to people who were inundated with Greek philosophy. As we have learned, one of the most significant revelations of the New Covenant is that God is our Father. As a Father, He desires a family. God's eternal purposes are bound up in His family. Consequently, sonship, fatherhood, and family have important implications for the church. Using the Hebraic model, our family is our reality check. It serves as our laboratory, or better yet our real-life seminary. Each family may be likened to a small church. The father/husband in the family serves as the elder/pastor or spiritual leader of the home. The mother/wife in the family would be likened to a deaconess (female deacon). The children would be the saints, or the congregation. If our methods and practice work successfully at home, it is likely they will work in the church and society.[1]

Two of the most serious problems in the world today are renegade fathers and rebellious children. The patriarchal (Hebraic) model has the potential to address both of these issues. The restoration of responsible fathers and obedient children is a much-needed remedy for many of the ills facing our current society. Church life, therefore, becomes relevant and offers genuine solutions to the problems of the world. This model allows the church to present an alternative to society instead of simply a critique of society. Unfortunately, I have yet to see the keynote speaker for a national Christian conference simply profiled in the advertisement as a great husband, successful father, and family man. In many circles intellectualism, gifting, style, and charisma have replaced Biblical truth. When we profile a person whose life and family are out of order, it can lead to serious problems, especially for those awed by his ministry. Jesus admonished us to focus on one's fruit, not one's gifts.

Many theologians link the prophecies in the book of Daniel to the end times. During a paranormal episode while Daniel was fasting, he was told that the prince of Greece (Hellenism) was about to come.[2] Most believe, and I concur, that the prince of Greece came physically in the person of Alexander the Great. However, the Bible indicates that Michael the archangel had fought with the prince of Persia, implying that the princes mentioned here were not simply physical beings, but were fallen angelic beings. Therefore, the prince of Persia and the prince of Greece would be supernatural spirit beings. I believe that the prince of Greece came, is still here, and that his influence has permeated the

---

[1] 1 Timothy 3:4-5
[2] Daniel 10:20

church and society. The Hellenistic influence of the ancient Greeks has been felt in every aspect of Western civilization, including the family and the church. Today, in the church as well as society in general, we battle against the philosophical problems inherent in ancient Hellenistic thinking.

A further danger of Hellenistic influence is the subtle shift of loyalty or allegiance from the family (the organic) to the institution (the organization). Evidence of this is when we use people to build up our structure (program or organization), rather than our structure to build up our people. Although I am aware that the following is an extreme example, perhaps it can serve to illustrate my point: By the turn of the 20th century, Germany had a tremendous spiritual legacy. Consider the contributions of such men as Gutenberg (gave common people access to the Bible), Luther (restored the truth of salvation by faith), and Count von Zinzendorf (gave impetus to worldwide missions). But Adolph Hitler took the Hellenistic model and turned the "Fatherland" into the "Third Reich." Allegiance to the state replaced family loyalty. The results were catastrophic! What is most frightening about this shift in focus is that it took less than a generation to do it. The psalmist wrote, "If the foundations are destroyed, what can the righteous do?"[1]

To properly contextualize what I have written, I am reminded of Paul's words. "For Christ did not send me to baptize, but to preach the gospel, not in cleverness of speech, that the cross of Christ should not be made void. For the word of the cross is to those who are perishing foolishness, but to us who are being saved it is the power of God. For it is written, 'I will destroy the wisdom of the wise, and the cleverness of the clever I will set aside. Where is the wise

---

[1] Psalm 11:3

man? Where is the scribe? Where is the debater of this age? Has not God made foolish the wisdom of the world? For since in the wisdom of God the world through its wisdom did not come to know God, God was well pleased through the foolishness of the message preached to save those who believe. For indeed Jews ask for signs, and Greeks search for wisdom; but we preach Christ crucified, to Jews a stumbling block, and to Gentiles foolishness.' "[1] The DNA of all culture and structure must recover and restore its genesis, relevance and its significance in the context of the gospel message, which culminates in the message of the life, death, burial and resurrection of our Lord and our Savior, Jesus Christ. Jews ask for signs, and Greeks search for wisdom, but we preach Christ crucified, resurrected and ascended to the throne room of His Father.

---

[1] 1 Corinthians 1:17-23

40
The DNA of Leadership

Many who have made the effort to read the Bible from beginning to end have stalled when they hit the genealogical lists in the book of Numbers. Tribal and family identities were extremely important in the Old Covenant and have always played a significant role in the history of Israel. Even religious duties were linked to the genealogical line. God appointed Aaron and his sons through Moses to perpetuate the priesthood.[1] This is significant in light of our subject. In the Old Covenant, the priesthood was limited to sons in a family line. If you were not one of the sons of Aaron, you could not be a priest. It mattered not how gifted or talented you might be. The priesthood was limited to Aaron's sons and only that family line. When Aaron was anointed as a priest, the oil was poured over his head, but not the heads of his four sons. Later, his sons were clothed in his robes. This might indicate that at least at the beginning, his sons were operating out of his anointing. Perhaps Aaron and his four sons were a shadow of the five-fold ministry laid out in the New Covenant. Isaiah wrote, " 'As for Me, this is My covenant with them,' says the Lord: 'My Spirit which is upon you, and My words which I have put in your mouth, shall not depart from your mouth, nor from the mouth of your

---

[1] Exodus 28:1

266 | Sonship: The Word Made Flesh

offspring, nor from the mouth of your offspring's offspring,' says the Lord, 'from now and forever.' "[1]

Under the Old Covenant, perpetuation of the Levitical priesthood was also exclusively limited to genealogical lineage. Levi and his sons were given responsibility for the care and keeping of the tabernacle.[2] If you were not a son and descendant of Levi, you could not even sweep the temple floor. We see this clearly demonstrated during the rebuilding of Jerusalem in the time of the prophets Ezra and Nehemiah. With the restoration of the priesthood, people were excluded from religious service, because they were not able to give proof of their genealogical history.[3] The order of God made sonship the single qualifying factor for ministry in the Old Covenant.

Genealogies play a significant role not only in the Old Covenant, but they have an important role in the New Covenant as well. The New Covenant begins with the genealogy of Jesus Christ. His lineage was of the tribe of Judah. Matthew, who wrote the first book of the New Covenant, calls Him the son of David. Being of the lineage of David made Jesus of royal blood. As a "son of David," Jesus was in line to be king. Matthew refers to Jesus as the son of Abraham. Abraham was God's choice of a spiritual father.[4] As I have mentioned, Luke refers to Jesus as the "supposed" son of Joseph (Mary's husband), and then goes on to trace His lineage to Adam, the first recorded father, and finally to God the Father, Himself.[5]

Now let us examine the issue of sonship in ministry as

---

[1] Isaiah 59:21
[2] Numbers 3:6-7
[3] Nehemiah:7:64; Ezra 2:62
[4] Matthew 1:1
[5] Luke 3:23 & 38

we move into the New Covenant. Since Jesus ushered in the New Covenant, and He is the archetype for ministry, we will begin with Him. With the exception of His conversation in the temple when He was but a teenager mistakenly left in Jerusalem by his parents, we know very little about Jesus until His baptism. Most scholars place the beginning of His public ministry after His baptism and temptation in the wilderness. I like to think that His Father spoke at His ordination, which was also His baptism. Here is what His Father said, "This is my beloved Son, in whom I am well-pleased."[1] Notice, God the Father refers to Jesus as His Son – not His Apostle, Prophet, Evangelist, Pastor or Teacher. At the ordination of Jesus, the recognition of His Sonship was the authorization for His ministry.[2] I contend that the example of Jesus sets the DNA for New Covenant ministry, as well.

I am convinced that the order of God for ministry, as well as family, was to build primarily upon our own children, more specifically sons. In the family, we build on natural children; in the church, on spiritual children. If we desire to leave a legacy in the family or the church, it behooves us to consider leaving it to the children whom we have raised up and equipped. Paul, who wrote a large part of the New Covenant, referred to his ministry disciples Timothy and Titus as his children rather than his students.[3]

If we choose the Hebraic model for building, we turn now to the qualifications for ministry leaders. As mentioned, the primary training center for ministry is the home. Although we know that Paul studied under Gamaliel, one of the noted rabbis of his day, Paul wrote nothing of certificates

---

[1] Matthew 17:5
[2] Matthew 3:17
[3] 2 Timothy 1:2; Titus 1:4

and degrees. Writing to Timothy, he said that a man's reputation in the community was of far greater importance than certificates or diplomas. As stated previously, the Hebraic model sees the home as proof of one's capacity to lead. A man's wife and children are his first disciples. What works in the home will probably work in society. That is to say, if one could successfully lead and disciple his wife and children, he is better prepared to lead in the community or the congregation of God's people. In regards to this, Paul wrote to Timothy, "An overseer, then, must be above reproach, the husband of one wife, temperate, prudent, respectable, hospitable, able to teach, not addicted to wine or pugnacious, but gentle, peaceable, free from the love of money. He must be one who manages his own household well, keeping his children under control with all dignity (but if a man does not know how to manage his own household, how will he take care of the church of God?); and not a new convert, so that he will not become conceited and fall into the condemnation incurred by the devil. And he must have a good reputation with those outside the church, so that he may not fall into reproach and the snare of the devil."[1]

Using the Hebraic model, appointing or acknowledging elders was extremely practical. Men who were successful in leading their own households were free to sit at the gates. They had proven that they could leave the confines of their own home without all sorts of confusion and disorder erupting there. Thus, having ordered their own homes, they could assist others who might be encountering problems doing such. Notice that in the ode to the virtuous woman, found in Proverbs, the writer describes the woman's husband

---

[1] 1 Timothy 3:2-7

as one free to sit in the gates.[1]

I do not wish to imply that higher learning is to be resisted or ignored. Paul was born a Jew in the city of Tarsus, and had been a student of Gamaliel, who was a teacher respected by all the people.[2] It is simply to say that university or seminary credentials were not mentioned among the qualifying factors for overseers in the early church. Paul saw Christianity as relational, not philosophical.[3] As a Pharisee, Paul knew of God; but after his conversion on the road to Damascus, he knew God.

Existing before creation, the DNA of the order of God is fatherhood and sonship. Tampering with the order, the rank and file of God, is a dangerous activity. It is like spiritual genetic engineering. Altering the DNA of something can create a monster. The imprint of God is found in the DNA of ministry. God and his order are unchangeable. If we modify or change the order of God, we touch God Himself. We do so at our own peril. Even when it appears that there is fault within the order of God, we must approach the issue with severe caution.

Now let us look at how the failure of spiritual fathers and the sins of the ministry sons affected the history of Israel. We begin with Eli and his two sons, Hophni and Phineas. The Bible says, "Now the sons of Eli were worthless men; they did not know the Lord."[4] Tragically, the man of God, Eli, failed to raise his sons in the knowledge and fear of God. Toward the end of his life, the Bible describes Eli as fat, fleshy and blind. The ministry had degenerated into being opulent, carnal and without vision. Conceivably this is a precursory warning to

---

[1] Proverbs 31:23
[2] Acts 5:34; Acts 22:3
[3] Philippians 3:8-10
[4] 1 Samuel 2:12

the church throughout the ages. A prophet came to Eli on behalf of God and asked, "...why have you honored your sons above me?"[1] The prophet went on to curse the sons of Eli, saying that the two of them would die on the very same day—which they did.[2] Upon hearing that the Ark of God had been taken and both his sons were dead, Eli fell over and died, as well. Upon hearing of the death of her husband, Phineas's widow gave birth to a son whom she named Ichabod. This would be Eli's grandson. Notice here the effect of the failure of a father and son on the third generation. The Ark of the Covenant was lost, and both father and grandfather died. By the way, the name Ichabod translates as "the glory has departed."[3]

But not all is lost, because God had given Eli a spiritual son. His name was Samuel. Some scholars have described Samuel as an Old Covenant type of John the Baptist. As Samuel was used as a forerunner to King David, John the Baptist was a forerunner to Christ. They continue this analogy by referring to David as a type of "Christ the King." Samuel was an anointed and powerful man of God. As a child, he had been dedicated to the Lord, and through his adult years he served the Lord faithfully. Samuel was a spiritual father to Israel, and God used him mightily. Nevertheless, there was one serious problem. Ironically, Samuel followed in the steps of Eli and failed to raise his natural sons to follow the God of Israel. As Samuel approached old age, the elders of Israel came to him and said, "You have grown old, and your sons do not walk in your ways. Give us a king to judge us like all the nations."[4] Samuel's failure as a natural father caused

---

[1] 1 Samuel 2:29
[2] 1 Samuel 4:11
[3] 1 Samuel 4:21
[4] 1 Samuel 8:5

Israel to reject the order of God, desiring instead to be "like all the nations." The response of God to this request requires some consideration.

The Lord said to Samuel, "Listen to the voice of the people in regard to all that they say to you, for they have not rejected you, but they have rejected Me from being king over them."[1] Notice that rejecting the order of God was considered equivalent to rejecting God. The order of God was that sons would perpetuate the ministry. Israel was not saying, We want another God; they were saying, We want another order. Instead of crying out to God that the sons of Samuel come to repentance, Israel demanded that there be a change in how they were to be ruled.

There are numerous other incidents where the order of God was tested, but for our purposes it will be sufficient to mention a couple. In Numbers 12 we read, "Then Miriam and Aaron spoke against Moses because of the Cushite woman whom he had married (for he had married a Cushite woman); and they said, 'Has the LORD indeed spoken only through Moses? Has He not spoken through us as well?' And the Lord heard it."[2] It is conceivable that Aaron and Miriam had a just complaint. Moses, born a Levite, had married a foreign woman; something forbidden under the law. Aaron and Miriam rose up against Moses. Aaron and Miriam decided to question Moses's authority. Even though they were correct in their position regarding marrying an outsider, God struck Miriam with leprosy for the attempted insurrection.[3]

Just four chapters later, Korah followed the path of Aaron

---

[1] 1 Samuel 8:7
[2] Numbers 12:1-2
[3] Numbers 12 1-16

and Miriam, questioning the order of ministry by suggesting that Moses had appointed himself. Korah was of the tribe of Levi but had ambitions to be a priest.[1] God's verdict and punishment was to open up the earth and swallow Korah, his followers and his family. Korah's rebellion against God's order and Moses's leadership resulted in a verdict more severe than most capital punishments. Korah was buried alive.

Saul of Tarsus went about persecuting the church, and Jesus took it personally. "And it came about that as he journeyed, he was approaching Damascus, and suddenly a light from heaven flashed around him; and he fell to the ground, and heard a voice saying to him, 'Saul, Saul, why are you persecuting Me?' "[2] Jesus said that when Paul touched the church, he was touching Him. Finally, the Bible mentions that even when angels broke ranks they were put into "eternal bonds under darkness for the judgment of the great day."[3]

---

[1] Numbers 16:8-10
[2] Acts 9:3-4
[3] Jude 6

41
The Goal of Sonship

A motto of the United States Army is "Be all that you can be." Jesus said, "Therefore you are to be perfect, as your heavenly Father is perfect."[1] In our lifetime here on earth, we shall never reach that level of perfection that exists in the eternal. Therefore, I believe that the perfection spoken of here encourages us to advance into the fullest maturity possible. We are born as children, we are built as sons, and then we mature into fathers. That was the progression of Jesus, and that is our journey.[2] As we become fathers, in both the natural and the spiritual realm, this process replicates when we reproduce sons. Both Jesus and the apostle Paul quote Moses, "For this cause shall a man leave his father and mother, and cleave to his own wife."[3] The cellular structure of the family is reproduced into a new setting, thus advancing the life of the extended family in the community. The Kingdom is advanced in this manner, through the reproduction of sons that become fathers and reproduce the same.

As mentioned earlier, a parable is a story, told as a riddle, that contains hidden meaning. "And the disciples came and

---

[1] Matthew 5:48
[2] Isaiah 9:6
[3] Genesis 2:24; Matthew 19:5; Mark 10:7; Ephesians 5:31

said to Him, 'Why do You speak to them in parables?' And He answered and said to them, 'To you it has been granted to know the mysteries of the kingdom of heaven, but to them it has not been granted. For whoever has, to him shall more be given, and he shall have an abundance; but whoever does not have, even what he has shall be taken away from him. Therefore I speak to them in parables; because while seeing they do not see, and while hearing they do not hear, nor do they understand."[1]

The parable of the four soils is given in three of the four gospel accounts.[2] Here is a portion from the book of Matthew. "He spoke many things to them in parables, saying, 'Behold, the sower went out to sow; and as he sowed, some seeds fell beside the road, and the birds came and ate them up. And others fell upon the rocky places, where they did not have much soil; and immediately they sprang up, because they had no depth of soil. But when the sun had risen, they were scorched; and because they had no root, they withered away. And others fell among the thorns, and the thorns came up and choked them out. And others fell on the good soil, and yielded a crop, some a hundredfold, some sixty, and some thirty. He who has ears, let him hear.' "[3] Later, Jesus goes on to explain to His disciples the meaning of the parable. "Hear then the parable of the sower. When anyone hears the word of the kingdom, and does not understand it, the evil one comes and snatches away what has been sown in his heart. This is the one on whom seed was sown beside the road. And the one on whom seed was sown on the rocky places, this is the man who hears the word, and immediately receives it

---

[1] Matthew 13:10-13
[2] Matthew 13; Mark 4: Luke 8
[3] Matthew 13:3-9

with joy; yet he has no firm root in himself, but is only temporary, and when affliction or persecution arises because of the word, immediately he falls away. And the one on whom seed was sown among the thorns, this is the man who hears the word, and the worry of the world, and the deceitfulness of riches choke the word, and it becomes unfruitful. And the one on whom seed was sown on the good soil, this is the man who hears the word and understands it; who indeed bears fruit, and brings forth, some a hundredfold, some sixty, and some thirty."[1] Permit me to highlight a few things from these passages. First, Jesus was speaking about the mysteries of the kingdom of God, so the Kingdom is our context. The four soils represent the hearts of men. Notice that three of the four— seventy-five percent—are shallow, infertile and unproductive. The seed sown in each soil type is the same; it is the Word of the Kingdom, not simply the Word of God. The purpose of sowing the seed would be to grow and harvest a crop, which the parable refers to as fruit.

Now let us look at a second parable, which relates back to the parable of the soils. "He presented another parable saying, 'The kingdom of heaven may be compared to a man who sowed good seed in his field. But while men were sleeping, his enemy came and sowed tares also among the wheat, and went away. But when the wheat sprang up and bore grain, then the tares became evident also. And the slaves of the landowner came and said to him, 'Sir, did you not sow good seed in your field? How then does it have tares?' And he said to them, 'An enemy has done this!' And the slaves said to him, 'Do you want us, then, to go and gather them up?' But he said, 'No, lest while you are gathering up the tares, you may root up the wheat with them. Allow both to grow together

---

[1] Matthew 13:18-23

until the harvest; and in the time of the harvest I will say to the reapers, first gather up the tares and bind them in bundles to burn them up; but gather the wheat into my barn.' "[1] In speaking of maturity, Jesus says that once the wheat and the tares grow, you will recognize the difference. As I have already mentioned, when wheat comes to maturity, the weight of the grain will cause the head of the stalk to bow. The heads of tares are light; therefore, they do not have the bowed heads and are easy to spot.

Later, Jesus' explanation of this parable came, which is the purpose of my including it. "He left the multitudes, and went into the house. And His disciples came to Him, saying, 'Explain to us the parable of the tares of the field.' And He answered and said, 'The one who sows the good seed is the Son of Man, and the field is the world; and as for the good seed, these are the sons of the kingdom; and the tares are the sons of the evil one; and the enemy who sowed them is the devil, and the harvest is the end of the age; and the reapers are angels. Therefore just as the tares are gathered up and burned with fire, so shall it be at the end of the age. The Son of Man will send forth His angels, and they will gather out of His kingdom all stumbling blocks, and those who commit lawlessness, and will cast them into the furnace of fire; in that place there shall be weeping and gnashing of teeth. Then the righteous will shine forth as the sun in the kingdom of their Father. He who has ears, let him hear."[2] In this passage, Jesus refers to the sower as the Son of Man, and the field as the world. In heaven, Jesus was always the Son of God; but on earth, He became the Son of Man. As the Son of Man, He was both the sower and the original seed. He says that the good

---

[1] Matthew 13:24-30
[2] Matthew 13:36-43

seed sown was the sons of the kingdom. In the previous parable, the seed that was sown was the Word of the Kingdom. Obviously, the seed of the Word of the Kingdom was to produce sons of the Kingdom. That is what our journey has attempted to establish. The kingdom of God is to be advanced by the sowing of Kingdom sons into the field of the world.

April 22, 1968, is the day that I was introduced to Jesus Christ. Within days of finishing the first draft of this manual, I had journeyed a generation with my Lord. Today, the reality of sowing Kingdom sons into the next generation has become even more real to me. God called my younger son Matthew, along with his family, to the eastern coast of Florida. Most of Matt's adult life was spent within ten miles of Kathy and me. Now, he is ten hours away. Of course, this has caused mixed emotions within me. Nevertheless, I have leaned upon this concept to steady me on my journey. I have had the privilege of sowing one of my sons into a different field. Sean continues to live within ten miles of us. Sean is now in his early forties. If we see a generation as forty years, both Sean and Matt literally represent a second generation. There could be no greater blessing on earth for me, than to see Sean and Matt continuing to build upon the legacy that I had hoped to leave. Then this legacy would be one that would unfold their destinies and the destinies of my eight grandchildren. That is, that by walking as sons they would become genuine fathers. Sonship is the path to fatherhood. Raising and sowing sons has been the goal of our journey.

Epilogue
My Personal Journey

*T*he scarcity of genuine fatherhood was graphically exhibited and confirmed for me in the early 1980's. However, before we look at that period, permit me to give you a little background and personal history. In 1966, I accepted a position to coach and teach in Marlette, Michigan. In July of that year, while doing graduate work at Western Michigan University, I met a nurse named Kathy Smith. Two weeks later, we were engaged to be married; yes, I did say two weeks. We were wed in November on the only weekend I had free between football and basketball season.

Kathy had met Jesus Christ as a young girl but had not been encouraged in her faith or in her walk with God. Although I was the son of a pastor, I did not know Jesus Christ as my Savior. In April of 1968 I was dramatically converted. I made the decision to become a devoted follower of Jesus Christ. Within three months of my conversion, Kathy and I were looking to relocate to another community. We call it "the week that was." In July of 1968, in one week's time, I signed a contract to teach and coach in Marcellus, Michigan, we rented a house there, I moved our belongings, and Kathy gave birth to our first son Sean. Yes, I was a new Christian with a new job, a new house, in a new town, with a new baby, all in a week's time. Two years later Matt was born, and that completed our family. Thus it was that this part of our journey began in Marcellus, Michigan.

Marcellus was a wonderful, safe and serene setting to raise the boys. The population of Marcellus, if you counted live pets, was perhaps 1,000 inhabitants. We joked that they could place the village limit signs back to back. Kathy, the boys and I settled down quickly into this tiny typical Michigan community. We began to search for a church and eventually ended up as members of a wonderful little rural Baptist congregation. The church was very conservative; jokingly I would say, "...just to the right of the National Rifleman's Association." In due course, their doctrinal position on dispensationalism would cause us some major conflict.

As Baptists, they held the position that the gifts of the Holy Spirit ceased with the apostolic age. As God would have it, I was supernaturally baptized in the Holy Spirit during a meeting of the local Baptist presbytery, and then the trouble began. Our pastor received the left foot of fellowship out of the Baptist church. Reluctantly, along with a handful of families, we left the Baptist church with him. Let me make this clear that I have a great love and appreciation for my Baptist heritage. Even though my father had been a Methodist pastor, I met Christ because a Baptist pastor introduced Him to me. Something I shall always treasure is that the Baptists gave me a sincere love and respect for the Word of God.

By 1972, I had backed into pastoral ministry simply attempting to fill the role vacated by our pastor, who moved to another community. In less than four years after I had received Christ, and without the benefit of any formal training, Bible school or seminary, I inherited a small congregation. I resigned my position as a football and basketball coach in 1973, but continued teaching high school English until 1978. For me the decade of the 1970's was awesome, while at times very turbulent and unsettling.

For five consecutive years, I was elected by the students of the local high school to receive the award of "Teacher of the Year." Ironically, during this time some in our community portrayed me as some kind of Dr. Jekyll and Mr. Hyde. It has been said, "What people don't understand they fear, and what they fear they fight." Rumors and gossip flourished about our little congregation mostly as a result of our charismatic beliefs, our worship style and ministry practices. We merely wished to recover and practice some of the elements of New Covenant Christianity. One principle that I teach is, "If we can't mobilize our followers, we're probably not their leaders." The fact that there was a tremendous sense of commitment on the part of our congregation caused some folks in our small town great suspicion and consternation. Some precious folks in the community were threatened by our ability to mobilize and act. It was impossible in this small village to be incognito. It is difficult for three dozen men gathering in one of the two restaurants for a fellowship breakfast to go unnoticed. Besides, as we began to help one another restore our houses, with three dozen men hammering shingles to replace a roof, it was impossible to go unnoticed. Being carefully scrutinized, we lived, so to speak, in a glass house.

During this season, we had been swept into the river of the charismatic renewal, and in particular what came to be known as the "Covenant Stream." Thankfully, a few months prior to taking the reins of Marcellus Christian Fellowship I met Dan Wolfe. With the help of his wisdom and guidance, we were able to navigate the waters of that era.

There were a number of church leaders in southwest Michigan who looked to Dan Wolfe for oversight. A local presbytery consisting of the elders of these congregations met regularly. In 1982 at the close of one of these meetings, my life took a mammoth twist. Erik Krueger, a guest at one of these presbytery meetings, led a large congregation of believers in East Lansing, Michigan. At that time both Dan Wolfe and Erik were under the personal oversight of Derek Prince. This alone would give each of them a measure of stature and credibility. I will never forget this moment. As I went to say goodbye to Erik, he said, "I'd like to speak to you." The tone of his voice and the look on his face sobered me, and for good reason. What he had to share with me dramatically changed the course of my life. He challenged me to consider prayerfully a move from Marcellus to Benton Harbor. I am sorry to admit, even when I am certain that God is speaking to me, I do not always respond immediately in joyful submission and obedience. During the forty-five minute drive from Kalamazoo to Marcellus, I must have thought of a hundred ways to broach this subject with Kathy. As I arrived home and entered our kitchen, I was surprised to face a teary-eyed wife. Her words struck me as a bolt of lightning; "We're moving, aren't we?" I am certain that my eyes resembled the eyes of a frog when you squeeze it.

To give you a greater insight into the trepidation I felt at that moment, let me share a couple of things. First, we had just finished the task of completely refurbishing and remodeling our home from basement to attic. Every niche and corner of the house reflected Kathy's personal touch and taste. For us, our home was a dream come true. Secondly, not long before, Kathy and I had sat in our car parked across from G.W. Jones Exchange Bank; we had been weeping for joy. We were elated and basking in the freedom of "owing no man anything." We were debt free! Our automobile, our mortgage, our newly remodeled house, yes everything was paid off. Selling our house, packing up and relocating were the furthest things from our minds.

What's more, in 1982 Benton Harbor was receiving national media coverage as the single most impoverished city in the United States. The vast majority of the downtown store windows were covered with plywood. Weeds flourished at the base of metal pipes that previously held parking meters. The cracked and potholed cement of empty streets and parking lots were littered with empty cans, plastic bags, and yellowed newspapers. What once had been a popular harbor and resort city nestled on the shores of Lake Michigan now appeared like a grey concrete skeleton. Days later, when Kathy and I drove through the downtown on our very first visit, the Scripture that occupied my mind was the account of the valley of dry bones. I had the impression that God was asking me, "Can these dry bones live again?" Reminiscent of Ezekiel, I answered cautiously, "Only you know, Lord!"[1] Kathy and I had come face to face with God's desire to strengthen the weak, the poverty-stricken and the disenfranchised. This only made it more evident to us that the idea of relocating to Benton Harbor came from our heavenly Father.

After a time of seriously seeking the Lord, discussing and praying with Kathy and the boys, and making numerous phone calls to Dan Wolfe, I succumbed to the obvious as the inevitable. Somewhat resembling the experience of Israel in the wilderness, I knew the cloud of His presence was moving for us. Kathy and I announced to the congregation our decision to move our family to Benton Harbor.

By this time, the Marcellus congregation had grown to represent around forty households. Imagine my alarm, dismay and apprehension when one by one the members of the congregation began to make known to Kathy and me

---

[1] Ezekiel 37:3

their intentions to relocate with us. Between 1982 and 1987, nearly every one of these forty households moved to the Benton Harbor area. Take a moment simply to consider the logistics of selling that many homes in a town of a thousand people that had no industrial base or job market. Then consider the dilemma of finding housing and new jobs in our nation's most impoverished city. Amazingly, we experienced God's supernatural intervention almost daily during this period of transition.

Let me attempt to illustrate what this move was like. A few years ago, my oldest brother's wife Betty Jo underwent surgery for a liver transplant. I vividly remember standing in the intensive care unit of a Florida hospital with my brother Dick looking at Betty Jo. Her face was grey, her breathing was labored and her heartbeat was faint. Tubes and electrical cords hung from her frail body like so many threads from a pair of worn out jeans. With the surgery completed, all we could do was to hope and pray that she would survive such an insult and trauma to her body. For me, transplanting the congregation from Marcellus to Benton Harbor could be likened to a congregational heart transplant. At first, it appeared that the transplant was an absolute success. Eventually, we saw how weak, delicate and frail one who undergoes a transplant could be. Tearfully, I watched men and families with whom we had walked for over a dozen years lose heart. As the storms mounted in our new environment, many were unable to find their bearings; they slipped from the deck of our fellowship and plunged into the raging waves of disillusionment. I am certain that a more capable captain could have navigated these troubled waters more skillfully. Perhaps a more seasoned professional than I could have saved more of these people. To this day, I often think back with pain and sorrow about those precious people who at one time had been so vibrant, so valiant, so dedicated and focused, who were unable to survive the trauma of the transplant.

In 1987, in an effort to help Dan Wolfe establish a church plant in Reston, Virginia, Kathy and I, along with the boys, left the congregation of Benton Harbor in the capable and skilled care of Dan and Glenda Head. More than two decades have passed since then, and I remain forever grateful for the selfless leadership of Dan and Glenda, who have pains-takingly cared for those who did survive. Thanks to them, and several other courageous families, Covenant Christian Church of Benton Harbor, Michigan lives on. Oh, by the way, with tremendous gratitude to God our Father, Betty Jo survived the liver transplant and to date, along with my brother Dick, she has continued to lead an active life.

Perchance you are curious as to why I would share the above in a book about restoring fathers and sons. The answer is simple. I wanted to dispel any preconception that the boys had grown up in some kind of "greenhouse atmosphere." It has been said, "Anyone can steer a ship on a calm sea." Yes, Sean and Matt spent their early and formative years in Marcellus. However, when our family moved to Benton Harbor, Sean was in the eighth grade and Matt was in the sixth grade. Benton Harbor High School alone had more students than the entire population of Marcellus. The overwhelming majority of the population of the city of Benton Harbor, and therefore of the schools, was African-American. Matt was the only Caucasian in his sixth grade class. A couple of years later, he was the only white kid on the football team. Amusingly, his teammates nicknamed him "Ghost."

Our home was within four blocks of the high school, and on any given day, we would find kids skipping school to play basketball in our driveway. Many of Sean and Matt's classmates were members of street gangs. Illegal drugs were readily available and regularly used inside the school building. Having been a teacher and an assistant principal responsible for school discipline, I could not imagine working in this kind of environment. Uniformed guards, including city police, roamed the hallways to quell the frequent fistfights. There were incidents of gunfire in the halls. A murder took place in broad daylight in the school parking lot. The junior high principal told me that fifty percent of his students would drop out of school before their senior year graduation. In this setting, Sean graduated in the top ten of his class, but when I mention it, he smiles and rolls his eyes. No, Sean and Matt were not homeschooled; neither did Kathy and I send them to a private or Christian school—not that I am against these alternatives. Perhaps if we had, it would have afforded them a much better academic education, but I doubt that they would have learned more about real life. Therefore, having spoken about Sean and Matt throughout the book, you now have a little insight into their journey.

In 1987 Kathy, Sean, Matt and I moved to Reston, Virginia. Sean had just graduated from high school, and Matt would finish his final two years at Herndon High School in Virginia. For six years, I served as an assistant to Dan Wolfe on the pastoral staff of New Covenant Christian Church. During this period, I was privileged to serve on the staff of Intercessors for America. Soon, I began to travel and minister with my good friend Gary Bergel, the president of Intercessors for America. Gary opened the door for me to do a number of healing seminars, under the banner of I.F.A. This was the spark that would ignite Jim McNally Ministries, now known as Harvest International Ministries.

I thoroughly enjoyed sharing with people about physical

healing, and I have been privileged to witness numerous miracles. The healing or gift of faith that God gave me opened up many doors. In nearly every place I went, I tried to encourage and equip the audience to exercise "the power of the casual touch." I had come to believe that there is little evidence that Jesus prayed for the sick. In nearly every incident of healing recorded in the Gospels, Jesus simply touched those afflicted. That is what I did, and I challenged others to do the same. But I never felt that the ministry of healing was my true passion. Whenever I had opportunity to do so, I would steer private conversations with anyone who would listen toward the subject of sonship and fatherhood. This subject truly captivated my mind and heart. I now believe that God used this gift to confirm this message.[1] As a result of sharing this message at home and abroad, I began to receive requests to be a spiritual father to various leaders around the world.

In 1990, Sean married Wendy Carder and the two of them relocated to Virginia Beach. They worked with a church affiliated with "People of Destiny." The church had a large youth ministry and Sean and Wendy had been targeted as potential leaders for it. In 1991 Bob Hughes, the youth pastor, asked Sean this question: "If you could do anything with your life, what would that be?" Sean answered, "I would work in the ministry with my dad." Bob's sagacious response was, "Well, that's what you need to do then." This meeting prompted Sean and Wendy to attempt to move to Reston, but housing costs in Northern Virginia made this impossible. Having exhausted every possibility of relocating nearer Kathy and me, in time Sean and Wendy were able to purchase a small home in Stafford, Virginia, about fifty miles south of

---

[1] Acts 14:3

Reston. Despite the distance, they quickly became the youth leaders at New Covenant Christian Church, commuting over an hour each way to do so. Eventually, it became increasingly apparent that working with the youth in Reston was not a viable option.

Finally, in 1993 New Covenant Christian Church faced the need to downsize its leadership. I looked at the situation as a boat with too many captains and not enough passengers. Someone needed to take the plunge, and I felt that someone was "yours truly." Therefore, in April of 1993 along with Kathy, Sean, Wendy and Matt as my apostolic team, we ventured out to plant a congregation in Stafford, Virginia. The result of this mission is known as Harvest Christian Fellowship. Planting a church while simultaneously attempting to oversee spiritual sons in the United States and abroad has been somewhat of a juggling act.

Using as a model my relationship with Dan Wolfe as a spiritual father, and with Sean and Matt as both natural and spiritual sons, I attempted to structure Harvest Christian Fellowship as a spiritual family. Eventually, both Sean and Matt were ordained into the ministry. Since 1993, many have come and gone, but some have remained. For a season, Matt took on the responsibility of the local church to assist and support me in my endeavors to take this message to the nations. As I mentioned in the previous chapter, a couple of years ago, Matt felt the call to move to Palm Coast, to assist in a church plant under the auspices of Church of the Nations. Sean and his family continue to lend their support to Kathy and me here in Stafford.

The journey from productive fatherhood to procreating children to building sons has no destination. It is cyclical in nature and will continue until the end of this age. With that in mind, as we part from our brief walk together, I will close with a custom introduced to me by two Native Americans, Jay Swallow and Nigel Bigpond. They told me that their people never say goodbye. Instead, they say, "Our paths will cross again, and we will be happy." Then they turn and go, and they do not look back.

Made in the USA
Charleston, SC
25 August 2013